Launching the Imagination

A Comprehensive Guide to Two-Dimensional Design

sixth edition

Mary **Stewart**

McGraw Hill Education

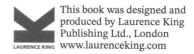

This book was designed and produced by Laurence King Publishing Ltd., London www.laurenceking.com

Commissioning Editor: Kara Hattersley-Smith
Production Controller: Simon Walsh
Design: Robin Farrow/Jo Fernandes (cover)
Picture Researcher: Alison Prior
Copy-editor: Rosie Fairhead

LAUNCHING THE IMAGINATION: A COMPREHENSIVE GUIDE TO TWO-DIMENSIONAL DESIGN, SIXTH EDITION
Published by McGraw-Hill Education, 2 Penn Plaza, New York, NY 10121. Copyright © 2019 by McGraw-Hill Education. All rights reserved. Printed in the United States of America. Previous editions © 2015, 2012, and 2008. No part of this publication may be reproduced or distributed in any form or by any means, or stored in a database or retrieval system, without the prior written consent of McGraw-Hill Education, including, but not limited to, in any network or other electronic storage or transmission, or broadcast for distance learning.

Some ancillaries, including electronic and print components, may not be available to customers outside the United States.

This book is printed on acid-free paper.

2 3 4 5 6 7 8 9 LWI 21 20 19

ISBN 978–1–26–040221–6
MHID 1–26–040221–5

Portfolio Manager: *Sarah Remington*
Product Developer: *Beth Tripmacher*
Marketing Manager: *Meridith Leo*
Content Project Managers: *Sandy Wille, Emily Windelborn*
Buyer: *Sandy Ludovissy*
Designer: *Egzon Shaqiri*
Senior Content Licensing Specialist: *Carrie Burger*
Cover Image: *Top: Suzanne Stryk, Journey Work (detail), 2011. Mixed media (paper, plant stains, gesso, topographic map, map pin, book pages, acrylic, pencil), 12 × 12 in. (30.5 × 30.5 cm). © Suzanne Stryk. Bottom: Sarah Mast, New Earth 11 (detail), 2016, oil and graphite on paper, 6 × 6 in (15.2 × 15.2 cm) © Sara Mast.*
Compositor: *Laurence King Publishing*

All credits appearing on page or at the end of the book are considered to be an extension of the copyright page.

Library of Congress Cataloging-in-Publication Data

Names: Stewart, Mary, 1952- author.
Title: Launching the imagination : a comprehensive guide to basic design /
    Mary Stewart.
Description: Sixth edition. | New York : McGraw-Hill Education, 2018. |
    Includes bibliographical references and index.
Identifiers: LCCN 2017030838| ISBN 9781259603631 (pbk.) | ISBN 1259603636
Subjects: LCSH: Design.
Classification: LCC NK1510 .S74 2018 | DDC 745.4--dc23
LC record available at https://lccn.loc.gov/201703083810

The Internet addresses listed in the text were accurate at the time of publication. The inclusion of a website does not indicate an endorsement by the authors or McGraw-Hill Education, and McGraw-Hill Education does not guarantee the accuracy of the information presented at these sites.

mheducation.com/highered

Launching the Imagination:

A Comprehensive Guide to Two-Dimensional Design

is dedicated to

Nancy Callahan, MFA

Launching the Imagination treats design as both a verb and a noun—as both a process and a product. Through an immersion in 2D, 3D, and 4D concepts and possibilities, students develop visual thinking strategies that will serve them throughout their studies and their careers. They discover that design is deliberate—a process of exploring a wide range of solutions and choosing the most promising option for development. They are encouraged to analyze each resulting solution thoughtfully in order to produce the clearest and most inventive solution to each assignment. And they find inspiration in the work of others, analyzing the art of the past and the present for insights.

LAUNCH YOUR IMAGINATION WITH CONNECT

Connect helps students better understand and retain these basic concepts. Connect is a highly reliable, easy-to-use homework and learning management solution that embeds learning science and award-winning adaptive tools to improve student results.

SmartBook

DESIGNED FOR

- Preparing for class
- Practice and study
- Focusing on key topics
- Reports and analytics

SUPPORTS

- Adaptive, personalized learning
- Assignable content
- Smartphone and tablet via iOS and Android apps

eBook

DESIGNED FOR

- Reading in class
- Reference
- Offline reading
- Accessibility

SUPPORTS

- Simple, elegant reading
- Basic annotations
- Smartphone and tablet via iOS and Android apps

Included in Connect, LearnSmart is an adaptive learning program designed to help students learn faster, study smarter, and retain more knowledge for greater success by distinguishing what students know from what they don't, and focusing on concepts they are most likely to forget, An intelligent adaptive study tool,

LearnSmart is proven to strengthen memory recall, keep students in class, and boost grades. Connect also includes additional assessments.

Instructors can access a database of images from select McGraw-Hill Education art and humanities titles, including *Launching the Imagination*. Instructors can access a text's images by browsing its chapters, style/period, medium, and culture, or by searching on key terms. Images can easily be downloaded for use in presentations and in PowerPoints. The download includes a text file with image captions and information. Instructors can access Connect Image Bank under the library tab in Connect.

Launching the Imagination now offers two reading experiences for students and instructors: SmartBook and eBook. Fueled by LearnSmart, SmartBook is the first and only adaptive reading experience currently available. SmartBook® creates a personalized reading experience by highlighting the most impactful concepts a student needs to learn at that moment in time. The reading experience continuously adapts by highlighting content based on what the student knows and doesn't know. Real-time reports quickly identify the concepts that require more attention from individual students—or the entire class. eBook provides a simple, elegant reading experience, available for offline reading.

Homework & Adaptive Learning

- Contextualized assignments
- SmartBook
- Time-saving tools
- Customized to individual needs

Robust Analytics & Reporting

- Easy-to-read reports
- Individual and class performance data
- Auto-grading

Quality Content & Learning Resources

- eBook available offline
- Custom course content
- Resource library
- Consolidated resources
- Easy course sharing
- Customized to-do list and calendar
- Lecture capture

Trusted Service & Support

- Seamless LMS integration
- Training
- In-product help and tutorials
- 1:1 or group help

HALLMARKS OF OUR NEW EDITION OF *LAUNCHING THE IMAGINATION*

Building on the strengths of the previous five editions, *Launching the Imagination*, sixth edition, is even more

- **Concise.** Content has been refined so that maximum content can be communicated as clearly and concisely as possible.

- **Colorful.** In addition to the full color used throughout the book, the writing is livelier than that in most textbooks. Analogies expand communication, and every visual example has been carefully selected for maximum impact.

- **Comprehensive.** *Launching the Imagination* is the only foundational text with full sections devoted to critical and creative thinking and to time-based design. The photo program is global, represents a myriad of stylistic approaches, and prominently features design and media arts as well as more traditional art forms.

- **Contemporary.** More than half of the visual examples represent artworks completed since 1970, and over 100 represent works completed since 2000.

- **Compelling.** Interviews with exemplars of creativity have always been an important feature of this book. Three of the best past profiles have been revised and a new profile has been added. Now inserted into the body of the text, each interview deliberately builds on its chapter content. In Chapter 5, designer Steve Quinn describes the seven-step sequence he uses in developing websites, logos, and motion graphics. In Chapter 8, Jim Elniski describes *The Greenhouse Chicago,* an innovative home that is both highly energy efficient and elegant. In Chapter 11, ceramicist David MacDonald describes his influences and work process. And, in the new profile in Chapter 6, artist Sara Mast describes an ambitious art and science collaboration begun in celebration of the ideas of Albert Einstein.

- We have also added a new feature called Success Stories. These short interviews explore connections between foundational coursework and career success. In Chapter 5, Elizabeth Nelson discusses her wide-ranging design work at the Shedd Aquarium in Chicago. In Chapter 6, Jane Parkerson Ferry describes her work as Curator of Education at the Orlando Museum of Art. Jason Chin's interview in Chapter 7 connects directly to his self-designed project in the Self Assignment feature earlier in the chapter. As a freshman at Syracuse University, he completed this ambitious illustration project as the final project in a Two-Dimensional Design course. In the Chapter 7 interview, he describes his current work as a professional illustrator. In Chapter 8, Dennis Montagna describes connections between his art and design major and his current historical preservation work for the National Park Service.

- Almost fifty new images have been added, representing major contemporary artists and designers including Wolfgang Buttress, Do Ho Suh, Garo Antreasian, Janet Ballweg, Phoebe Morris, Alain Cornu, and Natalya Zahn.

To suit a variety of design curricula, *Launching the Imagination* is offered in three versions: a comprehensive version containing all four parts; a 2D-only version containing Parts 1 and 2 covering 2D design; and a 3D-only version containing Parts 2 and 3. You have the 2D version, which includes the following eight chapters: Chapter 1: Basic Elements; Chapter 2: The Element Of Color; Chapter 3: Principles of Two-Dimensional Design; Chapter 4: Illusion of Space, Illusion of Motion; Chapter 5: Problem Seeking and Problem Solving; Chapter 6: Cultivating Creativity; Chapter 7: Developing Critical Thinking; and Chapter 8: Constructing Meaning.

CHAPTER-BY-CHAPTER CHANGES

Each chapter has been updated and, where needed, reorganized to maximize clarity. Improvements include the following:

Chapter 1: Examples of architectural design sketching and computer-aided design help to connect traditional and contemporary uses of line. A witty new tromp l'oeil image provides an engaging example of this technique.

Chapter 2: Diagrams have been updated and definitions have been further clarified.

Chapter 3: Witty new examples have been added and the writing has been further clarified.

Chapter 4: New examples have been added and the writing has been further clarified.

Chapter 5: The Steve Quinn interview is woven into the body of the chapter, and a *Success Story* with designer Elizabeth Nelson has been added.

Chapter 6: An interview with Sara Mast has been embedded into the chapter and a *Success Story* with Curator of Education Jane Parkerson Ferry has been added.

Chapter 7: The new Jason Chin Success Story clearly demonstrates connections between his foundational coursework and his current career as an illustrator.

Chapter 8: The interview with Jim Elniski has been updated and the Dennis Montagna Success Story has been added.

ACKNOWLEDGMENTS

Every new edition of *Launching the Imagination* is a significant challenge that requires work by a supportive and experienced team. At McGraw-Hill, senior editor Sarah Remington provided oversight for the project as a whole. At Laurence King Publishers, editor Donald Dinwiddie helped strengthen and clarify the writing and provided all kinds of helpful advice. Sandy Wille and Egzon Shaqiri from the McGraw-Hill production team made this new edition possible behind the scenes. Photo researcher Alison Prior was remarkably tenacious in pursuing each permission and was wonderfully inventive in suggesting alternatives when necessary. Robin Farrow worked tirelessly to develop the best possible layouts. Mat Kelly of Central College and A. Scott Baine of East Mississippi Community College contributed their expertise to assessments in Connect.

Images are at the heart of this book. I would like especially to thank all the artists and designers who granted permission for their artworks and the galleries, museums, archives, and private donors who provided the high-resolution images.

This edition is dedicated to four master educators. Dr. Dan Collins at Arizona State University has been an exemplar of innovation in education throughout his career. He is founding Co-Director of the PRISM lab (a 3D visualization and prototyping facility) and heads the foundation program in the School of Art (artCore). Through his leadership at the Telluride Institute in Colorado and as a Senior Sustainability Scholar at Arizona State, he continually seeks new ways to use art to advance the greater good. As past Director of the First-Year program at The School of the Art Institute of Chicago and co-founder of Integrative Teaching International, Jim Elniski has been a consistent and compelling voice for innovation in higher education. His community-based art projects, in conjunction with various human-service organizations, educational sites, and neighborhood associations, explore the dynamic interplay of the aesthetic experience, human behavior, and the social and natural environment. The two-dimensional design version of this book is dedicated to Nancy Callahan, a brilliant and versatile educator from the State University of New York at Oneonta. Callahan has inspired both students and professional book artists through her teaching, workshops, and exhibitions. The three-dimensional design version is dedicated to Anne Stagg, now serving as Associate Chair of the Florida State University Art Department. A versatile and inventive educator, Stagg is renowned for her honesty and strong commitment to students. All of these remarkable people are exemplars of the very best in higher education.

The following reviewers provided valuable insights and suggestions for the sixth edition:

Emily Beck, *The University of Notre Dame*
Narine Kchikian, *Henry Ford College*
Kevin W. Hughes, *Missouri State University*
Roxana Corradino, *Florida International University*
Susan E. Dodge, *Frostburg State University*
Genevieve Chaitra Linehan, *El Centro College*
Kevin Brooks Griffith, *The University of New Orleans*
Rae Goodwin, *University of Kentucky*
Michael Arrigo, *Bowling Green State University*
James Wade, *University of Kentucky*
Shannon Lindsey, *University of South Carolina*

Part One

Two-Dimensional Design

Part Two

Concepts and Critical Thinking

chapter seven
Developing Critical Thinking 141

Author, artist, and educator Mary Stewart is a professor in the Department of Art at Florida State University. Her drawing, prints, and visual books have been shown in over 90 exhibitions nationally and internationally, and she has received two Pennsylvania Arts Council grants for collaborative choreography. A cofounder of Integrative Teaching International, she has given over 60 lectures and workshops on creative inquiry, curriculum design, educational leadership, and storytelling.

As shown below, her *Continuum Series* connects the macroscopic with the microscopic. Fragments of towering trees are juxtaposed with images that suggest activity at a cellular level. In this series, Professor

Author Mary Stewart with *Labyrinth* book.
Courtesy the author

Stewart seeks to explore ways in which we construct and express knowledge, both of ourselves and of the world around us.

Mary Stewart, *Continuum #4*, 2012. Digital collage, 44 × 44 in. (111.7 × 111.7 cm).
Courtesy the author

Mary Stewart, *Continuum #8*, 2012. Digital collage, 44 × 44 in. (111.7 × 111.7 cm).
Courtesy the author

What is *Launching the Imagination* about, and how can it be useful to you?

In this book, we will explore

- the components of visual construction,
- ways that these components can be used,
- characteristics of creative and of critical thinking,
- ways to increase your creativity,
- the physical characteristics of various materials,
- ways in which you can use materials to express ideas,
- the components and power of visual storytelling,
- contemporary approaches to visualization.

Stephen Knapp installing *First Symphony*, 2006. Lightpainting installation, Ball State University, Muncie, IN.
© Stephen Knapp. Photograph by Satoshi Yamamoto

Because studio courses require hands-on work, we will treat design as a noun *and* as a verb.

As a noun, design may be defined as

- a plan or pattern, such as the blueprint for a house;
- an arrangement of lines, shapes, colors, and textures into an artistic whole, as in the composition of a painting.

As a verb, design can be defined as
- to plan, delineate, or define, as in designing a building or a functional object;
- to create a deliberate sequence of events, as in designing a film storyboard;
- to organize disparate parts into a coherent whole, as in designing a brochure.

Design is deliberate. Rather than simply hoping for the best and accepting the result, artists and designers explore a wide range of solutions to every problem, and then choose the most promising option for further development. Inspiring examples and informative text can help accelerate your learning process. In this book, over 625 images supply visual examples from many cultures and in all areas of art and design. Nine lively interviews with living artists provide insight into the creative process. Idea generation and critical thinking are thoroughly discussed in Part Two, and key questions (posted at the end of various sections of text) provide a way for you to self-assess your projects as they develop.

How high can you fly? How far can you travel? Will you work traditionally, in a specific discipline such as painting, printmaking, or ceramics? Or will you combine disciplines to create new forms of expression? Having mastered the basics of visual thinking, you will have the versatility and critical judgment needed to pursue a personal path.

Launching the Imagination

A Comprehensive Guide to Two-Dimensional Design

Lilian Garcia-Roig, *Water and Rock Flows,* **2010**. Oil on canvas, 48 × 48 in. (121.9 × 121.9 cm).
© Lilian Garcia-Roig. Private collection. Courtesy of Valley House Gallery & Sculpture Garden, Dallas

Two-Dimensional Design

Creating art in any form can be engrossing and exhilarating. Through our studio work, we can heighten our attention, engage our emotions, and build a sense of accomplishment. These personal rewards make art one of the most popular hobbies.

A *career* in art and design demands more from us. As art and design professionals, we must translate our personal insights into public communication. The ideas and emotions a professional wishes to express must engage an audience, whether the encounter occurs in the silence of a museum or in the chaos of a city street.

This ability to communicate visually is developed through years of study plus relentless practice. As professionals, we must develop our visual awareness, create new concepts, and master various techniques. We spend hours in the studio, refining ideas and inventing alternative solutions to each visual problem. A professional identifies the potential in a preliminary idea and develops it fully.

The elements and principles of design are the building blocks from which we create images and express ideas. Chapter One presents point, line, shape, texture, and value. Chapter Two is devoted to the characteristics and compositional impact of color. Chapter Three introduces a wide range of basic organizational strategies, known as the principles of design. Chapter Four expands these basic principles and devotes attention to the illusion of space and the illusion of motion.

Part One

Basic Elements

Point, line, shape, texture, value, and color are the building blocks that make up two-dimensional designs. Just as oxygen and hydrogen are powerful both individually and when combined as H_2O, so these visual **elements** operate both independently and in combination. In this chapter, we explore the unique characteristics of the five most basic elements and analyze their uses in art and design. We discuss color, the most complex element, in Chapter Two.

POINT

Defining Point

A **point** is a basic mark, such as a dot, a pixel, or a brushstroke. When we add a point to a blank sheet of paper, we create a dialog between this basic visual element and the surrounding space. This dialog sets a compositional game in motion. In this section, we explore two types of point. A **focal point** is the primary point of interest in a composition. By its size, compositional location, orientation, or color, a focal point activates the design and thus attracts the attention of the viewer. A collection of points is called an **array**. We can create rich textures and entire images using an array.

Using Point

Because points are both simple and powerful, they are often used in logo design. Logos must read clearly in both small and large scale, and must be easy to remember. For example, the Think Point Design logo in figure 1.1 is dominated by a circle combined with three words. The addition of the small point at the top

1.1 Andrew Beard and Sharon Sandercock, Think Point Design logo, **2012.** Dimensions variable.
© Andrew Beard, Think Point Design, www.thinkpointdesign.co.uk

1.2 Pentagram Design, Corella Publishing logo, **2006.** Dimensions variable. Courtesy of Pentagram Design

mohawk

1.3 Michael Bierut, lead designer, Pentagram Design, Mohawk Paper logo, 2012. Digital media, dimensions variable.
Courtesy of Pentagram Design

1.4 Charis Tsevis, *Obama*, 2007. Photo mosaic, dimensions variable.
© Charis Tsevis

of the logo adds a splash of darker green and suggests movement. This quickly communicates a simple message: "Think Point Design is an innovative company and always on the move." By contrast, the point in figure 1.2 transforms a simple black-and-gray shape into a cheerful parrot's head. We immediately want to find out more about Corella Publishing, the business this logo represents. Our final example is a logo for Mohawk Paper (1.3). Green, orange, violet, blue, and aqua points combined with lines of various colors create an energetic M. This combination of lines and points also refers to the process by which paper is produced and printed as it moves past the inked cylinders. Using a series of colorful points and lines, lead designer Michael Bierut provided a fresh identity for a well-established company.

An array of points can create an entire image while retaining the energy of the individual parts. Magazines often use this approach for their covers or posters. In figure 1.4, Charis Tsevis combined images of hundreds of everyday people to create the image of American president Barack Obama. Many wear blue or hold blue signs, further stating their support for his Democratic Party agenda. The image suggests that Obama is a man of the people rather than a remote politician. In our second example of an array,

Paddy Japaljarri Stewart has created an Australian landscape from hundreds of colorful dots. Using a traditional Aboriginal approach, *Bush Cabbage Dreaming at Ngarlu* (1.5) presents an imagined aerial view of the outback. Based on Dreaming, a spiritual practice that is uniquely Aborigine, each mark records the journey of an ancestral presence across the earth.

1.5 Paddy Japaljarri Stewart, *Bush Cabbage Dreaming at Ngarlu* (detail), Yuendumn, Central Australia, 1986. Acrylic on canvas, full size 47½ × 93½ in. (120.5 × 237.5 cm).
South Australian Museum. © 2017 Artists Rights Society (ARS), New York/VISCOPY, Australia

LINE

Defining Line

Line is one of the simplest and most versatile elements of design. Line may be defined as

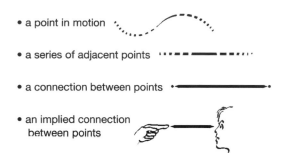

- a point in motion
- a series of adjacent points
- a connection between points
- an implied connection between points

1.6 Line definitions.

The first definition emphasizes the unique dynamism of line. The remaining three definitions emphasize its connective power. Lighter and more fluid than any of the other visual elements, line can add a special energy to a design. Simply by drawing a line, we can activate a space, define a shape, or create a compositional bridge.

Line Quality

Each line has its own distinctive quality. This quality is largely determined by the line's orientation, direction, and degree of continuity, and by the material used.

Orientation refers to the line's horizontal, vertical, or diagonal position. Diagonal lines and curving lines are generally the most dynamic (1.7A, 1.7D). Charged with energy, they suggest action and movement. Horizontal lines are typically the most stable, or static (1.7B). Vertical lines imply *potential* change. When verticals adhere to the edge of the design, they become tethered and thus lose mobility. Free-floating verticals, on the other hand, seem ready to topple at any moment (1.7C).

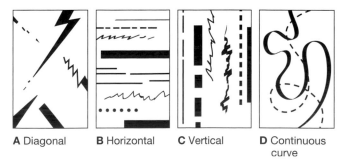

A Diagonal   **B** Horizontal   **C** Vertical   **D** Continuous curve

1.7A–D Line orientation and continuity.

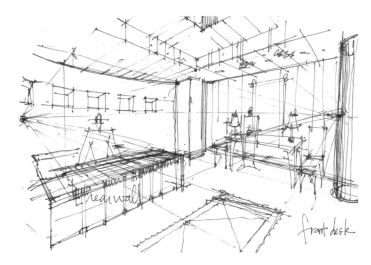

1.8 Jim Dawkins, concept sketch exploring view compositions for the front desk area of a hotel lobby, 2009. © Jim Dawkins

Direction refers to the implied movement of a line. We can use line weight to accentuate direction. Generally, a swelling line suggests forward or outward movement, and a shrinking line suggests inward movement. Notice how the top and bottom diagonal lines in figure 1.7A seem to push forward as they become thicker.

Continuity, or linear flow, can enhance direction. Figure 1.7D shows that a continuous line tends to generate a stronger sense of direction than a broken or jagged line.

As our fourth aspect of line, each material produces a range of distinctive marks. We can use a metallic graphite pencil to produce modulating lines of varying thickness. A felt pen produces a crisp, clean, emphatic line. Charcoal and chalk are soft and highly responsive to each change in pressure and direction. Brush and ink offers even wider variation in line width, continuity, and darkness. By experimenting with the range of marks each instrument can produce, we can use any material more expressively.

Artists and designers use line as the most direct means of translating an initial thought into a preliminary image. In figure 1.8, architect Jim Dawkins laid out a rough plan for a hotel lobby. He needed only a few lines to record the essential idea. As shown in figure 1.9, computer-aided design (CAD) can then be used to create a much more detailed wire-frame drawing. And, in figure 1.10, painter Kevin Haran used vertical, horizontal, and diagonal lines to map out the positions of objects in a still life. Spheres, cones, and the detailed skull move our eyes around and through the shifting space.

1.9 Computer-aided design (CAD) utilizing a wire frame drawing for a collection of buildings. © nadia/Getty Images

1.10 Kevin Haran, *Still Life with Skeleton*, 2004. Charcoal, ink, and acrylic wash on Arches paper, 30 × 22 in. (76.2 × 55.9 cm).
© Kevin Haran

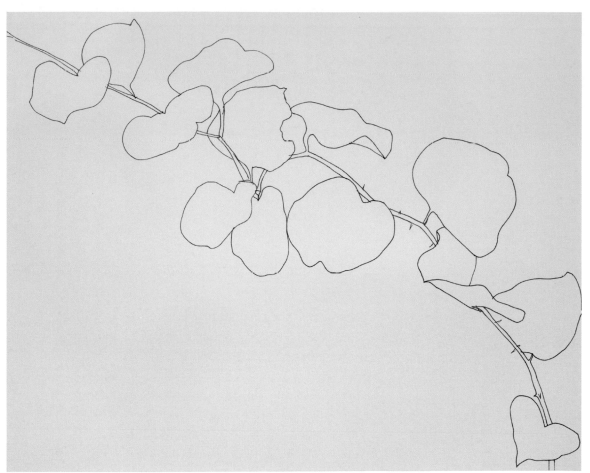

Actual Lines

Actual lines can describe forms simply and eloquently. In figure 1.11, Ellsworth Kelly used **contour lines** to define the edges of each leaf and locate them along a simple stalk. As this artwork demonstrates, essential shapes can be as eloquent as photographic detail. Similarly, Rico Lebrun's **gesture drawing** of a hand (1.12) captures essential action rather than describing every anatomical detail. We focus on what the hand is *doing* rather than on what the hand *is*. And, as figure 1.13 shows, Rembrandt often used economical lines to describe the spheres and cylindrical volumes from which figures are made. Because it communicates information using basic volumes, we often call this type of line drawing a **volume summary**.

    Calligraphic lines can add even more energy to a drawing or a design. The word *calligraphy* is derived from two Greek words: *kalus*, meaning "beautiful," and *graphein*, meaning "to write." Like handwriting, the calligraphic line is both personal and highly expressive. For example, in figure 1.14, painter

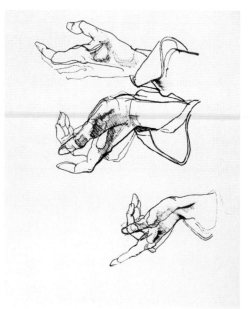

Tawaraya Sōtatsu and calligrapher Hon'ami Kōetsu used variations in line weight and continuity to suggest the graceful motion of birds.

    Artists often use **organizational lines** to create the loose linear "skeleton" on which to build a composition.

1.13 Rembrandt van Rijn, *Two Women Helping a Child to Walk*, c. 1635–37. Red chalk on paper.
© The Trustees of the British Museum/Art Resource, New York

1.14 Attributed to Tawaraya Sōtatsu, calligraphy by Hon'ami Kōetsu, *Flying Cranes and Poetry*, Edo period (1615–1868). Ink on gray-blue paper, gold flecked, 7⅝ × 6⅜ in. (19 × 16 cm).
The Nelson-Atkins Museum of Art, Kansas City, MO.
Gift of Mrs. George H. Bunting, Jr., 73-27. Photograph by Mel McLean

Kevin Haran's drawing in figure 1.10 shows that these skeletal drawings have great energy and can be presented as artworks in themselves. Similarly, Jim Dawkins's sketch in figure 1.8 provides just enough detail as he begins to design an interior. In other cases, organizational lines provide the framework for elaborate compositions. When we analyze Alfred Leslie's *The Killing Cycle* (1.15), we can see an underlying

1.15 Alfred Leslie, *The Killing Cycle #5: Loading Pier*, 1975.
Oil on canvas, 9 × 7 ft. (2.7 × 1.8 m).
© Alfred Leslie, courtesy of Bruce Silverstein Gallery, New York

framework. A dead man on a diagonal board connects a single woman in the lower left corner to the four figures in the upper right. A horizontal line supports these four figures, while their bent arms and legs create even more diagonal lines. The diagonal lines add energy to the composition, while the horizontal line adds stability.

Implied Lines

Lines can play a major role in a design even when they are implied rather than actually being drawn. Because **implied lines** simply *suggest* connections, the viewer becomes actively involved in compositions that use this type of line.

Fortunately, we have a natural inclination to seek visual unity. Given enough clues, we will connect separate visual parts by filling in the missing pieces. The visual clues may be quite obvious. For example, we can easily link the circles in figure 1.16 to create a linear spiral. In other cases, the clues are subtle. In Minor

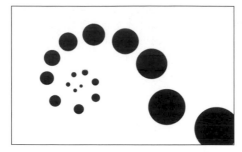

1.16 A series of dots can create an implied line.

1.17 Minor White, *Sandblaster, San Francisco,* **1949.** Gelatin silver print, 10⁷⁄₁₆ × 11⁷⁄₁₆ in. (26.5 × 29.1 cm).
© Minor White, San Francisco, 1949. The Minor White Archive, Princeton University Art Museum, bequest of Minor White (MWA 49-78.1).
© Trustees of Princeton University

White's *Sandblaster* (1.17), the white arrow implies a connection between the numbers in the foreground and the worker's helmet.

This inclination to connect fragmentary information is called **closure**. "Lost and found" contours require an elegant form of closure. In a "lost and found" composition, the edges of some shapes are clearly defined, and other shapes appear to merge with the background. When presented with such an image, the viewer must create a mental bridge between the resulting islands of information.

Caravaggio's *The Deposition* (1.18A) uses closure extensively. A contour drawing of this image has many gaps, as details are lost in the shadows (1.18B). Used skillfully, this loss of definition becomes a strength rather than a weakness. Connections made through closure can stimulate the viewer's imagination and encourage a more personal interpretation.

Linear Networks

Multiple lines can add detail to a design and create a convincing illusion of space. **Hatching** produces a range of grays through straight parallel lines. We can produce an even wider range of grays through **cross-hatching**. Many layers of lines at various angles

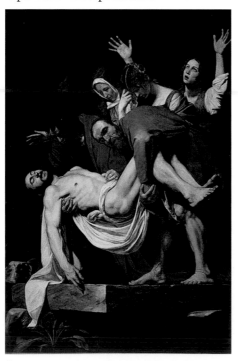

A

B

1.18A–B Caravaggio, *The Deposition,* **1604.** Oil on canvas, 9 ft 10⅛ in. × 6 ft 7⅞ in. (3 × 2.03 m).
Vatican Museums, Vatican State. Scala/Art Resource, New York

1.19 Jacques Villon, *Baudelaire*, c. 1918. Etching, printed in black, plate 16⅝₆ × 11 in. (41.4 × 28 cm). Gift of Victor S. Riesenfeld. The Museum of Modern Art, New York. Digital image © The Museum of Modern Art/Licensed by SCALA/Art Resource, New York. © 2017 Artists Rights Society (ARS), New York

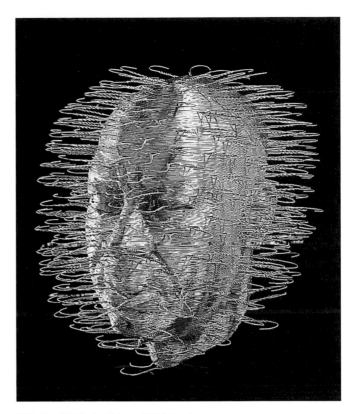

1.20 David Mach, *Eckow*, 1997. Coat hangers, 2 ft 2¼ in. × 1 ft 11½ in. × 2 ft 5½ in. (67 × 60 × 75 cm). © David Mach

are used in cross-hatching. Jacques Villon used both hatching and cross-hatching in his portrait of poet Charles Baudelaire (1.19). The head is divided into a series of faceted planes. Hatching defines each shift in the surface of the head, and cross-hatching creates the shadows.

Cross-contours can create an even more powerful illusion of three-dimensionality. Often created using curving parallel lines, cross-contours "map" surface variations across shapes or objects. In figure 1.20, David Mach created a cross-contour sculpture by bending coat hangers into the shape of a human head. In two-dimensional design, we can use drawn lines to produce a similar effect.

Hatching, cross-hatching, and cross-contours are often combined. In *Head of a Satyr* (1.21), Michelangelo used all these techniques to visually carve out the curves and planes of the head.

Linear networks play an equally important role in more abstract or conceptual art. As we will see in Chapter Six (which includes a full interview), Sara Mast is fascinated by humanity's connection to the cosmos. She has noted that our bodies and the stars

1.21 Michelangelo, *Head of a Satyr*, c. 1620–30. Pen and ink over chalk, 10⅝ × 7⅞ in. (27 × 20 cm). Photograph by Michèle Bellot. © RMN-Grand Palais/Art Resource, New York

1.22 Sara Mast, *Orion's Gift*, **2010.** Detail plus full-sized painting.
Encaustic on paper mounted on panel, 22 × 30 in. (50.8 × 76.2 cm).
© Sara Mast

are ultimately made from the same materials. Orion is one of the most visible of the constellations. In *Orion's Gift* (1.22), Mast connects the branching growth of biological forms to the atomic particles in this mysterious constellation. Black and gray lines of varying width reach out from clusters of points, creating pathways that are also reminiscent of neurons in the brain.

Using Line

We can use line to define, enclose, connect, or dissect. Line serves all these purposes in a New York City subway map (1.23). A curved line has been combined with an angular line to define the wheelchair logo. Another line encloses this logo within a square, emphasizing its importance. Diagonal lines connect the subway entrance to the elevators, and vertical lines dissect the drawing to highlight the location of the elevators. Using this map, a person in a wheelchair can navigate through a busy station and catch the right train.

In a sense, the first line we draw is actually the *fifth* line in a rectangular composition. In his *Self-Portrait* (1.24), Joel Peter Johnson used drawn lines to echo the four pre-existing edges of the composition. His head breaks out of this linear boundary. As a result, the portrait appears to extend beyond the painting's edge and into the world of the viewer.

Lines can serve many purposes at once. In an advertisement for the American Institute of Graphic Arts

1.24 Joel Peter Johnson, *Self-Portrait*, 1999. Oil on board, 9 × 8 in. (22.9 × 20.3 cm).
© Joel Peter Johnson

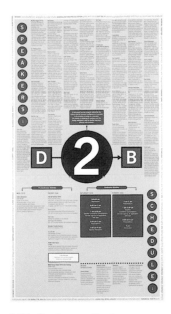

1.25 Pentagram Design, brochure from the American Institute of Graphic Arts "Design 2 Business" conference, 1996.
Courtesy of Pentagram Design

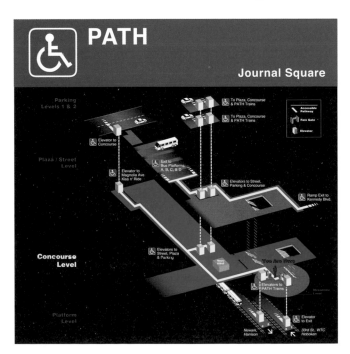

1.23 Louis Nelson Associates, Inc., PATH Station Maps, 1993.
Graphic designer: Jennifer Stoller.
© Louis Nelson Associates for the Port Authority of New York & New Jersey

(1.25), vertical dotted lines at the upper left and lower right highlight the speakers' schedule. A horizontal line creates a connection between the *D* and *B* in the "design to business" logo, and separates the top and bottom of the overall layout. We can even read the columns of text as vertical and horizontal lines.

When orientation, direction, continuity, and medium are effectively employed, line can be used to create compositions that are both sophisticated and thoughtful.

key questions

LINE

- What is the dominant orientation of the lines in your design—diagonal, vertical, or horizontal? What is the expressive effect?

- What happens when you repeat lines or when lines intersect?

- How would the composition change if you removed one or more lines?

- Consider using line to direct attention to areas of compositional importance.

SHAPE
Defining Shape

A **shape** is a flat, enclosed area (1.26A–D). You can create shapes by:

- Enclosing an area within a continuous line
- Surrounding an area with other shapes
- Filling an area with solid color or texture
- Filling an area with gradated color or texture

A three-dimensional enclosure is called a **volume**. Thus, circles and squares are shapes; spheres and cubes are volumes. We can use **gradation** or **shading** to make a two-dimensional shape appear three-dimensional, or volumetric. For example, in figure 1.27, a flat, circular shape becomes a faceted polyhedron when we add a series of gray tones.

Both flat and gradated shapes can be used to create an arresting image. In Aaron Douglas's *Aspects of Negro Life: From Slavery Through Reconstruction* (1.28), flat silhouettes combined with transparent

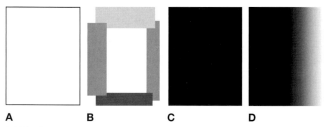

A   **B**   **C**   **D**

1.26A–D Any form of enclosure can create a shape.

1.27 Variations in shading can transform a shape into an illusory volume.

1.28 Aaron Douglas, *Aspects of Negro Life: From Slavery Through Reconstruction*, 1934. Oil on canvas, 5 ft × 11 ft 7 in. (1.52 × 3.5 m).
Schomburg Center for Research in Black Culture, The New York Public Library. Schomburg Center/Art Resource, New York/ Art © Heirs of Aaron Douglas/ Licensed by VAGA

1.29 Diego M. Rivera, *Detroit Industry, North Wall* (detail), 1932–33. Fresco, full size 17 ft 8½ in. × 45 ft (5.4 × 13.7 m).

1.30 Cecilia Sorochin, SoroDesign, cover for *Fearless Beauty*, 2008. 8.5 × 5.5 in. (21.6 × 14 cm).
Courtesy of Cecilia Sorochin, SoroDesign, www.SoroDesign.com

1.31 Gustav Klimt, *Salomé*, 1909. Oil on canvas, 70⅛ × 18⅛ in. (178 × 46 cm).
Galleria Moderna Venice, Italy. Cameraphoto Arte, Venice/Art Resource, New York

targets create an energetic panorama. We can almost hear the speaker in the center and feel the movement of the crowd. In Diego Rivera's *Detroit Industry* (1.29), a combination of size variation and shading suggests volume and increases the illusion of space.

Graphic designers are equally aware of the expressive power of flat and gradated shapes. In a cover design for *Fearless Beauty* (1.30), Cecilia Sorochin combined a model's volumetric head with a headdress composed from swirling flat shapes. While rooted in reality, the woman seems empowered by her lively imagination.

Gustav Klimt also combined flat and volumetric shapes to create *Salomé* (1.31). In this horrific tale from the biblical New Testament, John the Baptist has been imprisoned for his criticism of the royal family. Salomé, the king's niece, performs a stunning dance and the delighted king grants her a single wish. In revenge, Salomé asks for John's head. The tall, vertical shape of the painting is similar to the size and shape of a standing viewer. Flat patterns and color surround the volumetric figures, while two curving lines add a sinuous energy to the center of the design.

Types of Shape

The size and shape of a soccer field are very different from the size and shape of a tennis court. In each case, the playing area defines the game to be played. It is impossible to play soccer on a tennis court or to play tennis on a soccer field.

Similarly, the outer edge of a two-dimensional design provides the playing field for our compositional games. The long, horizontal rectangles used by Douglas and Rivera create an expansive panorama, while Klimt's vertical rectangle compresses a sordid drama into a claustrophobic column. Thus, creating a dialog between compositional shapes and the surrounding format is our first concern.

Figure and Ground, Positive and Negative

As shown in figure 1.32A, a shape that is distinguished from the background is called a **positive shape**, or **figure**. The surrounding is called the **negative shape**, or **ground**. Depending on its location relative to the ground, the figure can become dynamic or static, leaden or buoyant (1.32B–D).

In traditional paintings such as Caravaggio's *The Deposition* (see figure 1.18A), the artist treats the entire composition like a window into an imaginary world. To increase this illusion, Caravaggio lightly sanded the canvas before he applied the paint, and he kept heavy brushstrokes to a minimum. We are invited to see *into* the painting, rather than focusing on its surface.

When an artist uses a shaped format, we become more aware of the artwork's physicality. The 9-foot-tall teacup in Elizabeth Murray's *Just in Time* (1.33) is monumental in size and loaded with implication. The painted shapes connect directly to the shaped edge, emphasizing the crack running down the center of the composition. This is no ordinary teacup. For Murray, this crack in everyday reality invites us to enter an alternative world that extends beyond a simple cup of tea.

1.33 **Elizabeth Murray,** *Just in Time,* **1981.** Oil on canvas, two sections, overall size 106 × 97 in. (269.2 × 246.4 cm).
Philadelphia Museum of Art: Purchased with the Edward and Althea Budd Fund, the Adele Haas Turner and Beatrice Pastorius Turner Memorial Fund. © The Murray-Holman Family Trust. Courtesy of Pace/Artists Rights Society (ARS), New York, 2017

When the figure and ground are equally well designed, every square inch of the composition becomes supercharged. In figure 1.34, illustrator Phoebe Morris used an aerial view of a fierce wolf to define the head of a young boy. In this Russian folk story, Peter manages to capture the wolf by dropping a noose over its head. He frees a duck the wolf has swallowed, and then a group of hunters transport the subdued animal to a zoo. Morris created a clever image that embodies various aspects of the narrative, including the negative shape creating Peter's head.

Figure/ground reversal pushes this effect even further. **Figure/ground reversal** occurs when first the positive and then the negative shapes command our attention. As this fragment from *Metamorphosis II* (1.35) shows, M. C. Escher was a master of figure/ground reversal. The organic shapes on the left become an interlocking mass of black-and-white

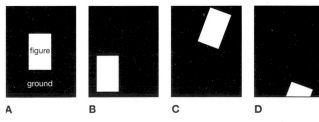

1.32A–D Various figure/ground relationships. When centered, the figure tends to be static. As it moves to the bottom left, it becomes more dynamic, and it becomes even more so when it is positioned diagonally near the top or bottom edge.

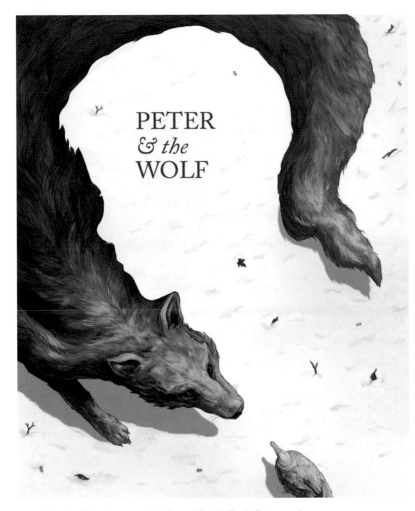

PETER
& the
WOLF

1.34 Phoebe Morris, poster for Sergei Prokofiev's *Peter and the Wolf,* **2013.** Graphite and digital, dimensions variable.

1.36 Sam Francis, *Flash Point,* **1975.** Acrylic on paper, 32¼ × 22⅞ in. (82 × 59 cm).

lizards. The lizards then evolve into a network of hexagons. Combined with the figure/ground reversal, this type of metamorphosis animates the entire 13-foot-long composition.

Figure/ground reversal requires a carefully balanced dialogue between opposing forces. Escher generally achieved this balance by using light and dark shapes of similar size. In figure 1.36, Sam Francis achieved a similar balance between a very small white square and a much larger red rectangle. The crisp boundary and central location strengthen the square. Despite its small size, it holds its own against the larger mass of swirling red paint.

Rectilinear and Curvilinear Shapes

Rectilinear shapes are composed from straight lines and angular corners. **Curvilinear shapes** are dominated by curves and flowing edges. Simple rectilinear shapes, such as squares and rectangles, are generally cooperative. When placed within a rectangular format, they easily connect to other shapes and can run parallel to the compositional edge (1.37A). Curvilinear shapes, especially circles, are generally less cooperative. They retain their individuality even when other

1.35 M. C. Escher, *Metamorphosis II* **(detail), 1939–40.** Woodcut in black, green, and brown, printed from 20 blocks on 3 combined sheets, full size 7½ × 153⅜ in. (19 × 390 cm).

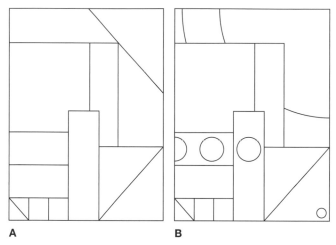

1.37A–B Rectilinear and curvilinear shapes. Rectilinear shapes can easily be fit together to create a unified design. Curvilinear shapes tend to be more individualistic.

A   B

1.38 Aubrey Beardsley, *Salomé with the Head of John the Baptist*, **1894.** Line block print, 11 × 6 in. (27.9 × 15.2 cm).
Creative Commons via the British Library

shapes partially conceal them (1.37B). As a result, we can use curvilinear shapes as targets that emphasize areas of special importance in a design.

Aubrey Beardsley (1.38) combined rectilinear and curvilinear shapes to create another interpretation of the Salomé story described on page 15. Using an internal boundary line, he emphasized the composition's rectangular shape. Within this boundary, curving black-and-white shapes create a series of complex visual relationships. A bubble pattern dominates the upper left corner. In the upper right corner, Salomé clutches Saint John's head. Extending from the head down to the flower, a white line follows the transformation of the dead saint's blood into a living plant. This line creates a conceptual and compositional connection between the top and bottom edges.

A very different combination of rectilinear and curvilinear shapes activates Robert Rauschenberg's *Brace* (1.39). The central image of three baseball players is surrounded by layered rectangles to the right, left, and bottom. A solid line extends from the catcher to the top edge. Vigorous brushstrokes add power to the painting. Occupying only a small fraction of the composition and surrounded by vigorously painted shapes, the circle *still* dominates the design: we *have* to keep our eyes on the ball!

Geometric and Organic Shapes

Geometric shapes are distinguished by their crisp, precise edges and mathematically consistent curves. They dominate the technological world of architecture and industry, and they appear in nature as crystalline structures and growth patterns. **Organic shapes** are more commonly found in the natural world of plants and animals, sea and sky. As Helen Frankenthaler's *Interior Landscape* shows (1.40), organic shapes can add unpredictable energy to a rectangular composition.

Using Shape

Artists and designers often use simple shapes when they seek clear, direct communication. In figure 1.41, I used just one gradated shape plus six words to visualize Hamlet's most famous soliloquy from Shakespeare's play. Commanded by the ghost of his murdered father to kill his uncle, Hamlet is distraught and indecisive. Should he become a murderer himself, based on his encounter with a ghost? What does it mean to be alive—or dead? "To Be," written across the top, offers one option. Along the bottom, "Or Not To Be" offers another.

More complex shapes are often used when the message is subtle or contradictory. **Collage** is one method of creating such complex shapes. Constructed from visual fragments initially designed for another

1.39 Robert Rauschenberg, *Brace*, 1962. Oil and silkscreen on canvas, 60 × 60 in. (152.4 × 152.4 cm).
Art © Robert Rauschenberg. Licensed by VAGA, New York

1.40 Helen Frankenthaler, *Interior Landscape*, 1964. Acrylic on canvas, 8 ft 8⅞ in. × 7 ft 8⅝ in. (266 × 235 cm).
San Francisco Museum of Modern Art, Gift of the Women's Board, © Helen Frankenthaler. © 2017 Artists Rights Society (ARS), New York. Photograph by Ben Blackwell

1.41 Mary Stewart, *Hamlet's Dilemma*, 2013. Digital study.
Courtesy of the author

1.42A Romare Bearden, *The Dove*, 1964. Cut-and-pasted paper, gouache, pencil, and colored pencil on cardboard, 13⅜ × 18¾ in. (34 × 47.5 cm).

1.42B Romare Bearden, *The Dove*, 1964, compositional diagram. Printed and cut shapes work together to create a complex composition.

purpose, a collage combines two kinds of shape: the shape of each piece of cut paper and the shapes created by the information printed *on* the paper.

In Romare Bearden's *The Dove* (1.42A), the outer edges of each cut fragment create a lively pattern of curvilinear and rectilinear shapes. The lines and textures printed on these photographic fragments create a second set of shapes. A linear diagram of this artwork demonstrates the complexity of the resulting composition (1.42B). Combining his perceptions of contemporary Harlem with childhood memories, Bearden used this interplay of cut edges and printed textures to create a rich composition from the shifting shapes.

In *Target with Plaster Casts* (1.43), Jasper Johns combined simple shapes with sculptural objects to create an equally complex composition. A series of concentric circles creates a clearly defined target at the center of the painting. Nine sculptural fragments of a human figure line the upper edge—an ear, a hand, a mouth, and so forth. To add further complexity, Johns embedded scraps of newspaper into the colored wax from which he constructed the painting. Equally attracted to the representational body parts above and the symbolic target below, we must reconcile two very different forms of visual information.

1.43 Jasper Johns, *Target with Plaster Casts*, **1955.** Encaustic and collage on canvas with objects, 51 × 44 × 2½ in. (129.5 × 111.8 × 6.4 cm).
Collection of David Geffen, Los Angeles. Art © Jasper Johns/Licensed by VAGA, New York

1.44 Albrecht Dürer, *The Knight, Death, and the Devil*, **1513.** Engraving, 11 × 14 in. (28 × 36 cm).
© NGA, Rosenwald Collection

TEXTURE

The surface quality of a two-dimensional shape or a three-dimensional volume is called **texture**. Texture engages our sense of touch as well as our vision, and can enhance the visual surface and conceptual meaning of a design.

Types of Texture

Physical texture creates variations in a surface. The woven texture of canvas, the bumpy texture of thickly applied paint, and the rough texture of wood grain are common examples. **Visual texture** is an illusion. We can create it by using multiple marks that simulate physical texture.

Albrecht Dürer's *The Knight, Death and the Devil* (1.44) employs both visual and physical texture. Dürer created the knight's armor, the horse's glossy hide, the dog's furry coat, and other details using cross-contours, cross-hatching, and patterns of dots called **stippling**. All are examples of visual texture. Furthermore, this print is an **engraving**. Each dot and line was carefully carved into a thin sheet of copper. Dürer then pressed ink into the grooves and wiped the surface metal clean. He then positioned the plate face up on a printing press and laid a damp sheet of paper over it. He cranked both through the press, transferring the ink and creating a subtle embossment. As a result, physical texture accentuates the visual texture in this image.

Invented texture is one form of visual texture. Using invented texture, the artist or designer can activate a surface using shapes that have no direct reference to perceptual reality. Bruce Conner used invented textures from many sources to construct his paper collage *Psychedelicatessen Owner* (1.45). He combined floral patterns, visual gemstones, and cross-contours to create a witty and improbable portrait. By contrast, Brad Holland drew all the textures in figure 1.46, using pen and ink. As the density of the marks increases, the face dissolves into dark masses of pure energy.

Creating Texture

When creating any type of texture, we must take two basic factors into account.

First, every material has its own inherent textural quality. Charcoal is characteristically soft and rich, while a linocut print, such as Beardsley's *Salomé* (see figure 1.38), creates crisp, distinct edges. It is very

1.45 Bruce Conner, *Psychedelicatessen Owner*, March 31, 1990. Paper collage, 8 × 6 in. (20.3 × 15.2 cm).
© 2017 Conner Family Trust, San Francisco/Artists Rights Society (ARS), New York

1.46 Brad Holland, *Literary Beast*, illustration for *Confessions of a Short-Order Artist*, *Persönlich*, 1997. Pen and ink.
© Brad Holland

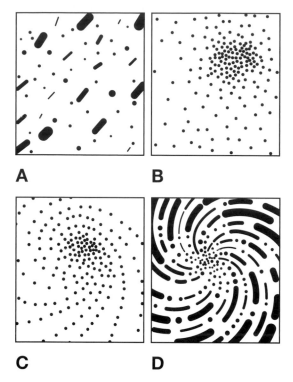

A   **B**

C   **D**

1.47A–D Examples of textural size, density, and orientation.

1.48 Douglas Smith, *No Turning*, 1986. Scratchboard and watercolor, 11¼ × 15 in. (29.2 × 38.1 cm).
© Douglas Smith, 2005. Courtesy of Richard Solomon Agency

difficult to create soft, atmospheric textures using linocut, or to create crisp textures using charcoal.

Second, the support surface contributes its own texture. This surface may be smooth, like most photographs, or quite bumpy, like the canvas and embedded collage that Jasper Johns used for his *Target* (see figure 1.43). Thus, work with texture requires a heightened sensitivity to both the support surface and the medium that the artist uses to create the design.

Texture and Space

Artists and designers create visual texture whenever they repeat lines, dots, or other shapes. Variations in the size, density, and orientation of these marks can produce different spatial effects. Larger and darker marks tend to advance outward (1.47A). Finer marks, tightly packed, tend to pull us inward (1.47B). In figure 1.47C, the marks have been organized into a loose spiral. The overall impact is strongest when size, density, and orientation are combined, as in figure 1.47D.

In figure 1.48, Douglas Smith combined texture and linear perspective to produce a dramatic illusion of space. The lines of mortar between the bricks all point toward the truck in the center, while the bricks themselves diminish in size as the distance increases. The truck at the bottom of the wall of bricks seems to be trapped in a claustrophobic space.

By contrast, Robert Indiana's *The Great American Dream: New York* (1.49) is spatially shallow. Indiana constructed a three-dimensional model of a coin or medallion from layers of cardboard. He then laid his drawing paper on top of the construction and made a rubbing, using colored pencils. We can interpret this seemingly simple composition in at least three ways. First, creating a design through rubbing can remind us of the coin rubbings we may have made as children. Second, in many cultures, rubbing coins evokes wealth or good luck. Finally, the rubbing itself creates the *illusion* of the coin or medallion, not the reality. Perhaps the Great American Dream of wealth and success for anyone is just an illusion, ready to dissolve during a stock market crash.

Both spatial and flat textures can be created using letters, numbers, or words. Variations in size, density, and orientation can strongly affect the meaning of these verbal textures. In figure 1.50, African-American painter Glenn Ligon repeatedly wrote, "I feel most colored when I am thrown against a sharp white background," on a gallery wall. As the density of the

1.49 Robert Indiana, *The Great American Dream: New York (The Glory-Star Version)*, **1966.** Wax crayon on paper sheet, 39¹³⁄₁₆ × 26⅛ in. (101.1 × 66.4 cm).

Whitney Museum of American Art, New York; Gift of Norman Dubrow 77.98. © 2017 Morgan Art Foundation Ltd./Artists Rights Society (ARS), New York

words increases, the words begin to fuse together, creating variations in the visual texture while reducing verbal clarity.

Trompe l'Oeil

Taken to an extreme, visual texture can so resemble reality that a deception occurs. We call this effect **trompe l'oeil**, from a French term meaning "to fool the eye." Trompe l'oeil can become a simple exercise in technical virtuosity or can significantly alter our perception of reality. By simulating architectural details, John Pugh created an amazing dialog between illusion and reality in figure 1.51. Originally painted on the side of Taylor Hall on the campus of Chico State University, *Academe* appears to peel away the surface of a conventional building to reveal four Greek columns underneath. This sly reference to the ancient source of many academic subjects is both arresting

1.50 Glenn Ligon, *Untitled (I feel most colored when I am thrown against a sharp white background)*, **1990.** Oilstick and gesso on wood, 6 ft 6 in. × 30 in. (200 × 76.2 cm).

Courtesy of the artist, Luhring Augustine, New York, and Regen Projects, Los Angeles

1.51 John Pugh, *Academe* on Taylor Hall, Chico State University, California, 1980. Mural painting.
Photo Barcroft/Getty Images

1.52 Claudio Bravo, *Blue Package*, 1967. Oil on canvas, 6 ft 2⅝ in. × 4 ft 10⅝ in. (190 × 149.5 cm). Courtesy Marlborough Gallery, New York. Photo © Christie's Images/Bridgeman Image

and thought-provoking. It was so popular that when Taylor Hall was demolished, the mural was re-created on a new Arts and Humanities building.

Combining Physical and Visual Texture

Each material has a distinctive physical texture, and each drawing method creates a distinctive visual texture. By combining physical and visual textures, we can unify a composition and add another layer of conceptual and compositional energy.

Blended graphite, pastel, or charcoal creates the smooth surface that is often favored for highly representational images. Claudio Bravo developed the visual textures in *Blue Package* (1.52) using pastel. By carefully drawing every fold, he created a convincing simulation of a three-dimensional object.

Cross-hatching creates a more active visual texture. Dugald Stermer constructed his portrait of mathematician Bertrand Russell (1.53) from a network of

1.53 Dugald Stermer, *Portrait of Bertrand Russell* (detail), for the *New York Times Book Review*, 2002. Colored pencil.
© Dugald Stermer

vigorous lines. The bumpy texture of the paper adds more energy to this lively drawing.

Anselm Kiefer combined physical and visual textures in *Wayland's Song (with Wing)* (1.54). In this myth, a metalsmith named Wayland is captured by the king of Sweden, then crippled and forced to create treasures on demand. In revenge, he murders the king's sons and makes drinking cups from their skulls. He then flees, using wings fashioned from metal sheets. By adding straw and a lead wing to the photographic base image, Kiefer was able to combine the illusionistic qualities of painting with the physical immediacy of sculpture.

Marks and Meanings

Every textural mark that we make can add to or subtract from the composition as a whole. When the texture is random or inappropriate, the composition becomes cluttered and confused. On the other hand, deliberate use of texture can enhance the illusion of space and increase compositional unity.

1.54 Anselm Kiefer, *Wayland's Song (with Wing)*, 1982. Oil, emulsion, straw, and photograph with lead wing, 110¼ × 149⅝ in. (280 × 380 cm).
© Anselm Kiefer. Courtesy of Gagosian Gallery, New York

1.55 Benjamin Marra, *Self-Portrait*, 1998.
Oil on canvas, 8½ × 11 in. (21.6 × 28 cm).
Courtesy of Benjamin Marra

1.56 Chuck Close, *Self-Portrait*, 1997. Oil on canvas,
8 ft 6 in. × 7 ft (2.59 × 2.13 m).
© Chuck Close. Photograph by Ellen Page Wilson. Courtesy of Pace Gallery,
New York

For example, each brushstroke in Benjamin Marra's *Self-Portrait* (1.55) describes a different facet of the face. Just as a sculptor carves out a portrait in plaster, so Marra used bold brushstrokes to carve out this portrait in paint. There are no random marks. Using both visual and physical texture, Marra increased the painting's immediacy and dimensionality.

Chuck Close's *Self-Portrait* (1.56) offers a very different interpretation of the head. Working from a photograph, Close methodically reduced the face to a series of squares within a grid. He then painted circles, diamonds, and other simple shapes inside each square. The grid provides structure, while the loosely painted interior shapes create an unexpected invented texture.

In Lilian Garcia-Roig's *Water and Rock Flows* (1.57), the texture of oil paint serves three distinct purposes. First, it creates a physical texture, suggesting the ripples and eddies in the moving water. Second, it brings great

1.57 Lilian Garcia-Roig, *Water and Rock Flows*, 2010.
Oil on canvas, 48 × 48 in. (121.9 × 121.9 cm).
© Lilian Garcia-Roig. Private collection.
Courtesy of Valley House Gallery
& Sculpture Garden, Dallas

energy to every painted shape: we feel the movement; we become mesmerized by the shifting and colorful patterns. Finally, we become connected to the artist herself. Often squeezing paint directly from the tube and onto the canvas, Garcia-Roig builds up vigorous layers of glistening color. As with the natural world, her paintings are both dazzling and highly tactile.

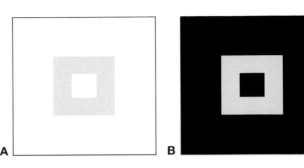

1.58A–B Relative value.

1.59 Value scale.

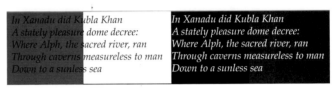

1.60 Contrast affects readability.

key questions

TEXTURE

- What physical textures can you create with the materials you've chosen?

- What visual textures can you create with the materials you've chosen?

- Can the marks you make enhance the spatial illusion or increase compositional unity?

- How large can the marks become, and how loosely can you draw them?

- What happens to your design when you combine solid shapes and textured shapes?

VALUE

Value refers to the relative lightness or darkness of a surface. The word *relative* is significant. The lightness or darkness of a shape is largely determined by its surroundings. For example, on a white surface, a gray square seems stable and imposing (1.58A). The same gray square has less visual weight and seems luminous when it is surrounded by a black ground (1.58B). A **value scale** further demonstrates the importance of context (1.59). The solid gray line appears luminous when it is placed on a black background. As it crosses over the middle grays and into the white area, it seems to darken.

Contrast

Both communication and expression are affected by **value contrast**, or the amount of difference in values. High contrast tends to increase clarity and improve readability (1.60). Artists and designers often use low contrast for shapes of secondary importance or when the message is subtle. The same text can be dramatic or incoherent, depending on the amount of contrast.

Photographers are especially aware of the importance of contrast. By using a filter, changing the print paper, or adjusting the image digitally, they can quickly modify contrast. High contrast gives Lewis Hine's *Powerhouse Mechanic* (1.61) a gritty immediacy. Each muscle and piece of machinery is clearly defined. By contrast, the city in Alfred Stieglitz's *The Terminal* (1.62) is quiet and atmospheric. This low-contrast photograph invites the viewer into a preindustrial world of horses and carriages.

Finally, value gradation can suggest a light source, create a sense of three-dimensionality, and enhance the illusion of space. Ray Burggraf's *Eternal Now* (1.63) demonstrates each of these effects.

Value Distribution

Value distribution refers to the proportion and arrangement of lights and darks in a composition. Careful use of value distribution can increase emotional impact. A composition that is 80 percent black simply has a different "feel" from a composition that is 80 percent white.

Artists and designers often use values to create a sense of mystery or increase dramatic tension. For

1.61 Lewis Hine, *Powerhouse Mechanic*, **1920.**
Photograph.
The National Archives

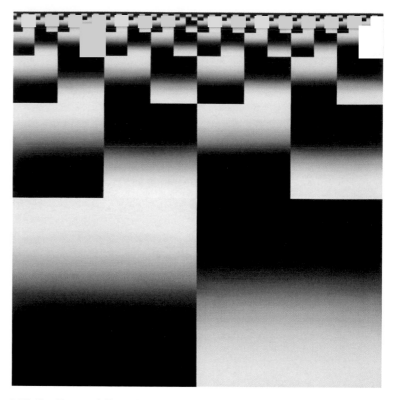

1.63 Ray Burggraf, *Eternal Now*, **1975.** Brushed acrylic on canvas, 40 × 40 in.
(101.6 × 101.6 cm).
© Ray Burggraf

1.62 Alfred Stieglitz, *The Terminal*, **c. 1892.** Chloride print, 3½ × 4½ in. (8.8 × 11.3 cm).
Courtesy of The Metropolitan Museum of Art/Gift of J. B. Neumann, 1958/Public Domain

example, *Ejecutado* (1.64) by Alice Leora Briggs combines split images of a seated man in the foreground and a crime scene in the background. The man in the foreground creates a visual and conceptual frame for the tragic scene at the center of the composition. Who is the man drinking coffee? Why was the other man killed? The combination of visual clues and the dark values creates a dramatic mystery.

Lighter values tend to suggest openness, optimism, and clarity. The layout of Kevin Fletcher's *Leaving Wittenberg by Afternoon Train* (1.65) is similar to that of

1.64 **Alice Leora Briggs**, *Ejecutado*, **2009.** Sgraffito drawing on panel, 15 × 24 in. (38.1 × 61 cm).
© Alice Leora Briggs. Courtesy of Davidson Galleries, Seattle, WA

1.65 **Kevin G. Fletcher**, *Leaving Wittenberg by Afternoon Train*, 2009. Monotype, 9¼ × 11¾ in. (23.5 × 29.8 cm).
© Kevin G. Fletcher. Courtesy of Davidson Galleries, Seattle, WA

1.66 From shape to volume through use of value.

1.67 Jan van Eyck, *Ghent Altarpiece* (closed), **completed 1432.** Oil on panel, approx. 11 ft 6 in. × 7 ft 7 in. (3.5 × 2.33 m).
© Lukas—Art in Flanders VZW/Hugo Maertens/The Bridgeman Art Library, New York

Ejecutado. The composition is divided down the center by an architectural beam, and other architectural details frame the left and right sides. Train tracks lead us into the background. However, in this image we move from a dark foreground to a brightly lit background. Rather than being trapped in a tragedy, we are liberated by the journey ahead of us.

Value and Volume

When we use a full range of values, a two-dimensional shape can appear three-dimensional, or **volumetric**. Figure 1.66 shows the transformation of a circle into a sphere. We begin with a simple outline, then add the **attached shadows**, or values that directly define the basic form. The addition of a **cast shadow** in the third image grounds the sphere. In the fourth drawing, the separation between the shadow and the sphere creates a floating effect.

This transformation of shapes through value is so convincing that objects can appear to extend out from a two-dimensional surface. The earliest oil painters often used **grisaille**, or a gray underpainting, to create the illusion of three-dimensionality. They then added color, using transparent glazes or layers of paint. A detail from Jan van Eyck's *Ghent Altarpiece* (1.67) shows both the grisaille painting and the full-color painting. Van Eyck painted the two statues in the center using a range of grays and then added color to the kneeling figures on the right and left. Variations in value give all the figures a remarkable dimensionality.

1.68 Thomas Moran, *Noon-Day Rest in Marble Canyon*, from *Exploration of the Colorado River of the West*, by J. W. Powell, 1875. Wood engraving after an original sketch by Thomas Moran, 6½ × 4⅜ in. (16.5 × 11 cm).
Courtesy of History Colorado, ID#10027120

Value and Space

When combined in a composition, very dark, crisp shapes tend to advance spatially, and gray, blurry shapes tend to recede. For example, in Thomas Moran's *Noon-Day Rest in Marble Canyon* (1.68), the dark values in the foreground gradually fade until the cliffs in the background become gray and indistinct. This effect, called **atmospheric perspective**, is one of the simplest ways to create the illusion of space.

Chiaroscuro (literally, "light-dark") is another way to create the illusion of space. A primary light source is used to create six or more values. A dark background is added to increase contrast. In *Judith and Her Maidservant with the Head of Holofernes* by Artemisia Gentileschi (1.69), the highlighted areas are clearly delineated, whereas darker areas seem to dissolve into the background. The resulting image is as dramatic as a theatrical stage.

Value and Lighting

Filmmakers and set designers are especially aware of the expressive uses of value. Working with a wide range of lights, including sharply defined spotlights and more diffused floodlights, they can increase or decrease the illusion of space, emphasize an object or an action, and influence our emotional response to a character.

Figure 1.70 shows four common forms of lighting. As described by Herbert Zettl in *Sight, Sound, Motion: Applied Media Aesthetics* (2004), a key light is the primary source of illumination. Placing this light at a 45-degree angle can enhance the illusion of space. Addition of a backlight separates the actor from the background and adds definition. When a fill light is added, the contrast between light and dark becomes less harsh, and the actor may appear less formidable. In theatrical performances, lighting designers often use powerful side lighting to increase drama while enhancing dimensionality.

Director Michael Curtiz used all these aspects of lighting expressively in the 1942 American classic film *Casablanca*. The lighting is fairly dark when we first enter Rick's Café Américain, the saloon where most of the action occurs. In this dark and mysterious place, a man will be shot, a seduction will be thwarted, and a romance will be rekindled.

The piano player, Sam, and the audience members closest to the stage are brightly lit as he sings an optimistic song (1.71A). The two villains in the film, Major Strasser and Captain Renault, are

1.69 Artemisia Gentileschi, *Judith and Her Maidservant with the Head of Holofernes,* **c. 1625.** Oil on canvas, 72½ × 54¾ in. (1.84 × 1.42 m).
Gift of Mr. Leslie H. Green. Photograph © The Detroit Institute of Arts/The Bridgeman Art Library

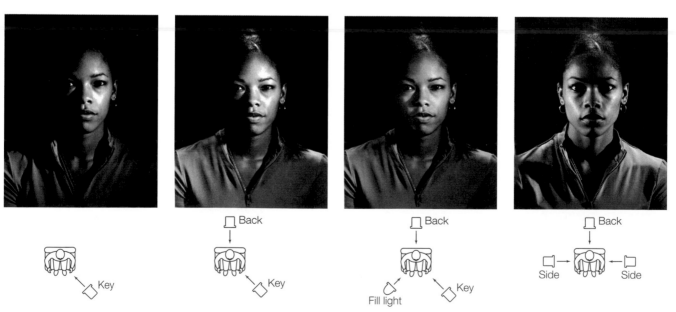

1.70 John Veltri, Lighting Techniques, from *Sight, Sound, Motion: Applied Media Aesthetics* by Herbert Zettl, 3rd ed., 1999.
© John Veltri, EarthAlive Communications

1.71A *Casablanca* **still.** Sam and Rick in the bar.
Pictorial Press/Alamy Stock Photo

1.71B *Casablanca* **still.** Major Strasser and Captain Renault hatch a plot.
Collection Christophel/Alamy Stock Photo

1.71C *Casablanca* **still.** Ilsa tries to explain to Rick why she abandoned him in Paris.
Courtesy of Photofest

1.71D *Casablanca* **still.** Rick persuades Ilsa to escape with her husband.
United Archives GmbH/Alamy Stock Photo

often strongly side-lit (1.71B), which makes them appear more formidable and enhances the texture in their faces. By contrast, Curtiz used much softer light for the face of the heroine, Ilsa, who is emotionally and politically fragile.

Curtiz also used value and lighting to accentuate Ilsa's emotions throughout the film. When she tries to explain to Rick the reason she left him in Paris two years earlier, Ilsa wears a pure white dress and enters the darkened saloon like a virginal beam of light (1.71C). Later, when she visits Rick in his apartment, shadows cover her face, accentuating her conflicted emotions as she tries to decide whether to remain with her freedom-fighter husband, Victor, whom she idealizes, or return to Rick, whom she loves. In the final scene at the airport, diffused lighting again emphasizes Ilsa's vulnerability (1.71D). She and Victor disappear into the foggy night, escaping from Casablanca, while Rick and a reformed Captain Renault stroll away together to join the Foreign Legion.

▶ key questions

VALUE

- What is the advantage of a wide value range? What is the advantage of a narrow value range? Which works better in your design?

- What happens when you invert the values—that is, the black areas become white and the white areas become black?

- Would your design benefit from a stronger illusion of space? If so, how can you use value to accomplish this?

summary

- The elements of two-dimensional design are point, line, shape, texture, value, and color.

- A point is a basic mark, such as a dot, a pixel, or a brushstroke. A focal point is the primary point of interest in a composition, while an array is a collection of points.

- Lines can contain, define, dissect, and connect. You can create line networks using hatching, cross-hatching, and cross-contours.

- A shape is created whenever an area is enclosed. The figure is the primary shape, while the ground, or negative shape, provides the surrounding context.

- When figure and ground shapes are equally strong, figure/ground reversal can occur.

- There are many types of shape, including rectilinear, curvilinear, geometric, organic, representational, nonrepresentational, and abstract. When gradated, shapes can appear three-dimensional.

- The surface quality of a two-dimensional shape or a three-dimensional volume is called *texture*. We can create visual texture through multiple marks, and use variations in the surface to create physical texture.

- Relative lightness or darkness in an artwork is called *value*. We can use value to create the illusion of space, suggest volume, shift compositional balance, and heighten emotion.

key terms

actual line
array
atmospheric perspective
attached shadow
calligraphic line
cast shadow
chiaroscuro
closure
collage
continuity
contour line
cross-contour
cross-hatching
curvilinear shape
direction
elements
engraving
figure/ground reversal
focal point
geometric shape
gesture drawing
gradation (shading)
grisaille
hatching

implied line
invented texture
line
negative shape (ground)
organic shape
organizational line
orientation
physical texture
point
positive shape (figure)
rectilinear shape
shape
stippling
texture
trompe l'oeil
value
value contrast
value distribution
value scale
visual texture
volume
volume summary
volumetric

The Element
of Color

Color immediately attracts attention. When presented with a collection of bottles filled with liquid in various colors, very young children group the objects by color rather than by size or shape. Color has great emotional power, and designers carefully choose a color palette that supports the mood of each project. An interior designer may use rose-red walls in a restaurant to increase emotional warmth, while using light blue walls in a day-care center to encourage calm.

Selecting the right colors can make or break a design. To assist their clients in project planning, the Neenah paper company produced a witty and informative brochure describing the effects of color (2.1). The company gave each color a personality as distinctive as an astrological sign. It then organized the colors in a booklet, creating an easy-to-use index of possibilities.

Although systems of this kind provide a shortcut to basic decision making, in this chapter we will see that color is an especially complex element. It defies easy formulas. We consider relationships between color and light, describe three major characteristics of color, explore harmony and disharmony, and analyze uses of color in various compositional contexts.

2.1 Brochure for Neenah Papers, 2009

Courtesy of Neenah Papers and Partners Design. Color Attributes courtesy of Dewey Color System®, deweycolorsystem.com

COLOR PHYSICS

To use color fully, we must understand the major types of color, how they are created, and how they interact. **Color theory** is the art and science of color interaction and effects. In *The Art of Color*,[1] Johannes Itten lists the following approaches to color theory:

- The *physicist* studies electromagnetic wavelengths in order to measure and classify color.
- Working with the molecular structure of dyes and pigments, the *chemist* seeks to produce highly permanent colors and excellent paint consistency.
- The *physiologist* investigates the effects of color and light on our eyes and brain.
- The *psychologist* studies the expressive effects of color on our mind and spirit.

Additive and Subtractive Color

Two major color systems are used in art and design. Beams of light create **additive color** (2.2A). Red, green, and blue, the familiar RGB on a computer screen, are the primary colors in this system. **Subtractive color** is created when white light is reflected off a pigmented or dyed surface (2.2B).

As children, we are taught that blue, red, and yellow are the subtractive primaries. As artists and designers, we become more specific. Cyan blue, magenta red, and yellow are the **process colors** commonly used in digital printing and mass production. Figure 2.3 provides an example of process printing. As viewers, we optically combine thousands of cyan, magenta, and yellow dots to create a coherent image. Black (abbreviated as *K* in the CMYK printing system) is then added to enhance detail and increase contrast (2.4A–G).

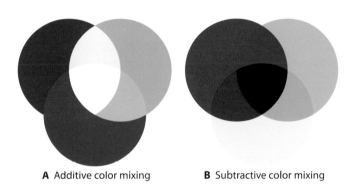

| **A** Additive color mixing | **B** Subtractive color mixing |

2.2A–B The two major color systems.

As artists and designers, we combine all these areas of knowledge. Like a physicist, we use color wavelengths to create visual effects. Like a chemist, we must be aware of the safety and permanence of dyes and pigments. We put into practice theories developed by physiologists, and our communication and expression are strongly affected by the psychological impact of color.

2.3 Color printing detail of *Wheel of Fortune*, showing dot pattern used in CMYK printing.
© Audrey Flack. Courtesy of Louis K. Meisel Gallery, New York

| **A** Yellow | **B** Magenta | **C** Yellow and magenta | **D** Cyan | **E** Yellow, magenta and cyan | **F** Black | **G** Full color |

2.4A–G Color separation in CMYK printing. Dots of yellow, magenta, cyan, and black are layered to create a full-color image.
© Audrey Flack. Courtesy of Louis K. Meisel Gallery, New York

1. Johannes Itten, *The Art of Color* (New York: Van Nostrand Reinhold, 1974), p. 16

Color and Light

These two systems exist because of the inseparable connection between color and light. When white light passes through a prism, it is refracted, or bent. This creates a wide spectrum of hues, which is dominated by red, orange, yellow, green, blue, blue-violet, and violet (figure 2.5). We define each hue, or separate color, by a specific electromagnetic wavelength. Red is the longest and violet the shortest. When white light hits a colored surface, some wavelengths are reflected, while other wavelengths are absorbed. As figure 2.6A shows, a red surface reflects the red wavelengths while absorbing the blue and green wavelengths. Similarly, a green surface reflects the green wavelengths while absorbing the red and blue (2.6B). All wavelengths are reflected off a white surface (2.6C); all wavelengths are absorbed by a black surface (2.6D). Color reflection and absorption are rarely total. As a result, we can often see hints of various colors within a dominant color.

Using Additive Color

Lighting designers, videographers, and website artists use additive color extensively. They use beams of red, green, and blue light to create a full-color video projection. The mixture of adjacent beams creates cyan, magenta, and yellow, which are the *secondary* colors in the additive system. When all three beams are combined, white light results.

We can quickly and easily create variations in additive color on a computer. In figure 2.7, the current color choice is shown in the center. Variations appear in the eight surrounding squares. Even a 10 percent increase in a given color produces a very different result.

Our perception of additive color is influenced by the following:

- The intensity (or wattage) of the projected light.
- The light source. Incandescent light tends to be warmer than bluish fluorescent light. Daylight provides the richest color balance.
- The surface quality of the illuminated object. Projected light behaves very differently on transparent, translucent, and textured surfaces.
- The overall amount of light in the environment. Even a dimly lit object will appear to glow if you place it in a very dark room.

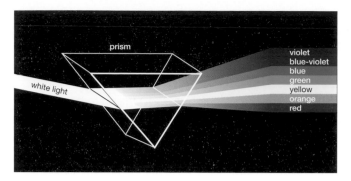

2.5 When white light passes through a prism, the spectrum becomes visible.

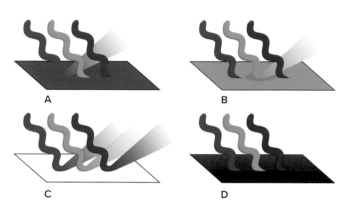

2.6A–D We see color when the additive primaries are reflected off a colored surface. A red surface absorbs the green and blue wavelengths, while reflecting the red. All wavelengths are reflected by a white surface. All wavelengths are absorbed by a black surface.

2.7 Color variations using a computer.
© Audrey Flack. Courtesy of Louis K. Meisel Gallery, New York

Using Subtractive Color

Painters, printmakers, and illustrators use subtractive color in various forms, including acrylics, oils, pastels, and inks. Each pigment or dye used in the manufacture of such materials is chemically unique. Quinacridone red and pthalocyanide blue are transparent and intense. The cadmiums and earth colors are generally opaque. **Color overtones** complicate matters further. Color theorist David Hornung defines an overtone as "a secondary hue bias in a primary color." For example, alizarin crimson is a red with violet overtones, while cadmium red has orange overtones. To create a wider range of mixtures, artists and designers often use a six-hue palette, including two reds, two yellows, and two blues, plus black and white. Black and white have no hue and are defined as **achromatic**.

Color Interaction

Color interaction refers to the way colors influence one another. We never see colors in isolation. The blue sheets of paper that we examine in an art supply store may remind us of the blue of the sky, the ocean, or the clothing worn by our favorite sports team. Lighting also affects our perceptions. Incandescent light creates a warm orange glow, and standard fluorescent lights produce a bluish ambience.

When we add our blue paper to a design, it is profoundly affected by the surrounding colors. **Simultaneous contrast** refers to this apparent change in a color when it is paired with another color. Figure 2.8A–C shows three principles of simultaneous contrast. The first pair of images shows a light/dark contrast. A blue-green square appears much lighter when it is placed on a black background. The second pair shows a complementary reaction. The same blue-green square appears to glow when it is surrounded by red rather than a neutral gray. In the third pair, the same blue-green square appears almost green when it is surrounded by solid blue, yet it appears almost blue when surrounded by green.

Color interaction becomes especially dramatic when we use complementary colors, such as red-orange and blue-green, in a composition. In the human eye, two types of cells, known as rods and cones, are arranged in layers on the retina. These cells serve as photoreceptors. The rods record lightness and darkness, while the cones distinguish the hues, such as red and blue. According to **opponent theory**, the

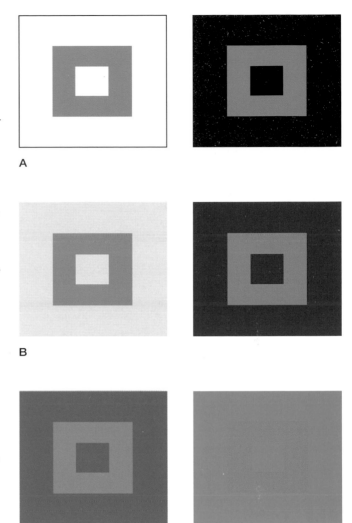

2.8A–C Examples of simultaneous contrast. Light/dark contrast is shown in A, a complementary reaction is shown in B, and subtle variations are shown in C. The blue-green square is the same color in all examples but appears different because of the surrounding colors.

cones can register only one color in a complementary pair at a time. Constant shifting between the opposing colors creates a visual overload at the edges of the shapes, resulting in an electric glow. In *Inner Lhamo Waterfall* (2.9), Pat Steir used this effect to suggest the majesty and mystery of the falling water.

We can use a similar characteristic of human vision to create an **afterimage**. If we stare at a red square for 20 seconds (2.10) and then stare at a white sheet of paper, a blue or green shape will seem to appear. This is caused by fatigue in the cones, the color sensors in our eyes. Overloaded by the intense red, our eyes revert to the blue and green cones, creating the afterimage.

2.9 Pat Steir, *Inner Lhamo Waterfall*, 1992. Oil on canvas,
114 × 90¼ in. (289.6 × 229.2 cm).
© Pat Steir. Courtesy of Cheim & Read, New York

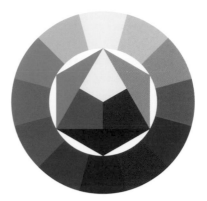

2.11 The 12-step Itten color wheel.

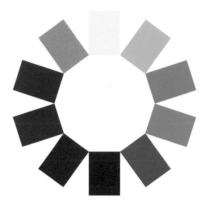

2.12 The 10-step Munsell color wheel.

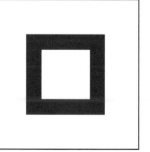

2.10 Afterimage exercise. Stare at the red square in the white box on the
left for 20 seconds, then stare at the white box on the right, and a blue or
green version of the red square from the left will seem to appear.
© Munsell Color

DEFINING COLOR

Hue

The **hue**, or name, of a color is determined by its
wavelength. For example, red, blue, green, and yellow
are all hues.

Physicists, painters, and philosophers have devised
numerous systems to organize hues. Johannes Itten's
12-step color wheel (2.11) is a clear and simple example. Cyan, magenta red, and yellow **primary colors**
are in the center. We can mix these colors to produce
many other colors. The **secondary colors** of green,

orange, and violet follow. These colors are mixed from
adjacent primaries. A circular spectrum of **tertiary
colors** completes the wheel. The mixture of a secondary color and the adjacent primary color creates a tertiary color.

The 10-step Munsell color wheel (2.12) provides
a more nuanced organizational structure, and the
three-dimensional Munsell color tree (2.13) provides
examples of changes in color value and intensity as
well as hue.

Artists often use a wide range of hues to capture
the richness of reality. In *Wheel of Fortune* (2.14),

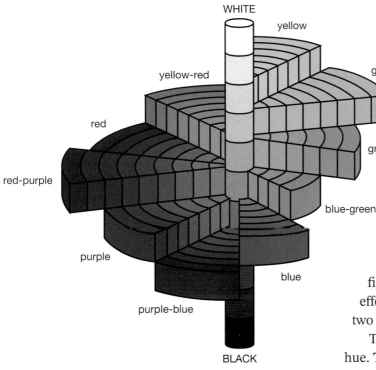

WHITE

yellow

yellow-red

green-yellow

red

green

red-purple

blue-green

purple

blue

purple-blue

BLACK

2.13 Munsell color tree diagram.

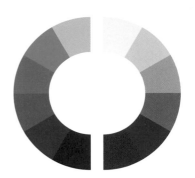

2.15 Separation of the color wheel by temperature.

Audrey Flack used a full spectrum of hues to define a collection of symbolic objects in meticulous detail. The makeup and mirrors symbolize vanity; the candles, hourglass, and skull suggest the passage of time; the grapes suggest passion. Cyan, magenta, and yellow

dominate the painting. Hints of orange, violet, and green complete the spectrum.

As demonstrated by Pat Steir's *Waterfall* (see figure 2.9), a limited range of hues can be equally effective. In this painting, interaction between just two hues creates an electric visual impact.

Temperature is an especially important aspect of hue. **Temperature** refers to the psychological heat a color generates. Figure 2.15 shows a simple division of the color wheel by temperature.

Color temperature can help to create the illusion of space. Under most circumstances, warm colors advance and cool colors recede. Kenneth Noland's *A Warm Sound in a Gray Field* (2.16) clearly demonstrates this effect. The red ring with its light yellow halo pushes toward us, while the blue-black circle

2.14 Audrey Flack, *Wheel of Fortune*, **1977–78.** Oil over acrylic on canvas, 8 × 8 ft. (2.44 × 2.44 m).
© Audrey Flack. Courtesy of Louis K. Meisel Gallery, New York

2.16 Kenneth Noland, *A Warm Sound in a Gray Field*, **1961.** Oil on canvas, 6 ft 10½ in. × 6 ft 9 in. (210 × 206 cm).
Art © Kenneth Noland/Licensed by VAGA, New York

2.17 Page from the *Book of Kells*, late 8th century. Illuminated manuscript, 13 × 8¾ in. (33 × 25 cm).
Print collector/Getty Images

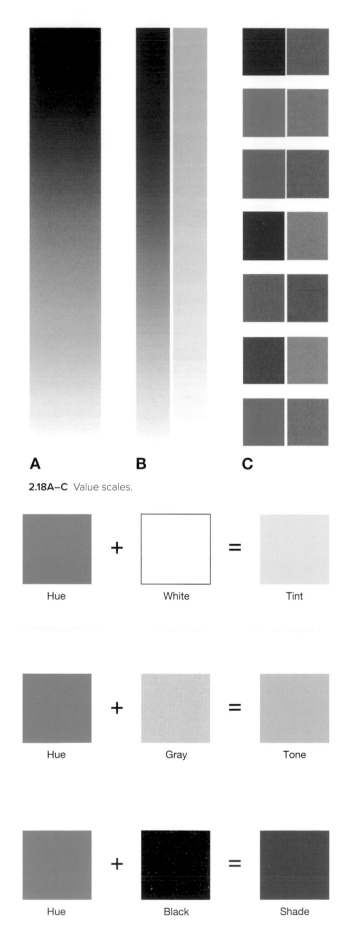

2.18A–C Value scales.

pulls us inward. The small red dot in the center of the composition further activates the void by creating another advancing shape. Temperature can also be used to create a strong emotional effect. In figure 2.17, the glowing colors create a radiant representation of the Christian gospel of Saint Luke.

Value

Value refers to the relative lightness or darkness of a color. By removing hue from the equation, we can create a simple value scale (figure 2.18A) that shifts from white to black through a series of grays. Figure 2.18B shows that hues such as violet, blue, and green are inherently darker in value than are pure yellow or orange. Figure 2.18C shows a translation of color into value. Despite the variety of hues, all the colors shown have nearly the same value.

Figure 2.19 shows three basic variations in value. When we add white to a hue, the resulting **tint** will be lighter in value. The addition of gray produces a **tone**.

Hue   +   White   =   Tint

Hue   +   Gray   =   Tone

Hue   +   Black   =   Shade

2.19 Tint, tone, and shade.

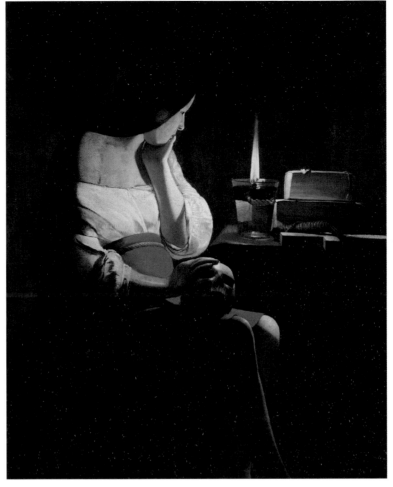

2.20 Georges de La Tour, *Mary Magdalene with the Smoking Flame*, 1630–35. Oil on canvas, 46⅟₁₆ × 36⅛ in. (117 × 91.76 cm).
Louvre, Paris, France/Giraudon/The Bridgeman Art Library

The addition of black creates a darker **shade**. One of the simplest ways to unify a design is to limit the colors that we use to the tints, tones, and shades of a single hue.

A full range of values can create a very convincing representation of reality. Using value, Georges de La Tour made *Mary Magdalene with the Smoking Flame* (figure 2.20) photographically realistic and emotionally powerful. The contemplative woman, a close companion of the Christian Jesus, looks at a burning candle and holds a skull, both symbols of death. Gradation in value makes all the forms seem rounded and three-dimensional.

Garo Antreasian's *Untitled* (2.21) combines strong value contrast in the dominant X shape, with low value contrast in the other diagonals. The complementary blue-violet and yellow-orange color scheme helps to unify the image, while gradation in all shapes add subtlety. Beyond the large X at the center of the

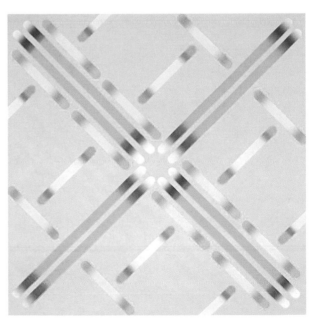

2.21 Garo Antreasian, *Untitled C.P. 236, 16/60*, 1970. Color lithograph, 24 × 24 in. (61 × 61 cm).
© 2017 Garo Antreasian, courtesy of Gerald Peters Gallery

design, the secondary diagonals almost dissolve into the background due to the reduced contrast.

By making a black-and-white photocopy or changing a digital image to grayscale, we can easily check the range of values in a design. The image will remain quite readable when the value range is broad. When we use a very narrow range of values, the photocopy or grayscale image will lose definition—and thus may lose visual impact.

Value is the dominant force in some paintings, while hue is a dominant force in others. Each approach has a distinctive emotional effect. Romaine Brooks's *Self-Portrait* (figure 2.22) is essentially a value painting. Blacks, whites, and grays dominate the image. The woman's eyes are concealed by the brim of her hat and the shadow it casts. Patches of red on her

2.23 Henri Matisse, *Green Stripe (Madame Matisse)*, **1905.** Oil on canvas, 16 × 12¾ in. (40.6 × 32.4 cm).
© 2017 Succession H. Matisse / Artists Rights Society (ARS), New York / Statens Museum for Kunst, Denmark

lips and coat add just a touch of color. She is wary and reserved. Value, rather than hue, is the appropriate choice for this image.

In contrast, hue dominates Henri Matisse's *Green Stripe* (2.23). Surrounded by large blocks of red, green, and violet, the woman seems bold and self-confident. The avocado-green dividing line separates blocks of pink on the right and lime green on the left half of her face, suggesting warmer and cooler aspects of her personality. Even her eyes and hair are painted in blue-black, adding yet more color to this expressive portrait.

Intensity

Intensity, **saturation**, and **chroma** all refer to the purity of a color. The primary colors are the most intense. Intensity generally diminishes when colors are mixed.

Figure 2.24A–C presents three intensity scales. Column A shows the most intense primary, secondary, and tertiary colors. Column B demonstrates the loss of intensity when we add black to a single color. The vibrant red at the top diminishes to a chocolate brown

2.22 Romaine Brooks, *Self-Portrait*, **1923.** Oil on canvas, 46¼ × 26⅞ in. (117.5 × 68.3 cm).
Smithsonian American Art Museum, Washington, DC/Art Resource, New York

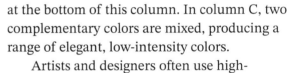

2.24A–C Intensity scales. The most intense primaries, secondaries, and tertiaries are shown in A. The addition of black reduces the intensity of the color red in B. Mixing the complements yellow and violet creates low-intensity colors in C.

A   B   C

at the bottom of this column. In column C, two complementary colors are mixed, producing a range of elegant, low-intensity colors.

Artists and designers often use high-intensity colors to maximize impact. In *Daphne II* (2.25), Cat Crotchett juxtaposed rich violet with glowing yellows and oranges to capture a moment of dramatic transformation. In a Greek myth, Daphne begs to escape capture by the god Apollo, and is turned into a bay laurel tree. Crotchett used encaustic, a paint made of colored wax, to make the hues even more brilliant.

2.25 Cat Crotchett, *Daphne II* (after *Apollo and Daphne* by Gian Lorenzo Bernini), 2004. Encaustic on canvas, 32 × 23⅞ in. (81.3 × 60.6 cm).
© Cat Crotchett. Photograph by Mary Whalen

2.26 Samantha Fields, *Nocturne #2: Overpass*, 2012. Acrylic on canvas on panel, 48 × 48 in. (121.9 × 121.9 cm).
© Samantha Fields. Courtesy of Western Project

Low-intensity colors can be equally effective. In figure 2.26, Samantha Fields combined grays, tans, and subdued violets to create a glowing representation of car headlights at night.

▶ key questions

DEFINING COLOR

- Which will work better in your design, a limited or a wide range of hues?

- What proportion of warm and cool colors best communicates your idea?

- What happens when you combine low-intensity colors with high-intensity colors?

HARMONY AND DISHARMONY

Relationships among colors are critical to the success or failure of a design, and many theories of **color harmony** help artists, architects, and designers to make good choices. A basic color wheel can illustrate five common approaches.

Monochromatic Color Schemes

Variations on a single hue are used in a **monochromatic** color scheme (2.27). The advantage of this system is a high level of unity: all the colors are strongly related. Boredom, caused by the lack of variety, is a potential hazard. Mark Tansey's masterful *Discarding the Frame* (2.28) is almost entirely composed of variations of blue. The mysterious activity depicted, combined with the monochromatic color,

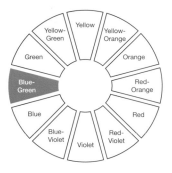

2.27 Monochromatic color system.

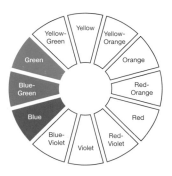

2.29 Analogous color system.

2.28 Mark Tansey, *Discarding the Frame*, 1993. Oil on canvas, 84 × 74½ in. (213.4 × 189.2 cm).
© Mark Tansey. Courtesy of Gagosian Gallery

2.30 *Chromatics Place Settings*, 1970.
Gerald Gulotta, shape designer; Jack Prince, pattern designer. Porcelain, linen, and stainless steel, dimensions variable.
Gerald Gulotta, Jack Prince, Arzberg, Porzellanfabrik. Block China Company, American, founded 1963. Porcelain, printed. Dallas Museum of Art, gift of Gerald Gulotta

raises questions rather than provides answers. Who are these men, and why are they hurling a large picture frame into the abyss? As we will see in Chapter Eight, highly realistic images often evoke metaphors, creating new and complex ideas.

Analogous Color Schemes

Adjacent colors on the color wheel are used in an **analogous** color scheme (2.29). As with monochromatic harmony, a high degree of unity is ensured, but

the wider range of hues offers greater variety and can increase interest. *Chromatics Place Settings*, shown in figure 2.30, is activated by a surprising variety of blues and greens.

Complementary Color Schemes

The palette dramatically expands in a **complementary** color scheme (2.31). Complementary colors are opposites on the traditional color wheel. When mixed together, they can lower intensity and produce a wide range of browns. When paired in a composition, complementary colors can become powerful partners. Each increases the impact of the other.

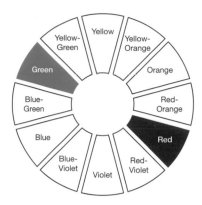

2.31 Complementary color system.

Francis Bacon's *Four Studies for a Self-Portrait* (2.32) is dominated by the complements red and green. The design is unified by browns, including the reddish brown filling the background. Vigorous slashes of pure green and red add visual energy and create the illusion of movement.

Chris Kienke used orange and pink to complement blue and green in *From the Hip* (2.33). Combining digital information with traditional painting, he created this image from subtle vertical lines, photographically realistic shapes, and fragmentary squares and rectangles. The blues and greens that dominate the composition heighten the power of the oranges and pinks we see in the shooter's hand.

Each complementary pair has its own distinctive strengths. Violet and yellow provide the widest value range, and orange and blue provide the widest range of variation in temperature. Red and green are closest in value and create extreme agitation when placed side by side. By mixing two complements plus black and white, we can create a range of colors that begins to suggest the power of a full spectrum.

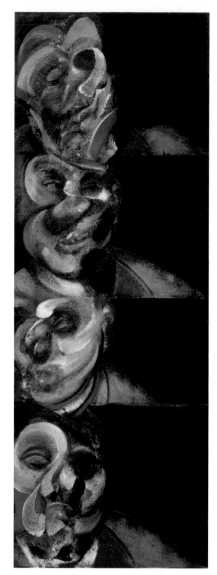

2.32 Francis Bacon, *Four Studies for a Self-Portrait*, 1967. Oil on canvas, 36 × 13 in. (91.5 × 33 cm).

2.33 Chris Kienke, *From the Hip*, 2013. Oil and digital pigment on canvas, 82 × 38 in. (208 × 97 cm).

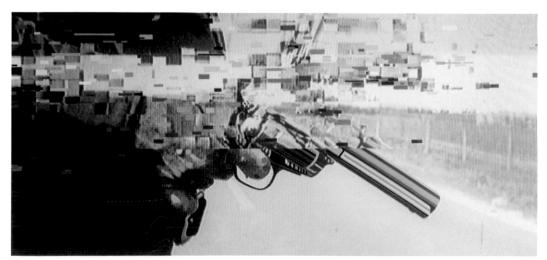

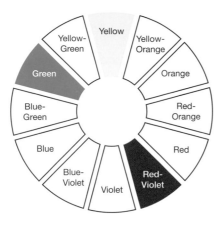

2.34 Split complementary color system.

Split Complementary Color Schemes

An even wider range of possibilities is offered by the **split complementary** color scheme (2.34). Rather than pair colors that are in opposite positions on the color wheel, the artist completes the scheme using the two colors on either side of one of the complements. Georgia O'Keeffe's *Jack in the Pulpit No. V* (2.35) is dominated by rich greens and violets, with accents of yellow at the top of the composition, and a vertical line of red just to the left of the center.

Triadic Color Schemes

The **triadic** color scheme pushes the choices even farther apart, so that they are now in a triangular position, equally spaced around the wheel (2.36). Artists and designers often use this scheme when variety and strong impact are needed. In a brochure for a UCLA Extension Open House (2.37), variations on yellow-green, red-orange, and blue-violet bring energy to the design, while the white areas provide openness.

2.36 Triadic color system.

2.35 Georgia O'Keeffe, *Jack in the Pulpit No. V*, **1930.** Oil on canvas, 48 × 30 in. (122 × 76 cm). Image courtesy of the Board of Trustees, The National Gallery of Art, Washington. Alfred Stieglitz Collection, Bequest of Georgia O'Keeffe. © 2014 Georgia O'Keeffe Museum

2.37 Tin Yen Studios, *UCLA Extension Open House,* **2013.**
Courtesy of TYS Creative

Chromatic Grays and Earth Colors

Although the basic color wheel can help us to identify many kinds of relationship, two important types of color are generally not included: chromatic grays and earth colors. A **chromatic gray** is made from a mixture of various hues, rather than a simple blend of black and white. The result is both subtle and vibrant. In *The Magpie* (2.38), the grays vary widely, from the purples and blue-grays in the shadows, to the golden-gray light in the foreground and the silvery grays for the snow-covered trees. This is not a dark, sullen winter day. Through the use of chromatic grays, Claude Monet made the warm light and transparent shadows sparkle in the crisp air.

Earth colors, including raw and burnt sienna, raw and burnt umber, and yellow ochre, are made generally from pigments found in soil. Often warm in temperature, when used together they create a kind of analogous harmony. For example, browns, oranges, and tans accentuate the gestural energy and organic shapes in *Bush Cabbage Dreaming at Ngarlu* (2.39) by Australian artist Paddy Japaljarri Stewart. This acrylic painting was inspired by traditional Aboriginal artworks, which are literally made from earth colors. The dark blue-greens in the background act as an elegant complement to the earth colors.

When used alone, earth colors can unify even the most agitated composition. When used in combination with high-intensity colors, they can provide an elegant balance between subdued and louder, more overt colors.

Using Disharmony

Selecting the right colors can make the difference between a visual disaster and a visual delight. As a result, color harmony is the subject of endless books

2.38 Claude Monet, *The Magpie*, **1869.** Oil on canvas, 35 × 51 in. (89 × 130 cm). Musée d'Orsay, Paris. PAINTING/Alamy Stock Photo

2.39 Paddy Japaljarri Stewart, *Bush Cabbage Dreaming at Ngarlu;* Yuendumn, Central Australia, **1986.** Acrylic on canvas, 47½ × 93½ in. (120.5 × 237.5 cm).
South Australian Museum. © 2017 Artists Rights Society (ARS), New York/ VISCOPY, Australia

offering advice to artists, architects, and surface pattern designers. As noted previously, monochromatic, analogous, complementary, split complementary, and triadic systems are traditional forms of color harmony.

However, cultural definitions of harmony are as changeable as popular music. In a search for eye-catching images, designers in all fields invent new color combinations each year. For example, the pink, gray, and black prized by fashion designers in one year may seem passé in the next. Consequently, definitions and uses of color harmony are quite fluid.

Furthermore, when skillfully used, color **disharmony** can be as effective as color harmony. Artists and designers often use disharmony when the subject matter is disturbing or when they require an unusual visual approach. In figure 2.40, Francis Bacon used tans, grays, pinks, yellow, orange, and blacks to produce a painting that is as disturbing as it is beautiful. The colors in the body suggest disease, while the areas of black, yellow, and gray create a room that is agitated and disorienting. Using similar pinks, gray, black, and yellow-orange, Steve Quinn created a gentle evocation

2.40 Francis Bacon, *Three Figures and Portrait*, **1975.**
Oil and pastel on canvas, 78 × 58 in. (198 × 147.5 cm).
© Estate of Francis Bacon. All rights reserved. ARS,
New York/DACS, London, 2017. Photo: Prudence Cuming Associates, Ltd

2.41 Steve Quinn, *A Christmas Memory,* **1991.**
Photoshop, 17 × 11 in. (43.2 × 27.9 cm).
Courtesy of Steve Quinn

2.42 Guerrilla Girls, *Do women have to be naked to get into the Met. Museum? Less than 5% of the artists in the Modern Art sections are women, but 85% of the nudes are female,* **1989.**
Poster, 11 × 28 in. (27.9 × 71.1 cm).
© Guerrilla Girls. Courtesy www.guerrillagirls.com

of memory in his Christmas poster (2.41). Here, the words and images shift back and forth in space, as fluid as a dream.

Figure 2.42 shows a third example. Bright yellow and hot pink add pizzazz to an eye-catching poster. Designed to call attention to a disparity in the number of exhibitions granted to male and female artists, this poster had to compete with other information displayed on walls around New York City. A witty image combined with jarring colors was just right in this case.

As these examples demonstrate, the degree and type of harmony that the artist uses must depend on the ideas behind the image and on the visual context in which an image will appear.

▶ # key questions

HARMONY AND DISHARMONY

- What are the advantages of each of the traditional color schemes?

- When we use a limited palette, how can a few colors produce the greatest impact? When we use a full palette, how can the colors become harmonized?

- What happens when your composition is dominated by earth colors or chromatic grays? How does it change when you add an intense color?

- Which is more suitable for the idea you want to express: traditional color harmony or some form of disharmony?

COMPOSING WITH COLOR

Composition may be defined as the combination of multiple parts into a harmonious whole. The effect of color on composition is profound. Color can shift visual balance, create a focal point, influence our emotions, and expand communication. In this section, we will consider four major compositional uses of color.

Creating the Illusion of Space

Pictorial space is like a balloon. When we "push" in on one side, the other side appears to bulge outward. Through our color choices, we can cause various areas in a composition to expand or contract visually. In most cases, cool, low-intensity colors tend to recede, while warm, high-intensity colors tend to advance. In Wolf Kahn's *The Yellow Square* (2.43), the greens and violets defining the exterior of the barn gently pull the viewer into the painting, while the blazing yellow window inside the barn pushes out as forcefully as the beacon in a lighthouse.

This effect can play an even more important role in nonobjective paintings. As described by painter Hans Hofmann, the "push and pull" of color can be a major source of energy in a nonobjective composition. For example, in Hofmann's *Sun at the Wall* (2.44), two

2.44 Hans Hofmann, *Sun at the Wall*, 1962. Oil on canvas, 48 × 36¼ in. (121.9 × 92.1 cm).
With permission of the Renate, Hans & Maria Hofmann Trust/Artists Rights Society (ARS), New York © Christie's Images/Bridgeman Images

2.43 Wolf Kahn, *The Yellow Square*, 1981. Oil on canvas, 44 × 72 in. (112 × 183 cm).
Art © Wolf Kahn/Licensed by VAGA, New York

2.45 Henri Matisse, *Icarus*, maquette for plate VIII from *Jazz*, **1946.** Gouache on paper, cut and pasted, mounted on canvas, 17¹/₁₆ × 13⁷/₁₆ in. (43.4 × 34.1 cm).
Photo: Philippe Migeat. Location: Musee National d'Art Moderne, Centre Georges Pompidou, Paris, France © CNAC/MNAM/Dist. RMN-Grand Palais / Art Resource, NY © 2017 Succession H. Matisse / Artists Rights Society (ARS), New York

large red rectangles and four yellow shapes frame the blue and green shapes near the center. As cool colors, the blue and green shapes "should" recede. However, their placement near the center of the design and the ambiguity of their spatial location give us pause. The blue and green shapes appear to overlap the red rectangle at the bottom, suggesting that they are on top spatially. As a result, the entire composition bounces back and forth, pulsating with unexpected energy.

Weight and Balance

The effect of color on visual weight and balance is equally dramatic. In *Icarus* (2.45), Henri Matisse visually tells the story of the boy who flew too close to the sun, melting his wax wings and plunging into the ocean. The heavy black body "falls" into the blue background, while a vibrant red heart seems to pull the figure upward, away from death. Six bursts of yellow surround the figure. Equally suggestive of the stars above the boy and of light shimmering on the water below, these simple shapes add energy to the composition, and meaning to the myth.

Distribution and Proportion

Through careful distribution, even the most disharmonious colors can work together beautifully. Four rectilinear gray shapes dominate Nancy Crow's *Double Mexican Wedding Rings 1* (2.46). Gradated values extend outward, creating a subtle glow. Four small multicolored squares accentuate the edges of the four large squares, and eight colorful rectangles frame up the composition as a whole. In most compositions, the earth colors, chromatic grays, and high-intensity reds, blues, and yellows would clash. In this work, an even distribution of colors creates a unified composition.

Color as Emphasis

Graphic designers often use color to emphasize critical information in a composition. The subway map in figure 2.47 provides a good example. Cooler areas of gray, green, and blue, placed on a black background, provide

2.46 Nancy Crow, *Double Mexican Wedding Rings 1*, **1990.** Hand-quilted by Marie Moore. 72 × 72 in. (183 × 183 cm).
© Nancy Crow. Photograph by J. Kevin Fitzsimons

2.47 Louis Nelson Associates, PATH Station Maps, 1993.
Graphic designer: Jennifer Stoller.
© Louis Nelson Associates for the Port Authority of New York & New Jersey

2.49 Vernon Fisher, *Objects in a Field*, 1986.
Acrylic on canvas, 8 × 8 ft (2.4 × 2.4 m).
© Vernon Fisher. Collection of Michael Krichman

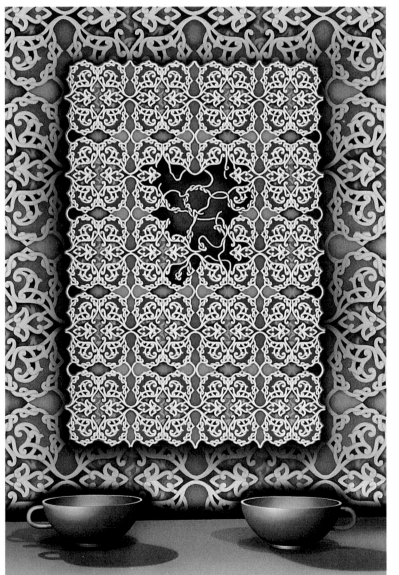

basic structural information. The bright yellow lines show the path through the subway. Red, which is used at only one point in the diagram, clearly locates the viewer on the map.

Simply combining vibrant color with grayscale is another way to emphasize a shape within the composition. In figure 2.48, Janet Ballweg combined a pattern dominated by tans and oranges with a surrounding pattern of grayish green. Two beautifully rendered cups are symmetrically balanced in the foreground. Just as a flawed human relationship may appear perfect, so this harmonious domestic scene is punctured in the center by the unraveling pattern.

Indeed, color is often used to create a very explicit focal point. A small red astronomical observatory dominates Vernon Fisher's *Objects in a Field* (2.49). Located just above the center of the painting, it commands our attention while echoing the curved shape of the white parachute in the foreground.

2.48 Janet Ballweg, *Frayed*, 2012. Lithograph, 25 × 16¾ in. (63.5 × 42.5 cm).
© Janet Ballweg

key questions

COMPOSING WITH COLOR

- How much space do you need in your composition, and how can color increase the illusion of space?

- How "heavy" is each of your colors? How does weight affect balance?

- Can color proportion or distribution shift, enhance, or unify your overall composition?

- Can color add emphasis to your design?

EMOTION AND EXPRESSION

Colors are never emotionally neutral. In Andrew Wyeth's *Wind from the Sea* (2.50), subtle browns and greens suggest the faded color of a nineteenth-century photograph. They evoke the slow pace and serenity of a countryside at rest. Richard Diebenkorn's *Interior with Book* (2.51), painted just 12 years later, provides a very different interpretation of a similar interior scene. The intense yellows and oranges in the background push toward us, while the solid blocks of blue pull inward, flattening the image. The tension and power thus generated create a California landscape that is a world apart from Wyeth's New England. The color in Sandy Skoglund's *Radioactive Cats* (2.52) creates yet another interpretation of an interior space. The gray walls, furniture, and clothing suggest a world that is lifeless and coated in ash. In contrast, the lime-green cats glow with an inquisitive energy that may be toxic!

2.50 Andrew Wyeth, *Wind from the Sea*, 1947. Tempera on hardboard, 18½ × 27½ in. (47 × 69.9 cm).
© Andrew Wyeth, National Gallery of Art, Gift of Charles H. Morgan, 2009.13.1

2.51 Richard Diebenkorn, *Interior with Book*, 1959. Oil on canvas,
70 × 64 in. (178 × 163 cm).
© The Estate of Richard Diebenkorn. The Nelson-Atkins Museum of Art, Kansas City, MO.
Gift of the Friends of Art, F63-15. Photograph by E. G. Schempf

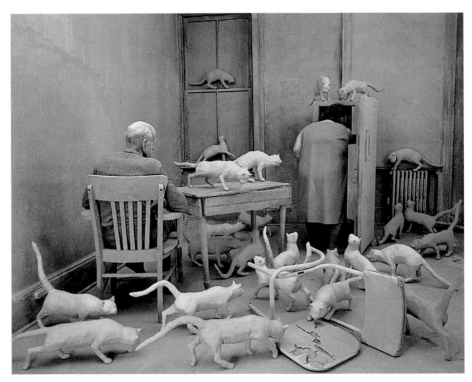

2.52 Sandy Skoglund, *Radioactive Cats*, 1980. Cibachrome print, 30 × 40 in. (76.2 × 101.6 cm).
© 1980 Sandy Skoglund

2.53 Joseph Spadaford, *Illustrated Man*, 1998. Acrylic, 10 × 8 in. (25.4 × 20.3 cm).
© Joe Spadaford

2.56 Chaz Maviyane-Davies, *Our Fear Is Their Best Weapon*, 2002. Offset poster.
© Chaz Maviyane-Davies

2.54 Egon Schiele, *Portrait of Paris von Gütersloh*, 1918. Oil on canvas, 55¼ × 43¼ in. (140.3 × 109.8 cm).
Gift of the P. D. McMillan Land Company, the Minneapolis Institute of Arts/ The Bridgeman Art Library

Color Keys

A dominant color, or **color key**, can heighten psychological as well as compositional impact. The blues that dominate Joseph Spadaford's *Illustrated Man* (2.53) suggest both magic and melancholy. Basing his image on a book by Ray Bradbury, Spadaford had to suggest the torment of a man whose tattoos come to life at night. At the other extreme, in Egon Schiele's *Portrait of Paris von Gütersloh* (2.54), the flaming orange around and within the figure places the anxious man in an emotional electric chair. Likewise, when color surrounds the viewer, as in Hiroshi Senju's installations (2.55), the emotional impact can be profound. When immersed in glowing color, we enter an alternative world. In each case, the artist used color to heighten emotion rather than represent reality.

Designers also use color keys. Blood red dominates Chaz Maviyane-Davies's *Our Fear Is Their Best Weapon* (2.56). The soldier's face is tightly cropped, highlighting his fierce red eyes. The powerful slogan, presented in faded black letters, is almost consumed by the red background. As the text says, the voice of the people will be lost if fear is allowed to prevail.

2.55 Hiroshi Senju, *New Light from Afar*, **exhibition at Sundaram Tagore Gallery, 2008.** Fluorescent pigment on rice paper on board, dimensions variable.

© Hiroshi Senju. Courtesy of Sundaram Tagore Gallery. Photograph by Nacasa & Partners Inc.

2.57 Butterfly Maiden, Hopi Kachina, 20th century. Carved cottonwood, height 13½ in. (35 cm).
© Museum of Northern Arizona Photo Archives, Negative number 83C.45, Catalog number E561

Symbolic Color

Colors are often assigned symbolic meaning. These meanings may vary widely from culture to culture. In *The Primary Colors*, Alexander Theroux writes:

> [Blue] is the symbol of baby boys in America, mourning in Borneo, tribulation to the American Indian and the direction South in Tibet. Blue indicates mercy in the Kabbalah and carbon monoxide in gas canisters. Chinese emperors wore blue to worship the sky. To Egyptians it represented virtue, faith, and truth. The color was worn by slaves in Gaul. It was the color of the sixth level of the Temple of Nebuchadnezzar II, devoted to the planet Mercury. In Jerusalem a blue hand painted on a door gives protection . . . and in East Africa, blue beads represent fertility.[2]

In Hopi culture, colors symbolize spatial location and geographic direction. The Kachina doll in figure 2.57 represents Butterfly Maiden, a benevolent spirit.

2.58 Rogier van der Weyden, *Deposition* (detail), from an altarpiece commissioned by the Crossbowman's Guild of Louvain, Brabant, Belgium, c. 1435. Oil on panel, full size 7 ft 2⅝ in. × 8 ft 7⅛ in. (2.2 × 2.6 m).
Museo del Prado, Madrid. Bridgeman Images

2. Alexander Theroux, *The Primary Colors: Three Essays* (New York: Henry Holt and Company, 1994), p. 6.

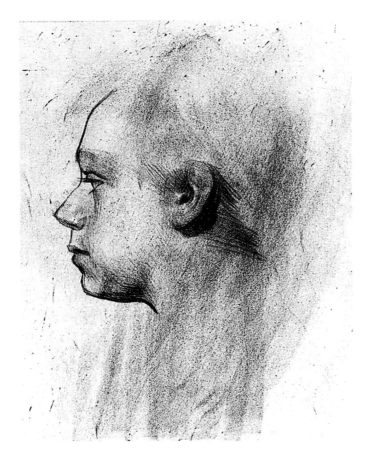

2.59 Käthe Kollwitz, *Self-Portrait in Profile, Facing Left, I* (detail), **1889.** Lithograph, full size 5⅞ × 5⅞ in. (15 × 15 cm).
© 2017 Artists Rights Society (ARS), New York/VG Bild-Kunst. Bonn. Staatliche Kunstsammlungen der DDR. Kupferstichkabinett Dresden

2.60 Käthe Kollwitz, *Self-Portrait in Profile Facing Right*, c. **1900.** Pastel on laid paper, 19 × 14⅜ in. (46.8 × 36.5 cm).
© 2017 Artists Rights Society (ARS), New York/VG Bild-Kunst. Bonn. Gift of Robert and Chris Petteys. Image courtesy of the Board of Trustees, National Gallery of Art, Washington, DC. 1956.1

Red represents a southerly direction; white, the east or northeast; blue or green, the west.

Similarly, in the Christian tradition, the Virgin Mary is typically shown wearing a blue cloak, as a symbol of both purity and grief. In this detail from Rogier van der Weyden's *Deposition* (2.58), Mary collapses as her dead son is lowered from the Cross.

The Power of Color

Color and value each have distinctive strengths. The black-and-white self-portrait by Käthe Kollwitz in figure 2.59 is simple and direct. Her profile is clearly defined, whereas the back of her head seems to dissolve into the surrounding space. In the second image (2.60), Kollwitz juxtaposed a full-color portrait with a blue-gray background. There seems to be a hint of vulnerability in the first portrait, and a solidity and strength in the second.

Color can increase the power of a given shape, shift compositional weight, and create a focal point. It can enhance the illusion of space, suggest volume, and heighten emotion. Well used, color is one of the most expressive elements of art and design.

▶ key questions

EMOTION AND EXPRESSION

- Sepia browns tend to evoke the past, while bright, high-contrast colors tend to suggest the present. What range of colors is appropriate for your design?

- Will a dominant color key increase the emotional impact of your design?

- Have you chosen colors with strong symbolic meaning? If so, how can such symbolic meaning enrich your composition?

- How much or how little color is needed for the ideas you wish to express?

summary

- Color immediately attracts attention. Its emotional and physiological impact strengthens communication and heightens expression.

- Red, green, and blue are the additive color primaries. Blue, red, and yellow are the subtractive color primaries.

- The three basic qualities of color are hue (the name of the color), value (its lightness or darkness), and intensity (its purity).

- Using a monochromatic, analogous, complementary, split complementary, or triadic color scheme can increase harmony in your design.

- The level of color harmony must match the expressive intent. In the right context, disharmony can be more expressive than harmony.

- In a composition, color can enhance the illusion of space, shift visual weight and balance, and help to emphasize compositional details.

- Distribution and proportion can help to unify disharmonious colors.

- Colors are never emotionally neutral. A dominant color key can heighten psychological impact, while a symbolic color provides a cultural reference.

key terms

achromatic	color overtones	opponent theory	split complementary
additive color	color theory	primary colors	subtractive color
afterimage	complementary	process colors	temperature
analogous	composition	saturation	tertiary colors
chroma	disharmony	secondary colors	tint
chromatic gray	earth colors	shade	tone
color harmony	hue	simultaneous contrast	triadic
color interaction	intensity		value
color key	monochromatic		

Principles of Two-Dimensional Design

Imagine yourself practicing jump shots on a deserted basketball court. By focusing all of your attention on the basket, you can master the sequence of moves needed to score. Now imagine yourself playing in a high-paced game. You are surrounded by skillful and cooperative teammates. The skills you practiced alone become heightened as you take passes and make shots. The complexities increase and the stakes rise when 10 players fill the court.

Developing a rich, complex composition can be equally exhilarating. We can define **composition** as the combination of multiple parts into a unified whole. In a well-composed design, point, line, shape, texture, value, and color work together, as a team. As one element becomes dominant, the other elements must adjust. This creates a dialog between positive and negative shapes, and multiple visual forces increase vitality rather than create confusion.

We begin this chapter with a discussion of unity and variety, the basis on which all design is built. We then define and discuss balance, scale, proportion, rhythm, and emphasis. Connections between concept and composition will be emphasized throughout.

UNITY AND VARIETY

Unity can be defined as similarity, oneness, togetherness, or cohesion. **Variety** can be defined as difference. Unity and variety are the cornerstones of composition. In the right combination, unity and variety can create compositions that are both cohesive and lively.

Mark Riedy used three major strategies to unify figure 3.1A. These strategies are diagrammed in figure 3.1B. First, all the major shapes are organized diagonally, from the lower left to the upper right. A series of parallel lines in the sand and sea emphasizes this diagonal structure. The cast shadows add another diagonal pattern, running from the upper left to the lower right. Second, the top third of the painting is filled with the blue water, while the beach fills the bottom two-thirds. This proportional relationship has been used since antiquity to create a dynamic form of balance. Third, one shape repeats 19 times, creating the graceful collection of umbrellas. Repetition in any form tends to increase unity.

A sailboat, nine groups of bathers, and especially the single red umbrella add variety. The red umbrella breaks the pattern set by the 18 white umbrellas. The resulting focal point attracts our attention to a particular spot on the beach. As we begin to notice the number of people clustered around this umbrella, we are pulled into the painting and the miniature world it represents. One small red circle

3.1A Mark Riedy, *Day at the Beach*, **1988.** Acrylic airbrush, 18 × 24 in. (45.7 × 60.9 cm).
© Mark Riedy. Courtesy of Scott Hull Associates

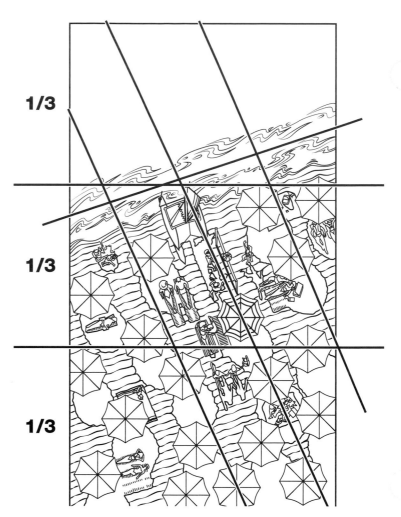

1/3

1/3

1/3

3.1B Compositional analysis of Mark Riedy's *Day at the Beach*.

3.2 Vija Celmins, *Untitled (Ocean)*, **1969.** Graphite on acrylic ground on paper, 14 × 18 in. (35.6 × 45.7 cm).
Philadelphia Museum of Art: Purchased with a grant from the National Endowment for the Arts and Matching Funds, Marion Boulton Stroud, Marilyn Steinbright, the J. J. Medveckis Foundation, David Gwinn, and Harvey S. Shipley Miller, 1991 © Matthew Marks Gallery

dramatically changes our visual and emotional response to the entire painting.

We face a new compositional challenge with each design we make. There are no simple formulas: each idea has its own expressive requirements. For example, in figure 3.2, Vija Celmins used a highly unified drawing to create a quiet, contemplative image. The size and shape of the waves are the only variations. At the other extreme, Michael Waraksa's *Sifted in the Annexed Scheme* (3.3) is crowded with conflicting images and fragmentary words. The six-armed central figure is both male and female, both chained and powerful. Just look at those bulging biceps, those gleaming pistols! A puffer fish pumps air into the funnel above a head encased in a gas mask; gloved and ungloved hands point in various directions. What does it

3.3 Michael Waraksa, *Sifted in the Annexed Scheme*, **2012.** Digital collage, dimensions variable.
© Michael Waraska

all mean? Celmins used a repetitive pattern of waves to suggest the ocean's hypnotic power, while Waraksa used a collection of conflicting images to generate a wealth of possible interpretations. Using very different approaches, each artist created an appropriate composition for the intended concept.

Every component of a composition must be balanced with every other component. Excessive unity can be monotonous, and excessive variety can be chaotic. In the following section, we explore ways to create an effective partnership between the two.

Unifying Forces

Artists and designers use many strategies to create unified compositions. **Gestalt psychology** offers a fascinating analysis of these strategies. According to this theory, we understand visual information holistically before we examine it separately. We first scan the entire puzzle, then analyze the specific parts. An image composed of units that are unrelated in size, style, orientation, and color appears chaotic and unresolved. The implications of Gestalt are complex, and there are many books on this subject. In this brief introduction, we focus on six essential aspects.

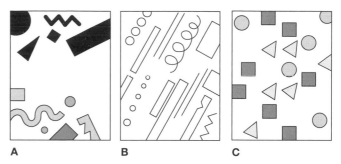

3.4A–C Examples of grouping by location, orientation, and shape.

Grouping

When presented with a collection of separate visual units, we immediately try to create order and make connections. **Grouping** is one of the first steps in this process. We generally group visual units by location, orientation, shape, and color. For example, the units in figure 3.4A form two distinct groups, despite their dissimilarity in shape. Orientation creates group cohesion in figure 3.4B. The diagonal placement of the various elements creates unity despite the variations in shape. Figure 3.4C shows grouping by shape. We mentally organize this set of units as circles, squares, and triangles in spite of their similarity in size and value.

3.5 Sahibdin and workshop, *Rama and Lakshmana Bound by Arrow-Snakes,* **from the** *Ramayana,* **Mewar, c. 1650–52.** Opaque watercolor on paper, 9 × 15⅛ in. (22.9 × 38.4 cm).
© The British Library Board/Bridgeman Images

Rama and Lakshmana Bound by Arrow-Snakes
(3.5) demonstrates the compositional and conceptual power of grouping. Multiple groups of humans and animals fill the long, horizontal rectangle. Next, we may notice that the composition is divided into three sections, each dominated by a distinctive background color. Blue and green dominate the section on the left; red and orange dominate the section on the right. A yellow background fills the center. Within these major groups, we can discern further subdivisions, including the two clusters of monkeys on the left, the four compositional boxes on the right, and the throng of horsemen in the center.

Like a graphic novel, this painting tells a complex story of prophecy, magical transformation, imprisonment, and escape. It begins in the rose-colored box on the right, as Indrajit devises a defense against Rama and Lakshmana, who are about to attack the palace. On the left, Indrajit's arrows turn into writhing snakes, binding the attackers. Indrajit's triumphal march dominates the center of the composition. By grouping the various events, the artist was able to present a complex visual narrative effectively.

Containment

As we can see from figure 3.5, groups are most easily created when visual units are placed inside a container. **Containment** is a unifying force created by the outer edge of a composition, or by a boundary within

3.7 Larry Moore, *Tattoo Face Man*, 1996. Pastel on paper, 15 × 10 in. (38.1 × 25.4 cm).
© Larry Moore, Winter Park, FL

a composition. A container encourages us to seek connections among visual units and adds definition to the negative space around each positive shape. The random collection of shapes in figure 3.6A becomes more unified when we add a simple boundary (3.6B). Any shift in the location of this boundary creates a new set of relationships. A vertical rectangle tends to create a rising or sinking effect, while a horizontal format can create an expansive effect (3.6C). The circular container in figure 3.6D draws our attention both to the center and to the outer edges of the composition.

Larry Moore's illustration in figure 3.7 uses containment in an especially inventive way. He uses three containers in this composition. The edge of the drawing provides the first container, the curtains provide the second, and the face itself provides the third. A variety of corporate logos cover the face. Logos must attract the viewer's attention, regardless of the context

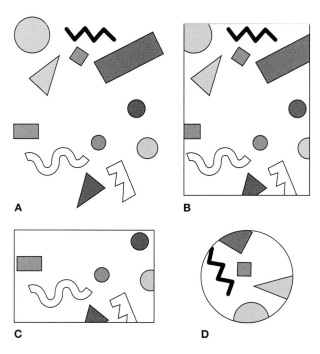

A   **B**

C   **D**

3.6A–D A container of any kind helps to unify disparate visual units.

Repetition

Repetition occurs when we use the same visual element or effect over and over. Wassily Kandinsky's *Several Circles* (3.8) is unified by shape. The repeated circles create a cohesive design despite the wide range of colors. Repeated textures unify many works, including the Villon portrait in figure 1.19, the Dürer engraving in figure 1.44, and the Moran landscape in figure 1.68.

In his *Repetition* series, French photographer Alain Cornu used the precise repetition of common objects to create a series of surprisingly powerful images. In *Repetition—Camera* (3.9), the 25 surveillance cameras are both elegant and unnerving. The green and black shapes in this highly unified composition at first seem unthreatening. As we consider them further, they suggest that our every move may be under constant observation.

Proximity

In design, the distance between visual elements is called **proximity**. Figure 3.10A shows how close proximity helps to increase unity. More distant shapes read as separate events (3.10B). **Fusion** occurs when shapes or volumes are placed so close together that they share common edges. When shapes of similar color and texture fuse, they can create new negative shapes as the surrounding area becomes more clearly defined (3.10C).

Careful use of proximity can create visual tension, adding energy to the design. A detail from Michelangelo's *Creation of Adam* (3.11) demonstrates the expressive power of visual tension. Jehovah's hand, on the right, nearly touches Adam's hand, on the left. As we gaze at the ceiling of the Sistine Chapel, less than 6 inches of space separates the two. In this cosmology, all of human history begins when the spark of life jumps this gap. If the hands had been placed too far apart or too close together, the spark that animates both the man and the painting would have been lost.

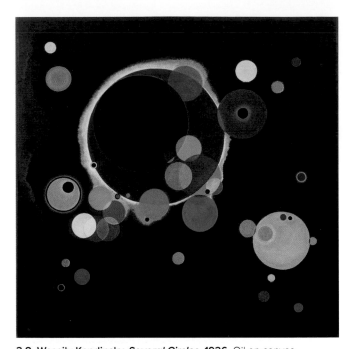

3.8 Wassily Kandinsky, *Several Circles*, 1926. Oil on canvas, 55¼ × 55⅜ in. (140.3 × 140.7 cm).
The Solomon R. Guggenheim Foundation/Art Resource, New York. © 2014 Artists Rights Society (ARS), New York/ADAGP, Paris

in which they are placed, and each of these logos was originally designed as a distinct visual unit. In this composition, however, the individualistic logos become a cooperative team. The connections created by the three levels of containment are stronger than the separations created by the individualistic logos.

3.9 Alain Cornu, *Repetition—Camera*, 2016. Digital photograph manipulated in Photoshop.
© Alain Cornu

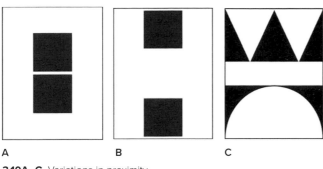

A   B   C

3.10A–C Variations in proximity.

Continuity

Continuity may be defined as a fluid connection among compositional parts. This connection can be actual or implied. With actual continuity, each shape touches an adjoining shape. With implied continuity, we mentally make the connections.

Skillful use of continuity can add visual movement to a design. **Movement** creates deliberate visual pathways and helps to direct the viewer's attention to areas of particular interest. In Frank Stella's *Lac Laronge IV* (3.12), curving lines and shapes flow from one circle to the next, creating actual continuity. Color distribution creates implied continuity, which enhances this visual flow. The upward curve of blue in the upper left corner is echoed by a quarter turn of

3.12 Frank Stella, *Lac Laronge IV*, 1969. Acrylic polymer on canvas, 9 ft ⅛ in. × 13 ft 6 in. (2.8 × 3.1 m).
Toledo Museum of Art, Toledo, OH. Purchased with funds from the Libbey Endowment, gift of Edward Drummond Libbey (1972.4). © 2017 Frank Stella/Artists Rights Society (ARS), New York

blue in the lower right corner. The violet curve on the left side is echoed by a quarter turn of scarlet in the upper right corner. The hints of olive and brown add a further spin to the wheel.

Movement can play an equally important role in a representational design. In *Raft of the Medusa* (3.13A), Théodore Géricault used a pattern of diagonal lines (3.13B) to direct our attention to a single **focal point**. The arms and legs of the sailors, the floorboards of

3.11 Michelangelo, *Creation of Adam* (detail), c. 1510. Fresco, Sistine Chapel, Rome.
EmmePi Images/Alamy Stock Photo

3.13A Théodore Géricault, *Raft of the Medusa*, 1818–19. Oil on canvas, 16 ft 1 in. × 23 ft 6 in. (4.9 × 7.2 m). Musée du Louvre, Paris. © Réunion des Musées Nationaux/Art Resource, New York

3.13B Diagram of *Raft of the Medusa*, showing eye movement toward focal point.

the raft, and even the angle of the sail all lead us toward the rescue ship in the upper right corner. This dramatic use of movement greatly increases the emotional power of this historical painting. Some 149 survivors from a sinking ship began a desperate journey on the raft. When rescued two weeks later, only 15 had survived. The pattern of bodies and extended arms pulls us irresistibly toward the sailor at the front of the raft, whose very life depends on the attention he can attract.

Closure

Closure refers to the mind's inclination to connect fragmentary information to produce a completed form. In figure 3.14, Kevin Curry created a self-portrait from paint samples he collected from a nearby store. This suggests that all of us may be defined by our surroundings, right down to the color of our skin. From close up, the image is simply a collection of evenly colored squares. From a distance, closure transforms them into a man's face.

Closure makes it possible to communicate using implication. Freed of the necessity to provide every detail, the artist or designer can convey an idea through suggestion, rather than description. When the viewer completes the image in his or her mind, it is often more memorable than an image that leaves no room for participation.

3.14 Kevin Curry, *Take Me as an Example*, 2012. Glidden paint sample chips, 42 × 42 in. (106.7 × 106.7 cm). © Kevin Curry

3.15 Morla Design, *Mexican Museum Twentieth Anniversary poster*, 1997.
© Morla Design, Inc., San Francisco

3.17 Illustrated page from *The Canterbury Tales*, 1896.
William Morris, designer; Edward Burne-Jones, illustrator.
Private collection/Bridgeman Images

Combining Gestalt Principles

Artists and designers often combine all the principles of Gestalt in a single composition. In figure 3.15, closure makes it possible for us to turn hundreds of dots into a face, and 15 letters in different fonts into words. The repeated dots in the face and the larger yellow and pink dots in the bottom section help to unify the design. Both the pink face at the top and the black-and-white face in the lower left corner lean to the left, increasing unity through orientation. Tightly contained within the rectangular format, the variety of visual components creates an exuberant yet cohesive composition.

Patterns and Grids

A **pattern** is created when any visual element is systematically repeated over an extended area. Many patterns are based on a module, or basic visual unit. A **grid** is created through a series of intersecting lines. We can fill in a simple grid with black and white squares, creating a checkerboard (3.16A). Gaps in this simple grid create a more complex composition (3.16B–C), and variations in grid density can add even more variety. Both patterns and grids increase compositional unity by creating containment, suggesting continuity, strengthening proximity, and encouraging closure.

Artists and designers often use patterns to decorate walls, books, or fabrics. In his page from *The Canterbury Tales* (3.17), designer William Morris used complex floral patterns to create multiple borders and backgrounds. The borders are filled with curving floral patterns. The flowing text at the top of the page echoes these curving shapes and creates an additional pattern.

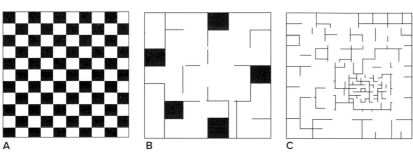

3.16A–C Grid variations. A simple checkerboard is a highly unified grid. Any variation on the basic structure increases variety, adding interest.

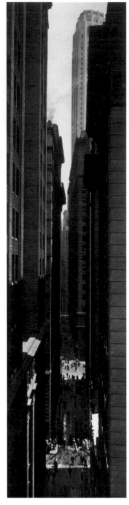

3.18 Dorothy LeBoeuf, Anna Williams–inspired quilt, 2011. Cotton fabric and batting, 40 × 40 in. (101.6 × 101.6 cm).
© Dorothy LeBoeuf. Photograph by Bruce Decker

3.20 Berenice Abbott, *Exchange Place, New York,* **1934.** Photograph.
© Berenice Abbott/Getty Images

Multiple fragments of visual information can also be unified through pattern. Dorothy LeBoeuf constructed the quilt in figure 3.18 from hundreds of fragments of cloth. She used solids, plaids, and patterns in a wide range of colors. The results could have been chaotic. However, by organizing all the pieces into square, modular units, she was able to unify this seemingly random collection of fabric scraps into a vibrant composition.

Compositional grids are most commonly created using vertical and horizontal lines. Their unifying power is so great that even the most disparate information gains cohesion when a grid is used.

► **key questions**

UNITY AND VARIETY

- What strategies have you used to unify your composition?

- What gives your composition variety?

- Is the balance between unity and variety appropriate for the ideas you want to express?

- What would happen if you constructed your composition using a pattern or a grid?

- What happens when some areas in a pattern are disrupted?

- What happens when some areas in a grid compress while others expand?

BALANCE

In design, **balance** refers to the distribution of weight or force within a composition. Negative and positive shapes can work together to create an equilibrium among compositional units, regardless of variations in their size, weight, or shape.

Weight and Gravity

We can define **visual weight** in two ways. First, *weight* refers to the inclination of shapes to float or sink. Second, *weight* can refer to the relative importance of a visual element within a design.

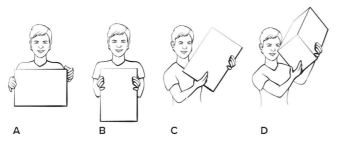

3.19A–D Which box is the most static? Which is the most dynamic?

The compositional forces that most influence visual weight are the size and type of shape, its texture or value, its location within the compositional frame, and its orientation.

As noted in figure 1.32A–D, a shape tends to gain stability when it is placed in the center of a composition, while it tends to become more dynamic when it goes off the edge.

The orientation of the composition as a whole also affects weight and balance. Try this simple experiment. Which is the most dynamic and which is the most stable position of the box in figure 3.19A–D? Most viewers find positions A and B the most stable. The box is at rest, with its vertical and horizontal edges reconfirming the stability we experience in daily life. By contrast, positions C and D place the box in an unstable or dynamic position. It is halfway between standing and falling. Likewise, a composition that is dominated by diagonals tends to be visually dynamic, while a composition that is dominated by horizontals tends to be stable.

The overall compositional format also affects balance. Using dramatic vertical shapes within a tall vertical format, Berenice Abbott captures the soaring energy of Wall Street in figure 3.20. The compositional dynamics change dramatically when a square format is used. In *Radical Acts* (3.21), Kathryn Frund combined the stability of a square with the dynamism of the diagonal lines that dissect the painting from upper left to lower right.

3.21 Kathryn Frund, *Radical Acts*, 2008. Mixed media with found objects and paper mounted on aluminum, 48 × 48 in. (121.9 × 121.9 cm).
© Kathryn Frund. Courtesy of Chase Young Gallery, Boston, MA

3.22 Ansel Adams, *Moonrise, Hernandez, New Mexico*, **1941.** Silver print, 18½ × 23 in. (47 × 58.4 cm).

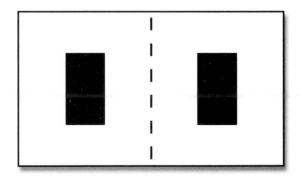

A

B

3.23A–B Examples of symmetrical balance.

Integrating flat painting and actual objects, she presents us with a puzzle. Why construct an image using actual journal pages, a plumb-bob weight, a tiny ladder, and large, dramatic blocks of color? Frund challenges viewers to reconcile these seemingly contradictory visual forces to create a wide range of possible meanings.

Visual weight can also refer to the relative importance of a visual element within a design. In *Moonrise, Hernandez, New Mexico* (3.22), Ansel Adams combined balance, gravity, and movement to create an image that is both tranquil and dramatic. A squarish format dominated by horizontal lines provides stability. The quiet village sinks to the bottom of the design. The tiny moon, positioned just to the left of the compositional center, pulls us into the velvety black sky in the top half of the image. As the focal point of the image, the tiny moon has the most visual weight in this photograph.

Symmetrical Balance

Symmetrical balance occurs when shapes are mirrored on either side of an axis, as in a composition that is vertically divided down the center (3.23A). A shift in this axis (3.23B) creates symmetry between the top and bottom of the design.

A symmetrically balanced design can appeal to our desire for equilibrium and communicate calm and stability. The Taj Mahal (3.24) was built by a seventeenth-century Indian emperor as a tomb for his beloved wife. The three white marble domes and the four flanking towers create architectural symmetry. In the reflecting pool, a mirror image appears, making it even more symmetrical. The building is both graceful and serene.

Approximate symmetry is created when similar imagery appears on either side of a central axis. For example, in Richard Estes's *Miami Rug Company* (3.25), actual and reflected light poles divide the space as decisively as a gate. Radiating from the center of the composition, a network of diagonal lines pulls us into the painting. At the same time, the large pane of glass on the left pushes toward us, shimmering with darkened reflections of the buildings on the right. The overall effect is unnerving. The seemingly symmetrical shapes are actually quite different, and the resulting image is disorienting rather than serene.

3.24 Taj Mahal, Agra, India, 1630–48.
© Pushp Deep Pandey/2kPhotography/Getty Images

3.25 Richard Estes, *Miami Rug Company*, 1974. Oil on canvas, 40 × 54 in. (101.6 × 137.2 cm).
© Richard Estes. Courtesy of Marlborough Gallery, New York

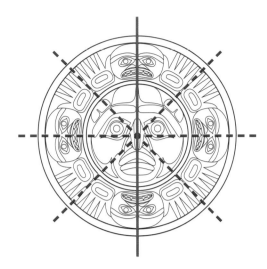

3.26 Diagram of Bella Coola mask. The central face is symmetrically balanced. The outer ring is an example of radial symmetry.

3.27 Zak Weinberg, *Square Series*, 2016. Masonite and wood, 4 ft 5 in. × 4 ft 5 in. × 5 in. (134.6 × 134.6 × 12.7 cm).
© Zak Weinberg

Radial Symmetry

With **radial symmetry**, lines and shapes are mirrored both vertically and horizontally, and the center of the composition acts as a focal point. For example, the center of the Bella Coola mask in figure 3.26 is symmetrically balanced. By contrast, the surrounding ring of faces and hands creates radial balance. Zak Weinberg's *Square Series* (3.27) presents sixteen variations on radial balance. Using a laser cutter, he was able to transform sheets of masonite and wood into a wide range of elegant designs.

An alternative to radial balance is a spiral. A spiral can increase energy within a circular format or add movement to a rectangular composition. In Christina Klein's *Kansas Winds* (3.28), a visual vortex pulls our eyes from the bottom of the composition to the top. The diagonals within this vortex contrast sharply with the more stable vertical and horizontal shapes that define the blue building in the background. On the left side and bottom, fragments of the composition seem to have exploded beyond the frame. It seems that the wind's energy simply cannot be contained!

Asymmetrical Balance

Asymmetrical balance creates equilibrium among visual elements that do *not* mirror each other on either side of an axis. Depending on the

3.28 Christina Klein, *Kansas Winds*, 2015. Acrylic on canvas and wood, 48 × 36 in. (121.9 × 91.4 cm).
© Christina Klein

degree of asymmetry, the resulting design may be quite stable, very dynamic, or nearly chaotic.

We can use many strategies to create asymmetrical balance:

- We can place a large shape close to the fulcrum, while placing a small shape farther away. Just as a child at the end of a seesaw can balance an adult near the center, so large and small shapes can be balanced in a design (3.29A).

- We can use several small shapes to balance a larger shape (3.29B).

- A small, solid square can balance a large, open circle. The solidity and stability of the square give it additional weight (3.29C).

- We can balance a textured shape near the fulcrum with a lighter open shape that we place farther away (3.29D).

Asymmetrical balance becomes even more interesting when we add a boundary. Because the negative space is as important as each positive shape, we can now create more complex compositions:

- A small shape placed near the bottom of the format balances a large shape placed along the top. Especially within a tall rectangle, shapes placed near the top tend to rise, and shapes placed near the bottom tend to sink (3.30A).

- When the small square intersects with the bottom edge and the large square moves away from the edge, the differences in weight become even more pronounced (3.30B).

- The top shape now gains energy through its diagonal orientation. We need three bottom shapes to create balance (3.30C).

- Finally, a small, aggressive triangle can balance a large, passive rectangle (3.30D).

Balance in a composition shifts each time we add or subtract a visual element. Piet Mondrian's *Composition II in Red, Blue, and Yellow* (3.31) is constructed from black vertical and horizontal lines, three brightly colored shapes, and four white rectangles. "Oh, my four-year-old cousin could make a painting like that," chortle our friends. Yet, notice how carefully the composition is balanced. Placed at the bottom of the painting, the tiny yellow rectangle in the lower

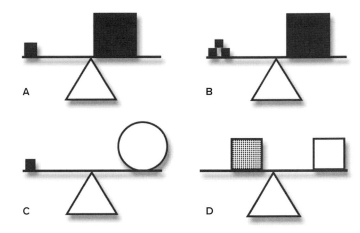

3.29A–D Creating asymmetrical balance.

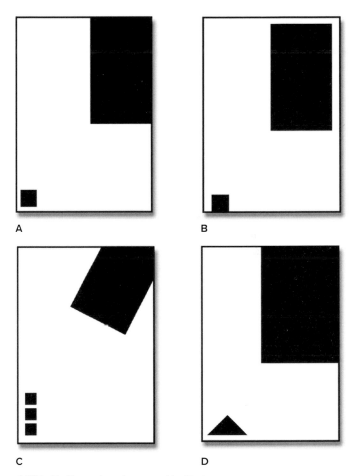

3.30A–D Examples of asymmetrical balance.

right corner provides an essential counterbalance to the larger shapes in the design.

In figure 3.32, designer Hans-Ulrich Allemann balanced multiple layers of text within a vertical rectangle. Returning to our earlier discussion of Gestalt, let's deconstruct this image step by step. A light-blue shape fills the top half of the image, then dissolves into the white shape at the bottom. A horizontal block of text is positioned slightly below the center, while

3.31 Piet Mondrian, *Composition II in Red, Blue, and Yellow*, **1930.** Oil on canvas, 18 × 18 in. (46 × 46 cm).
© 2017 ES Mondrian/Holtzman Trust

3.32 *Interaction/Motion*: a poster for the lecture series *Exposed*, sponsored by the Graphic Design Department, University of the Arts, Philadelphia, 2006.
Concept and design: Hans-Ulrich Allemann, Principal. Allemann Almquist & Jones, Design/Strategic Communications, Philadelphia. Digital image

along the right edge a vertical block of text pulls our eyes upward. The word *action* is enclosed by a fine line. Five lines of orange text connect the horizontal and vertical axes, with three near the bottom and two running parallel to the right edge. The tiny red logo positioned nearby creates a visual exclamation point.

Each type of balance has its advantages. The approximate symmetry that Frida Kahlo used for her double self-portrait (3.33) is symbolically appropriate and compositionally effective. Painted in response to her divorce from painter Diego Rivera, it presents the beloved Frida in a native costume on the right and the rejected Frida in European dress on the left. A linear vein connects the women's hearts. In figure 3.27, Zak Weinberg used radial symmetry to pull the viewer into each square in a nine-part series. And in figure 3.1A, Mark Riedy used asymmetrical balance to animate his beach scene and accentuate the red umbrella.

In some cases a degree of **imbalance** is necessary. Eric Fischl used distortion to create imbalance in *Barbeque* (3.34). The table in the foreground is tilted, and the bowl of fish seems impossibly large. Pulled by the diagonal lines leading to the house, the pool also seems skewed, while the tiny women are more like dolls than people. Manning the grill, the father looks on approvingly as his son engages in a little recreational fire-breathing. The entire scene seems to be

3.33 Frida Kahlo, *Las Dos Fridas*, **1939.** Oil on canvas, 69⅕ × 69⅕ in. (176 × 176 cm).
© 2017 Banco de México Diego Rivera Frida Kahlo Museums Trust, Mexico, D.F./Artists Rights Society (ARS), New York. Photo Schalkwijk/Art Resource, NY

3.34 Eric Fischl, *Barbeque*, 1982. Oil on canvas, 5 ft 5 in. × 8 ft 4 in. (1.7 × 2.5 m).
© Eric Fischl. Courtesy of Mary Boone Gallery, New York

slightly bowed. This spatial distortion combined with a bizarre collection of objects and events turns a family picnic into a suburban nightmare.

▶ key questions

BALANCE

- Which is the "heaviest" shape in your design? Does its weight match its importance?

- How does the outer shape of your design affect its compositional balance?

- In your composition, how does negative space affect overall balance?

- We described various forms of balance in this section. Which is most effective for the ideas and emotions you want to express?

PROPORTION AND SCALE

Proportion and scale create two types of size relationship. Both strongly affect compositional balance and emotional impact. **Proportion** refers to the relative size of visual elements *within* an image or within a figure. For example, figure 3.35A demonstrates proportional relationships within a human head. The eyes are roughly sixty percent above the chin, and the bottom of the nose is roughly halfway between the eyes and the chin. **Scale** commonly refers to the size of a form when compared with our own human size. For example, figure 3.35B shows a small-scale figure walking into an imposing large-scale building. Thus, a 50-foot-long painting is a large-scale artwork, while a 10-inch-square painting is an example of small scale.

Most designs distribute information fairly evenly within the format, with only modest size variation among the parts. Exaggerating these proportions can be eye-catching, because the image immediately stands out from the norm. Figure 3.36 shows the cover of an annual report for the Eaton Corporation. The

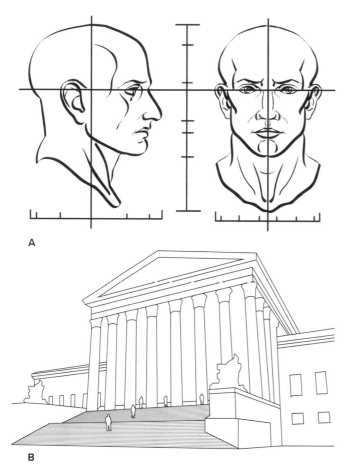

A

B

3.35A–B Proportion is an essential part of drawing, whether you are composing the different elements of a human head or whether you are drawing elements that are dramatically different in scale.

3.36 Mark Schwartz, Greg Oznowich, and Teresa Snow, Nesnadny + Schwartz Design, annual report for Eaton Corporation, "This is NOT business as usual," 2002.

Courtesy of Mark Schwartz and Greg Oznowich, Nesnadny + Schwartz, Cleveland, OH

bold yellow color and the asymmetrical balance in this design are eye-catching in themselves, but it is the oversized "not" that really distinguishes the design. The large white word is then repeated in the final tag line: "This is not business as usual."

Scale is also important when drawing figures in relation to each other. In the line drawing in figure 3.37, the woman, the chair she is sitting on, and the desk and the computer in front of her must all be carefully scaled so that they work well in relation to each other. Claes Oldenburg and Coosje van Bruggen have also used scale extensively in their artwork. Nearly 20 feet long, their four *Shuttlecocks* (3.38) add a whimsical note to the formidable exterior of the Nelson-Atkins Museum of Art in Kansas City.

The scale of the artwork itself also expands the expressive possibilities. Ken Stout's *Intermission* (3.39) is 50 feet long. As a result, we can view various aspects of the painting sequentially as we walk past. We visually enter the theater through the pink doorway at the far left. Cool blue light bathes the restless audience.

Two men in the balcony add to the action, as one aims a peashooter and the other launches a paper airplane. On the stage, a tiny actor creates a transition between the audience and the stage crew. The painting ends in a final burst of red, at the far right side. Taking advantage of each square inch, Stout created a swirling panorama of figures engaged in a variety of theatrical activities, on- and offstage.

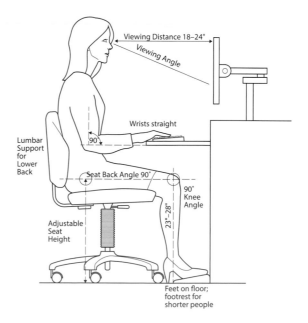

3.37 Scale drawing of woman sitting at computer.

3.38 Claes Oldenburg and Coosje van Bruggen, *Shuttlecocks*, **1994.** South facade of the Nelson-Atkins Museum of Art and the Kansas City Sculpture Park. Aluminum, fiberglass-reinforced plastic, and paint, 19 ft 29⅟₁₆ in. × 15 ft 11⅞ in. (585.63 × 487.36 cm).
Claes Oldenburg and Coosje van Bruggen. Donald J. Hall Sculpture Park at the Nelson-Atkins Museum of Art, Kansas City, MO. Purchase: acquired through the generosity of the Sosland Family, F94-1/3-4. Photograph by Louis Meluso

3.39 Ken Stout, *Intermission*, **1994.** Oil on canvas, 9 × 50 ft (2.7 × 15.2 m).
© Ken Stout. Photograph by Don House

key questions

RHYTHM

Rhythm is a sense of movement that is created by the repetition of multiple units in a deliberate pattern. Visual rhythm is similar to musical rhythm. In music, rhythm is created through the organization of sound in time. We can combine meter (the basic pattern of sound and silence), accents (which emphasize specific notes), and tempo (the speed at which the music is played) to create a dazzling array of compositional possibilities.

As with music, the rhythm in a visual composition can take many forms. In *Drift No. 2* (3.40), Bridget Riley repeated a simple line to create an undulating rhythm similar to waves on water. Vibrant words create a spatial rhythm in figure 3.41. Warm and cool colors in various values and intensities cause some words to advance while others recede.

3.41 A repeated word becomes a rhythmic design through color choices.
Courtesy of the author

3.40 Bridget Riley, *Drift No. 2,* **1966.** Acrylic on canvas, 7 ft 7½ in. × 7 ft 5½ in. (2.32 × 2.27 m).
Gift of Seymour H. Knox, 1967. Albright-Knox Art Gallery, New York/Art Resource, New York

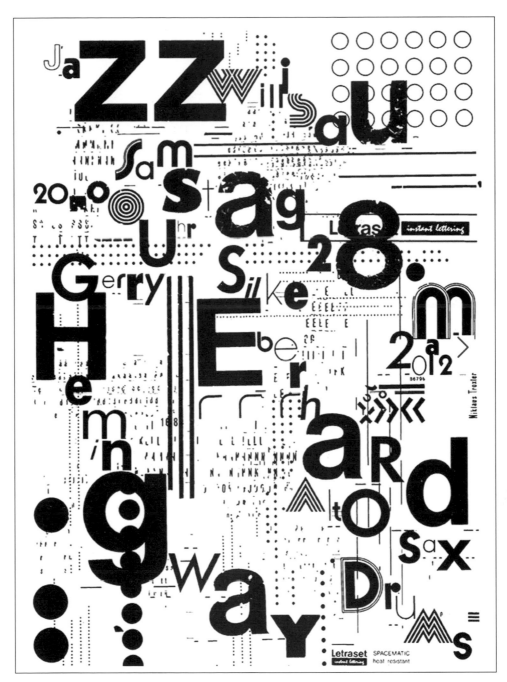

3.42 Niklaus Troxler, Willisau Jazz Festival poster, 1992.
© Niklaus Troxler

Niklaus Troxler used a looser and more layered approach to rhythm in his poster for the Willisau Jazz Festival (3.42). Breaking every rule of good design, he combined multiple fonts in various sizes. Seemingly random punctuation marks complicate matters further. Like a sophisticated jazz piece, the entire composition balances on the verge of chaos. It is held together by an underlying rhythm of dots, circles, and straight lines.

Visual rhythm can be as regular as a waltz or as syncopated as jazz. Multiplication, fragmentation, and superimposition propel the nude descending Marcel Duchamp's staircase (3.43). The jerking rhythm demonstrates the alternating stability and instability of human locomotion, rather than physical grace. When walking, we continually fall forward, then catch ourselves as we take the next step.

3.43 Marcel Duchamp, *Nude Descending a Staircase, No. 2*, **1912.** Oil on canvas, 58 × 35 in. (147.3 × 88.9 cm).
© 2017 Artists Rights Society (ARS), New York/ADAGP, Paris/Succession Marcel Duchamp. Philadelphia Museum of Art/The Bridgeman Art Library

EMPHASIS

Each player in a basketball game has a particular role to play. The guards primarily focus on defense, the forwards on offense. The point guard plays a dominant role, calling plays and controlling the action. Likewise, the various visual elements in a composition must work together as a team. In most cases, a few carefully selected visual elements dominate, or stand out, while others play a supporting role.

3.44 Pentagram Design, magazine, 2009. Publisher: ArtCenter College of Design, Pasadena, CA.
Publisher: ArtCenter College of Design, Pasadena, CA. Courtesy of Pentagram, New York

Emphasis gives prominence to part of a design. As noted in Chapter One, a focal point can be used to create emphasis. Both emphasis and a focal point attract attention and increase visual and conceptual impact.

Emphasis by Isolation

Any **anomaly,** or break from the norm, tends to stand out. Because we seek to connect the verbal and visual information that we are given, a mismatched word or an isolated shape immediately attracts our attention. In figure 3.44, Pentagram emphasized the word *design* through its separation from the word *magazine*. By placing this anomaly at the bottom edge of the composition, they made it even more eye-catching.

Just as a pattern tends to increase connection among visual elements, so any break in the pattern emphasizes isolation. In figure 3.1A, 18 white umbrellas establish the pattern that is so beautifully broken by the single red umbrella. Do Ho Suh's *Fallen Star* (3.45) is a three-quarter-size cottage based on an actual house in Providence, Rhode Island. When Suh traveled to the United States to study at the Rhode Island School of Design, he felt as though he had dropped from the sky into another world. If *Fallen Star* was placed on the ground in

3.45 Do Ho Suh, *Fallen Star*, 2012. House construction materials and furniture; approx. 15 × 18 ft (4.6 × 5.5 m).
© Do Ho Suh, Stuart Collection, University of California, San Diego, Photograph by Philipp Scholz Ritterman

3.46 Sam Francis, *Flash Point*, 1975. Acrylic on paper,
32¼ × 22¾ in. (82 × 59 cm).
© 2017 Sam Francis Foundation, California/Artists Rights Society (ARS), New York

a suburban setting, it would simply read as a very small house. Tilted and perched precariously on the side of a campus building seven stories up, it is a powerful anomaly.

Emphasis by Placement

Every square inch of a composition has a distinctive power. As a result, placement alone can increase the importance of a particular shape.

The compositional center is especially potent. In *The Power of the Center* (1982), psychologist Rudolf Arnheim discusses **centricity** (compressive compositional force) and **eccentricity** (expansive compositional force). Both centricity and eccentricity activate *Flash Point* (3.46). The central white square pulls us into the middle of the painting, while the explosive red rectangle pushes toward the outer edge.

This effect is even more pronounced in figure 3.47. Any representation of another human attracts our attention, and faces are of particular interest. Four major lines and a series of concentric circles

3.47 Jacey, *Untitled*, 1995.
Digital design.
© Jacey, Début Art Ltd

direct us inward, toward the man's left eye. Fragments of text extend outward, beyond the edge of the composition. Continually compressing and expanding, the seemingly simple image pulls the viewer inward while simultaneously appearing to extend outward, beyond the boundary.

Emphasis Through Contrast

Contrast is created when two or more forces operate in opposition. By reviewing the elements and principles of design discussed in this section, we can quickly create a long list of potential adversaries, including static/dynamic (3.48A), small/large (3.48B), solid/textured (3.48C), and curvilinear/rectilinear (3.48D).

When the balance is just right, we can create powerful compositions from any of these combinations. Devoting about 80 percent of the compositional space to one force and about 20 percent to the other is especially effective. The larger force sets the standard, while

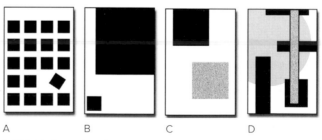

A   B   C   D

3.48A–D Examples of contrast: static/dynamic, small/large, solid/textured, curvilinear/rectilinear.

the smaller force creates the exception. Just as a single basketball player wearing a blue uniform will stand out if the other four players wear yellow, so a smaller force can dominate a design. Consider these examples:

- *Contrast in scale.* In figure 3.49, the small airplane and the moon become charged with meaning when combined with the image of the sleeping child. Dreams take flight.

3.49 Robert Crawford, *Jamie Sleeping*, 1988. Acrylic on canvas, 14 × 20 in. (35.5 × 50.8 cm).
© Robert Crawford

3.51 Steven Spielberg, still from *Schindler's List*, 1993.
Courtesy of Photofest

- *Contrast in shape.* Zurbarán's *Saint Serapion* (3.50) is a brilliant example of contrast by shape as well as emphasis by separation. The small note pinned at the right edge of the canvas gains so much power that it easily balances the large figure filling the rest of the frame.

- *Contrast in color.* One of the most compelling uses of emphasis by color occurs in *Schindler's List*, a film directed by Steven Spielberg (3.51). Midway through the black-and-white film, a small girl in a red coat is shown walking to her death. She breaks away from the line and runs back to hide under a bed in a nearby house. This is the only use of color in the main body of the film. When her red coat appears again, her body is being transported to a bonfire. This simple use of color creates one of the most emotional moments in a remarkable film.

3.50 Francisco de Zurbarán, *Saint Serapion*, 1628. Oil on canvas, 47½ × 41 in. (120.7 × 103.5 cm).
Photo Prudence Cuming Associates, Ltd. Ella Gallup Sumner and Mary Catlin Sumner Collection Fund, 1951.4. Photography by Allen Phillips/Wadsworth Atheneum

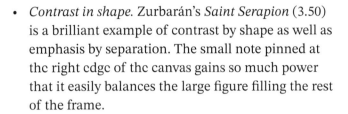

key questions

EMPHASIS

- Is there a dominant shape in your composition? If so, is it the shape you most *want* to emphasize?

- What would happen conceptually if you dramatically changed the scale, shape, or color of a crucial visual unit?

- Is there a focal point in your composition? If not, should there be?

- Contrast tends to add interest. Can a shift in contrast strengthen your composition?

summary

- Using composition, we can organize multiple parts into a harmonious whole. In a well-composed design, visual elements work together as a team.

- Gestalt psychology describes six unifying strategies: grouping, containment, repetition, proximity, continuity, and closure.

- Effective design requires a dialog between unity and variety. Too much unity can lead to boredom, while too much variety can lead to chaos.

- Any similarity between visual elements tends to increase unity; any difference between visual elements tends to increase variety.

- Symmetry, radial symmetry, and asymmetry are three common forms of balance. Visual balance creates equilibrium among compositional units, regardless of variations in their size, weight, or shape.

- Scale and proportion are two types of size relationship. Proportion refers to the size relationships within an image, while scale involves a size comparison to our physical reality.

- Emphasis is most commonly created through isolation, placement, or contrast. A focal point can strengthen emphasis.

key terms

anomaly	containment	grid	repetition
approximate symmetry	continuity	grouping	rhythm
asymmetrical balance	contrast	imbalance	scale
balance	eccentricity	movement	symmetrical balance
centricity	emphasis	pattern	unity
closure	focal point	proportion	variety
composition	fusion	proximity	visual weight
	Gestalt psychology	radial symmetry	

Illusion of Space,
Illusion of Motion

The Battle of Issus, fought by Alexander the Great of Macedonia and Darius III of Persia in 333 BCE, changed human history. Control of all of Asia Minor (present-day Turkey and the Middle East) was at stake. At age 47, Darius III ruled the greatest empire of its time. At age 23, Alexander was king of the small mountainous empire north of present-day Greece. Alexander began the battle on a rocky hillside and seemed doomed to fail. When Darius moved in for the kill, additional Macedonian troops swept in from the side, split the Persian army, and won the battle. This triumph launched Alexander's 10-year campaign to extend his empire from Greece to India, setting the stage for the subsequent Roman empire.

chapter four

In his *Battle of Issus* (4.1), Albrecht Altdorfer created an apocalyptic vision, combining the dramatic landscape and swirling armies with a crescent moon (representing Darius) and a blazing sun (representing Alexander). Commissioned by the Duke of Bavaria in anticipation of his own battle against Turkish forces, the painting was a clarion call to his countrymen. The illusion of space provides the setting for the desperate battle, and the illusion of motion captures both the movement of men and the shimmering sky.

In Chapter Three, we found that each image and idea presents unique challenges. Jasper Johns's *Target with Plaster Casts* (figure 1.43) demanded a confrontational approach. Johns chose to reaffirm the flatness of the canvas surface. Altdorfer, on the other hand, needed deep space for his epic battle. How can you best meet the challenges presented by your own ideas? In this chapter, we explore ways to create the illusion of space and of motion, and consider the conceptual implications of each.

4.1 Albrecht Altdorfer, *Battle of Issus*, 1529. Oil on limewood, 62¼ × 47¼ in. (158 × 120 cm). Alte Pinakothek, Munich, Germany/Bridgeman Images

CREATING THE ILLUSION OF SPACE

Linear Perspective

Linear perspective is a mathematical system for projecting the apparent dimensions of a three-dimensional object onto a flat surface. This surface, called the **picture plane**, is comparable to a window overlooking a city street. By tracing the outlines of the buildings on the pane of glass, you can make a simple perspective drawing.

Developed during the Renaissance, perspective offered a methodical approach to depicting the rational reality perceived by artists in the fifteenth century. It soon gained wide acceptance as a means of systematically diminishing the size of objects as they recede in space. Raphael's *School of Athens* (figure 4.2) is an example. A broad arch in the foreground frames the compositional stage. Three additional arches diminish in size, pulling us into the painting. The diagonal lines in the buildings and floor converge at a point in the center. The viewer is invited to enter an illusory world.

Even though many recent philosophical and aesthetic theories challenge this conception of reality, perspective remains the most pervasive Western system for suggesting three-dimensionality on the two-dimensional surface. Linear perspective is based on five concepts, shown in figures 4.3 and 4.4.

1. Objects appear to diminish in size as they recede into the distance. Perspective is possible because the rate at which objects appear to diminish is regular and consistent.

2. The point at which objects disappear entirely is called a **vanishing point**. Sets of parallel lines (such as train tracks) converge at a vanishing point as they go into the distance, creating an illusion of space.

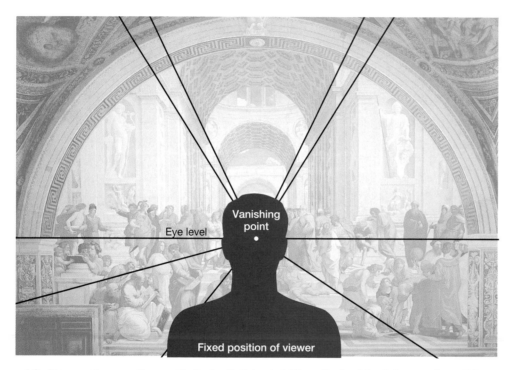

4.2 Diagram of perspective used in Raphael's *School of Athens* (for the full painting, see figure 7.4). History/Bridgeman Images

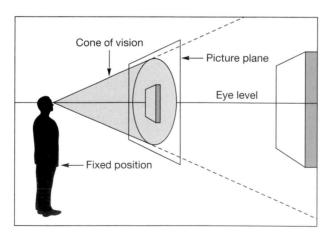

4.3 Fundamentals of linear perspective.

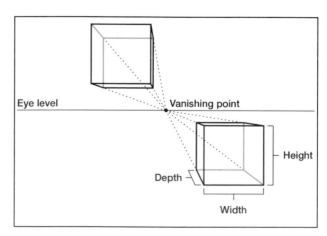

4.4 Example of one-point perspective.

3. In basic one- and two-point perspective, all vanishing points are positioned on the **eye level** or **horizon line**, which is level with the artist's eyes.

4. Because all proportional relationships shift with each change in position, a fixed viewing position is an essential characteristic of linear perspective.

5. Only a limited area is clearly visible from a fixed position. To accommodate a larger viewing area, you must move farther away from the object you are drawing. This expands the **cone of vision** and increases the viewing area.

We use **one-point perspective** to represent a straight frontal view of a scene (4.4). The lines representing depth are angled to converge on a single point at eye level, and the lines representing height are perpendicular to the horizon line. One-point perspective is relatively simple to master and can pull the viewer into the image with a single dramatic focal point (4.5).

Two-point perspective is effective for representing an object that is angled in space. A cube drawn in two-point perspective will not have any lines positioned parallel to the horizon line. Instead, the lines representing depth and width are angled to converge on two vanishing points (4.6). Because two-point perspective is effective in showing both the front and sides of a structure, it is often used for diagrams and architectural drawings (4.7).

In one- and two-point perspective, the lines representing height are perpendicular to the horizon line. In **three-point perspective** (4.8), these lines are tilted so that they converge on a third vanishing point, high *above*

4.5 Jan Vredeman de Vries, *Perspective Study*, from *Perspective*, Leiden, 1604.
Public domain

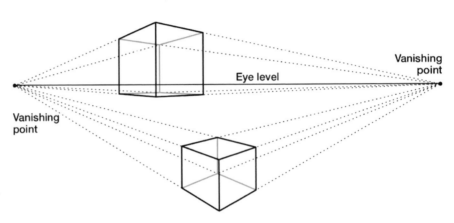

4.6 Example of two-point perspective.

4.7 Frank Lloyd Wright, detail of drawing for *Fallingwater* (Kaufmann House), Bear Run, Pennsylvania, 1936. Full size 15⅜ × 27¼ in. (39 × 69 cm).
© The Frank Lloyd Wright Foundation Archives (The Museum of Modern Art I Avery Architectural & Fine Arts Library, Columbia University, New York) ARS New York

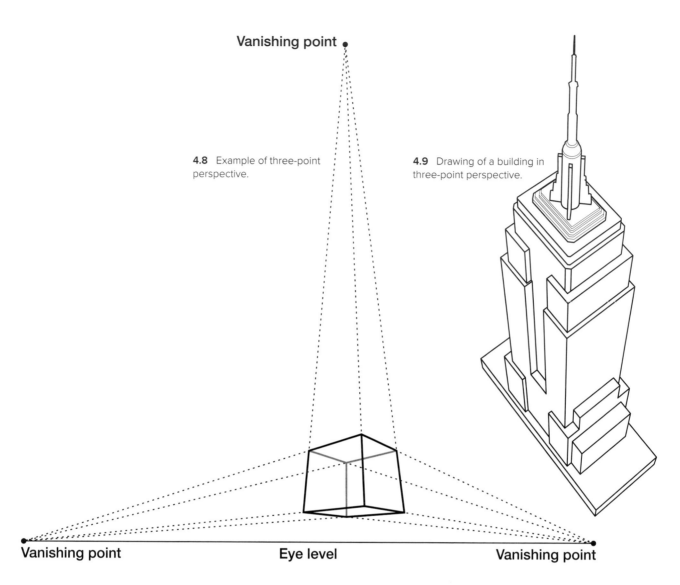

Vanishing point

4.8 Example of three-point perspective.

4.9 Drawing of a building in three-point perspective.

Vanishing point   Eye level   Vanishing point

or *below* eye level. The lines representing depth and width converge on two points at eye level, as in two-point perspective. We can use three-point perspective to exaggerate the sense of space and to present a unique "bird's-eye" or "worm's-eye" view, as illustrated in figure 4.9.

Other Ways to Create the Illusion of Space

- *Overlap.* Overlap is the simplest way to suggest space. It is especially effective when combined with size variation. In *Deposition* (4.10), Rogier van der Weyden used overlap combined with value to create a convincing drama within a crowded compositional space.

- *Size variation.* Because the diminishing size of distant objects is a basic characteristic of human vision, any systematic variation in size can enhance the illusion

of space. This effect is demonstrated most clearly when the distance is great, as in figure 4.1.

- *Definition.* Sharply focused shapes also tend to advance, while blurred shapes tend to recede. When we look at a landscape, dust and water droplets in the air blur outlines and add a blue-gray color to distant shapes. This effect is known as **atmospheric perspective**. In *The Rocky Mountains, Lander's Peak* (4.11), Albert Bierstadt combined dramatic lighting with atmospheric perspective to increase the illusion of space.

- *Location.* Visual elements placed near the top of the page tend to recede, and shapes placed at the bottom tend to advance. In *Landscape in the Style of Dong Yuan* (4.12), the mountains at the top of the scroll appear distant, despite their large size.

- *Color.* Dramatic contrast in hue, value, or color temperature can enhance the illusion of space.

4.10 Rogier van der Weyden, *Deposition*, from an altarpiece commissioned by the Crossbowman's Guild of Louvain, Brabant, Belgium, c. 1435. Oil on panel, 7 ft 2⅝ in. × 8 ft 7⅛ in. (2.2 × 2.6 m). Museo del Prado, Madrid. Bridgeman-Giraudon/Art Resource, New York

4.11 Albert Bierstadt, *The Rocky Mountains, Lander's Peak*, 1863. Oil on canvas, 6 ft 1¼ in. × 10 ft ¾ in. (186.7 × 306.7 cm).
The Metropolitan Museum of Art, Rogers Fund, 1907 (07.123). © The Metropolitan Museum of Art/Bridgeman Images

4.12 Wen Jia, _Landscape in the Style of Dong Yuan_, 1577. China, Ming dynasty (1368–1644). Hanging scroll; ink and light colors on paper, 65½ × 20½ in. (167 × 52 cm).
Kimbell Art Museum, Fort Worth, TX/Art Resource, New York

4.13 Salvador Dalí, _Christ of St. John of the Cross_, 1951. Oil on canvas, 80⅝ × 45⅝ in. (204.8 × 115.9 cm).
Art Gallery and Museum, Kelvingrove, Glasgow, Scotland/© Culture and Sport Glasgow (Museums)/Bridgeman Images/© Salvador Dalí, Fundació Gala-Salvador Dalí, Artists Rights Society (ARS), New York, 2017

Using the Illusion of Space

Through the illusion of space, artists invite viewers to enter an imaginary world. Expression can be heightened when this world is particularly intriguing or when the illusion is especially dramatic.

We call the exaggerated use of perspective **amplified perspective**. We can create amplified perspective by using an unusual viewing position, such as a bird's-eye view, exaggerated spatial convergence, or distortion.

In Salvador Dalí's _Christ of St. John of the Cross_ (4.13), amplified perspective changes our interpretation

4.14 Farrell Erickson, *Westcott #2*, **2017.** Photographic collage, 12½ × 8¹⁵⁄₁₆ in. (31.7 × 22.6 cm).
© Farrell Erickson

of the crucifixion of Jesus. Dramatic three-point perspective emphasizes the importance of the note pinned at the top of the cross. As we look down, the vulnerability of Jesus emphasizes his humanity, while the hovering position of the figure suggests his divinity.

By combining multiple viewpoints, we can also create **fractured space**. In his photographic collage (4.14), Farrell Erickson used multiple photographs to manipulate time and space. A central campus building and distinctive fountain seem to shimmer beneath the bright-blue sky. Passersby of various sizes enter and exit in surprising ways, suggesting that this image records multiple moments in time.

Layered space can be created when the foreground, middle ground, and background are clearly defined. Director Orson Welles used layered space many times in *Citizen Kane*, a film classic. In figure 4.15, young Charlie Kane plays in the background, while in the foreground his mother signs over his care to a lawyer. His father, who opposes this action, occupies the middle ground, caught between the mother and the child. The tensions in the family, the

4.15 Orson Welles, scene from *Citizen Kane*, 1941.
Three layers of space divide this shot: the mother in the foreground, the father in the middle ground, and the child in the background.
Courtesy of Photofest

▶ key questions

CREATING THE ILLUSION OF SPACE

- Which is more appropriate for your idea: a flat design or a spatial design?

- How can you increase or decrease spatial depth in your composition?

- If you use a spatial illusion, where will you place the viewer relative to the setting you create?

determination of the mother, and the innocence of the child are heightened when Charlie shouts, "The Union forever!" as part of his game. When the lawyer takes charge of Charlie, the family will be split apart forever. These three compositional layers communicate complex emotions while telling a story.

SPATIAL DYNAMICS

A Compositional Setting

Like a theatrical stage, the illusion of space creates a setting for compositional action. Objects can move within this illusory world, or the setting itself can begin to shift. Both create **dynamic space**, space that embodies movement. In *Inside Running Animals/Reindeer Way*, Robert Stackhouse combined diagonal lines with variation in definition and size to pull us into

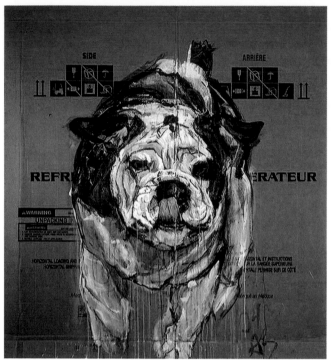

4.17 Ann Strassman, *Humphrey I*, **2004.** Acrylic on cardboard, 70 × 65 in. (177.8 × 165.1 cm).
© Ann Strassman

a mysterious tunnel (4.16). Ann Strassman's *Humphrey I* (4.17) comes charging out of the picture plane, ready to lick us or attack us. Cropping (cutting away part of the image) combined with vigorous brushstrokes helps to push the dog forward. Finally, Mark Messersmith activated *Vapid Visionaires* (4.18) using layer upon layer of visual information. A vertical pole compositionally dissects the painting, and six scarlet flowers seem to hover over the image. We then encounter a collection of windows and framed paintings in the foreground, followed by two figures clutching an alligator and a collection of tropical birds. A mysterious factory belching smoke fills the background.

4.16 Robert Stackhouse, *Inside Running Animals/Reindeer Way*, **1977.** Mixed media, 64 × 43¾ × 2 in. (162.6 × 111 × 5.1 cm).
© Robert Stackhouse. From the Collection of the John and Maxine Belger Family Foundation

▶ key questions

SPATIAL DYNAMICS

- What can the setting itself contribute to your design?

- When is a realistic setting most appropriate? When is an imaginary setting most appropriate?

4.18 **Mark Messersmith**, *Vapid Visionaires*, **2010.** Oil on canvas with carved wooden flowers and top pediment wooden pole plus mixed media predella box across bottom, 82 × 65 in. (208.3 × 165.1 cm). © Mark Messersmith

THE ILLUSION OF MOTION

Animated films are constructed from thousands of tiny frames. When run through a film projector, they create fluid movement. Animation is possible because we have the perceptual ability to integrate the sequential images into a continuous flow.

Substantial audience involvement is also required to create the illusion of motion within a static drawing or sculpture. When presented with multiple images on a single surface, we must feel the movement, complete the action, or anticipate the next event. Based on our day-to-day experience in an ever-changing world, we use our imagination to connect static images to create the illusion of motion.

The Kinesthetic Response

Kinesthetics is the science of movement. Through the very process of walking, we constantly engage in

4.19 Robert Longo, *Untitled*, from *Men in the Cities* series, **1980**. Crayon and graphite on paper, 28 × 40½ in. (71.1 × 102.9 cm).
Albright-Knox Art Gallery/Art Resource, NY. © Robert Longo.
Courtesy of Metro Pictures/ Art Resource, NY

4.20 Myron, *Discus Thrower* (*Diskobolos*). **Roman copy after the original bronze of c. 450 BCE.** Marble, height 5 ft 1 in. (1.54 m).
Museo Nazionale Romano delle Terme, Rome, Italy. Scala/Art Resource, New York

a complex balancing act as we fall forward, then catch ourselves with the next step. When we are confronted by a life-sized figure, such as the man from Robert Longo's *Men in the Cities* series (4.19), the lurching movement of the model resonates on a physical level: we feel as well as see the gesture. Capturing the gesture at the right moment is critical. In Myron's *Discus Thrower* (4.20), the athlete is caught at the moment *before* the whirling vortex of energy explodes, releasing the disc. By capturing this moment rather than the moment of release, the sculptor has trapped within the marble the implied energy of the throw.

The Decisive Moment

Photographer Henri Cartier-Bresson used his understanding of impending change to formulate a theory of photography that he called "the decisive moment." A pioneer in the use of the 35 mm camera, he specialized in capturing the most telling moment in time.

The following two shots from the Spanish town of Valencia demonstrate the difference between a photograph that is interesting and one that is unforgettable. In both cases, we are presented with three layers of space: a wooden door in the foreground framing the face of a policeman in the middle ground and a smaller figure in the background. In the first (4.21), the policeman looks to the right and a young man in the background looks to the left. In the second (4.22), the blurred figure in the background cautiously peers out from the darkness, while the policeman sternly confronts the photographer. While the first image is intriguing, the emotional charge in the second version created one of the most famous of Cartier-Bresson's photographs.

Before and After

The kinesthetic response and the perception of a decisive moment are based on our past experience and our ability to relate that experience to the images we see. Based on our physical experience, we can feel the awkward and unbalanced position of the Longo figure. Likewise, through our emotional experience, when we look at the Cartier-Bresson photograph, we realize that we are seeing a single moment in a more extensive story.

To create a story using a single image, many illustrators deliberately show the moment *before* or the moment *after* an actual event. This painting for *Lucille*

4.21 Henri Cartier-Bresson, *Inside the sliding doors of the bullfight arena, Valencia, Spain*, 1933. Photograph.
© Henri Cartier-Bresson/Magnum Photos

4.22 Henri Cartier-Bresson, *Inside the sliding doors of the bullfight arena, Valencia, Spain*, 1933. Photograph.
Another view of the famous image.
© Henri Cartier-Bresson/Magnum Photos

4.23   Debra Bandelin and Bob Dacey, preliminary painting for illustration in *Lucille Lost*, 2005. Watercolors.
© Debra Bandelin and Bob Dacey

Lost (4.23) is a great example. Illustrators Debra Bandelin and Bob Dacey created a close-up of a girl holding a squirming turtle. Given the size of the creature and its flailing feet, we know that it will soon be put back on the ground. Thus, we are seeing a moment that is charged with energy and meaning. Is this the lost Lucille, or a similar turtle?

Fragmentation

As an object moves, it sequentially occupies various positions in space. We can use visual fragmentation to simulate this effect in art. For example, the superimposed figures in Thomas Eakins's *Double Jump* (4.24) record the many positions the man occupies during an athletic event. Even when figures are simply repeated, as in Edgar Degas's *Frieze of Dancers* (4.25), movement is strongly suggested.

For Eakins, Degas, and Longo, the illusion of motion expanded both the conceptual and the emotional possibilities in an image. Always searching for more effective means of visual expression, any artist or designer can gain from the use of this powerful tool.

4.24   Thomas Eakins, *Double Jump*, 1885. Modern print from a dry-plate negative, 3⅞ × 4⅜ in. (9.8 × 11.1 cm).
Courtesy of the Pennsylvania Academy of the Fine Arts, Philadelphia. Charles Bregler's Thomas Eakins Collection, purchased with the partial support of the Pew Memorial Trust. Acc. No.: 1985.68.2.986

4.25   Edgar Degas, *Frieze of Dancers*, c. 1895. Oil on canvas, 27.6 × 79 in. (70 × 200.5 cm).
The Cleveland Museum of Art. Bequest of Leonard C. Hanna, Jr., 1946.83. Bridgeman Images

4.26 Jeremy Waltman, fight scene from *German***, 2010.** Graphic novel, size of page 8⅜ × 5½ in. (21.5 × 13.9 cm). © Jeremy Waltman

▶ key questions

ILLUSION OF MOTION

- Will the illusion of motion enhance the idea you want to express? If so, how can you create this illusion?

- To what extent is the illusion of motion affected by the illusion of space?

- What happens when you use static (unmoving) and dynamic (moving) shapes together in a design?

4.27 George Tooker, *Government Bureau***, 1956.** Egg tempera on gesso panel, 19⅝ × 29⅝ in. (50 × 75 cm). George A. Hearn Fund, 1956.
© The Metropolitan Museum of Art, New York. Art Resource, New York/DC Moore Gallery/Bridgeman Images

Multiplication

Multiplication can also play a role in visual story-telling. In this page from *German* (4.26) by Jeremy Waltman, we see four different images from a fight. This approach suggests movement and provides us with a surprising close-up at the bottom.

Multiplication creates a very different effect in George Tooker's *Government Bureau* (4.27). Repeated images of the central male figure combined with endless bureaucratic faces create a scene from a nightmare. No matter where the man goes in this hall of mirrors, he always returns to the beginning.

summary

- You can create the illusion of space using linear perspective, overlap, size variation, location, definition, atmospheric perspective, and use of color.

- Linear perspective is based on five fundamental concepts, listed on pages 92–93.

- Three common types of linear perspective are one-point, two-point, and three-point perspective.

- Overlap, size variation, definition, location, and color can also create the illusion of space.

- You can create the illusion of motion by selecting the most decisive moment in an event, through fragmentation, or through various types of multiplication.

key terms

amplified
  perspective
atmospheric
  perspective
cone of vision
dynamic space
eye level
  (horizon line)

fractured space
kinesthetics
layered space
linear
  perspective
one-point
  perspective
picture plane

three-point
  perspective
two-point
  perspective
vanishing
  point

Roger Shimomura, *Florence, South Carolina,* **from** *Stereotypes and Admonitions* **series, 2003.** Acrylic on canvas, 20 x 24 in. (50.8 × 61 cm).
© Roger Shimomura. Private collection.

Concepts and Critical Thinking

In *A Kick in the Seat of the Pants,* Roger von Oech identifies four distinct roles in the creative process.

First, the *explorer* learns as much as possible about the problem. Research is crucial. Ignorance may result in a compositional or conceptual cliché.

Second, the *artist* experiments with a variety of solutions, using all sorts of combinations, proportions, and materials. By creating 10 answers to each question, the artist can select the best solution rather than accepting the only solution.

Third, the *judge* assesses the work in progress and determines what revisions are required. Innovative ideas are never fully developed when first presented; most need extensive revision and expansion. Rather than discard an underdeveloped idea, the judge identifies its potential and determines ways to increase its strength.

Finally, the *warrior* implements the idea. When obstacles appear, the warrior assesses the situation, determines the best course of action, and then moves ahead decisively.

We explore each of these roles in the next four chapters. Chapter Five deals with concept development and visual problem solving. Strategies for cultivating creativity and improving time management are discussed in Chapter Six. Chapter Seven is devoted to critical thinking and provides specific ways to improve any design. In Chapter Eight, we expand our discussion of visual communication and consider ways to create more meaningful artworks.

Problem Seeking and Problem Solving

You can increase the visual power of your work by mastering the basic elements and principles of design described in Parts One and Three. Composition, however, is only part of the puzzle. With the increasing emphasis on visual communication, ideas have become more and more complex. In contemporary art and design, conceptual invention is just as important as compositional strength.

So, to help expand your creativity, we will now explore ways to better define and solve a variety of problems.

PROBLEM SEEKING

The Design Process

In its most basic form, we can distill the design process to four basic steps. When beginning a project, the designer asks:

1. What do we want?

2. What existing designs are similar to the design we want?

3. What are the differences between the existing designs and our new design?

4. How can we combine the best ideas from past inventions with our new ideas?

By studying the classic Eames chair, we can see this process clearly. Charles and Ray Eames were two of the most innovative and influential postwar era designers. Trained as an architect, Charles was a master of engineering. He continually combined "big picture" thinking with attention to detail. Trained as a painter, Ray contributed a love of visual structure, a sense of adventure, and an understanding of marketing. Combining their strengths, this husband-and-wife team designed furniture, toys, exhibitions, and architecture, and directed more than 80 experimental films.

Their first breakthrough in furniture design came in 1940, when they entered a chair competition that the Museum of Modern Art in New York City sponsored. Many architects had designed furniture, and the Eameses were eager to explore this field.

Many similar products existed. The most common was the overstuffed chair, which continues to dominate American living rooms. Extensive padding on a boxy framework supported the sitter. Another popular design was the Adirondack chair, constructed from a series of flat wooden planes. Of greatest interest, however, were designs by architects such as Marcel Breuer (5.1). Using modern materials such as plywood and steel, Breuer and Alvar Aalto had begun to re-define chair design.

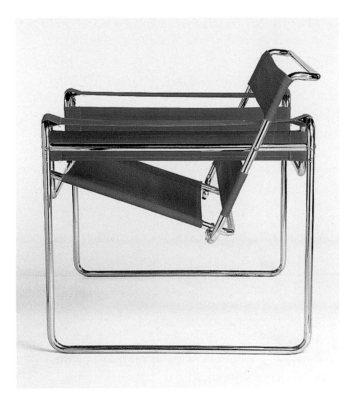

5.1 Marcel Breuer, *Armchair*, 1925. Tubular steel, canvas, 28$\frac{1}{16}$ × 30 × 26$\frac{3}{4}$ in. (72.8 × 77 × 68 cm).
Gift of Gary Laredo. Cooper-Hewitt National Design Museum, Smithsonian Institution/ Art Resource, New York

By comparing existing chairs with the chair that they wanted, Charles and Ray could identify qualities to retain, discard, or change. The familiar overstuffed chair (5.2) was bulky and awkward, but it was comfortable. The Adirondack chair (5.3) was easy to mass-produce, but too large for interior use. The modern chairs were elegant and inventive, but they were expensive to produce and often uncomfortable. The Eameses wanted to create a modern chair that was comfortable, elegant, and inexpensive.

During World War II, the Eames team had designed and manufactured molded plywood splints,

5.2 Overstuffed chair.

5.3 Adirondack chair.

which doctors in the U.S. Navy used. After extensive research and experimentation, they had mastered the process of steaming and reshaping the plywood sheets into complex curves. The resulting splints supported sailors' broken legs without using the precious aluminum and steel needed in the war effort.

So, to develop their competition entry, they combined their knowledge of splints, love of modern chairs, understanding of anatomy, and mastery of architecture. After their plywood chair won the first prize, they created a more refined model (5.4) that combined plywood with aluminum.

5.4 Charles and Ray Eames, *Side chair, Model DCM*, 1946. Molded ash plywood, steel rod and rubber shockmounts, 28$\frac{3}{4}$ × 19$\frac{1}{2}$ × 20 in. (73 × 49.5 × 50.8 cm).
Courtesy of Knoll, Inc.

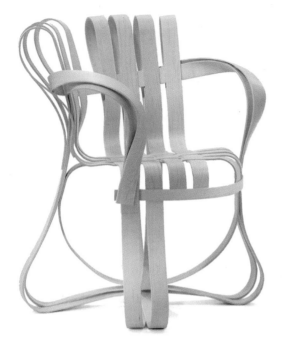

5.5 Frank Gehry, *Cross Check Armchair*, **1992.** Maple, 33⅝ × 28½ × 28½ in. (85.3 × 72.4 × 72.4 cm). Courtesy of Knoll, Inc.

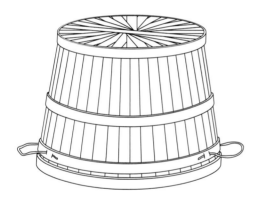

5.6 Wood-strip bushel basket.

A series of Eames designs followed, including numerous cast plastic versions. Variations on these stackable chairs are still being used in many schools. To create the plastic chairs, the Eames team invented a new manufacturing process. This led to a breakthrough in the field of furniture design.

By addressing a need, researching existing designs, making comparisons, and combining the best characteristics of existing chairs, the Eames team produced a new kind of chair and thus firmly established themselves as leaders in the design field.

The Fine Art Process

As this example demonstrates, the design process begins when a client requests help or the designer identifies a societal need. With the Eames chair, the museum competition provided the impetus for an experiment that reshaped an industry.

By contrast, contemporary sculptors, filmmakers, painters, and other fine artists generally invent their own aesthetic problems. Ideas often arise from personal experience. Combining self-awareness with empathy for others, many artists have transformed a specific event into a universal statement. For example, Pablo Picasso's *Guernica*, painted in response to the 1937 bombing of a Spanish village, is now seen as a universal statement about the horrors of war. Working more independently than designers, and with fewer deadlines, artists can more easily explore ideas and subjects of personal interest.

Sources of Ideas

Regardless of the initial motivation for their work, both artists and designers constantly scan their surroundings in a relentless search for images and ideas. As the interviews that appear throughout this book demonstrate, the most improbable object or idea may provide inspiration. Biological systems and architecture inspire sculptor Kendall Buster. Images from art history inspire painter Carrie Ann Baade. Jim Elniski and Frances Whitehead combined a commitment to their urban community with a fascination with solar and geothermal energy to create their "greenhouse." If you are at a loss for an idea, take a fresh look at your surroundings. Here are three strategies.

Transform a Common Object

Architect Frank Gehry based the exuberant armchair in figure 5.5 on the wood-strip bushel basket that farmers use (5.6). If you consider all the ideas that you can generate from a set of car keys, a pair of scissors, or a compass, you will have more than enough to start a project.

Study Nature

Natural forms such as seashells, stones, leaves, and nests have inspired many artists. Trained in scientific illustration, Suzanne Stryk is particularly attentive to both the visual nuances of natural forms and the wide range of ideas they may suggest. In *Journey Work* (5.7), she combined fragments of topographic maps, strips of text, plant stains, and paint. Two carefully drawn birds explore this elegant matrix of lines, shapes, and patterns. In figure 5.8, Vera Lisková used the fluidity and transparency of glass to create a humorous version of

5.7 **Suzanne Stryk, *Journey Work*, 2011.** Mixed media (paper, plant stains, gesso, topographic map, map pin, book pages, acrylic, pencil), 12 × 12 in. (30.5 × 30.5 cm).
© Suzanne Stryk

a prosaic porcupine. Through an inventive use of materials, both artists reinterpreted nature.

Visit a Museum

Artists and designers frequently visit all kinds of museums. Carefully observed, any culture's history and physical objects can be both instructive and inspirational. Looking at non-Western artwork is especially valuable. Unfamiliar concepts and compositions can stimulate creativity. Richard Hunt's Sisiutl mask (5.9) is one example. In Native American mythology, Sisiutl is a giant three-headed sea serpent whose glance can turn an adversary into stone. A benevolent and powerful presence, his image is often carved into the cross beams of clan houses. When he transforms himself into an invincible war canoe, or into a magic belt, Sisiutl becomes a powerful ally. By understanding the story and studying this mask, you

5.8 **Vera Lisková, *Porcupine*, 1972–80.** Flame-worked glass, 4¼ × 11 in. (10.8 × 28.2 cm).
Collection of the Corning Museum of Glass, Corning, NY, Anonymous gift (86.4.180)

5.9 Dr. Richard Hunt, *Raven and Sisiutl Transformation Mask,* **1988.** Red cedarwood, cloth, and string, painted black, red, and green, approximately 16 in. wide × 14 in. tall × 20 in. long (40.6 × 35.6 × 50.8 cm).
© Dr. Richard Hunt, www.richardhunt.com

5.10 Albrecht Dürer, *The Knight, Death, and the Devil* **(detail), 1513.** Engraving, full image 11 × 14 in. (28 × 36 cm).
Open Access Image from the Davison Art Center (Photo: R. Lee). Gift of George W. Davison, 1949.D3.1

can more readily design a mask based on your own experiences.

Historical examples such as Albrecht Dürer's *The Knight, Death and the Devil* (5.10) can be equally inspiring. Some 200 years before this print was made, the Black Death killed nearly half the population of Europe. This horrific disease remained a threat in Dürer's time. As a result, Renaissance conceptions of life and death were very different from our contemporary viewpoint. This difference can spark a new way of thinking and lead you to a fresh idea.

Characteristics of a Good Problem

Regardless of its source, the problem at hand must fully engage either the artist or the designer. Whether somebody commissions it or you invent it, a good problem generally includes the following characteristics.

Significant

Identifying and prioritizing your major goals can help you determine a task's significance. Is it truly essential, or just a distant dream?

Socially Responsible

With the human population exceeding 7 billion, it is unwise to pursue a project that squanders natural resources. What materials will you need, and how will you dispose of the resulting waste? Today, artists and designers often consider each project's environmental and economic implications.

Comprehensible

It is impossible to solve a problem that you don't fully understand. Ask questions if the assignment specifications and objectives are unclear to you.

Open to Experimentation

It is important to distinguish between clear definition and restrictive limitations. Consider the following two assignment descriptions:

1. Organize at least 20 photographs in such a way that they convey an idea or emotion.
2. Organize 20 photographs by American Civil War photographer Mathew Brady to tell a story about the life of Abraham Lincoln.

In the first case, the project requirements are clearly stated, but the solution remains open. The second case describes the *solution* as well as the *problem*.

For the professional artist or designer, there are no "bad" problems, only bad solutions. However, when limited to a narrow range of possible solutions, even the most inventive person will become frustrated. If you find yourself in a straitjacket, rethink the problem and try a new approach.

Authentic

Regardless of the source, every person approaches each problem in his or her own way. Each of us has a unique perspective, and the connections we make vary. As a student, you will learn more when you really embrace each assignment and make it your own. Ask questions so that you can understand each project's conceptual implications. When you reframe the *question* in your own terms, the creative possibilities will expand and your imagination can soar.

CONVERGENT AND DIVERGENT THINKING

Now, let's work our way through an actual assignment, using two problem-solving strategies.

> *Problem:* Organize up to 20 photocopies or prints from historical sources so that they tell a story. Use any size and type of format. You can enlarge, reduce, crop, or repeat any image.

Using Convergent Thinking

Convergent thinking involves the pursuit of a predetermined goal, usually in a linear progression and through a highly focused problem-solving technique. The word *prose* can help you remember the basic steps:

1. Define the *problem*.
2. Do *research*.
3. Determine your *objective*.
4. Devise a *strategy*.
5. *Execute* the strategy.
6. *Evaluate* the results.

In convergent thinking, the end determines the means. You know what you are seeking before you begin. For this reason, clear definition of the problem is essential: the most brilliant idea is useless if it doesn't solve the problem.

Convergent thinking is familiar to most of us in the scientific method, which follows the same basic procedure. It is orderly, logical, and empirical. There are clear boundaries and specific guidelines. Clearly focused on the final result, convergent thinking is a good way to achieve a goal and meet a deadline. Let's analyze each step.

Define the Problem

Determine all the assignment's physical and technical requirements and ask whether there are any stylistic limitations. Be sure that you understand the preliminary steps as well as the final due date.

Next, assess your strengths and weaknesses relative to the assigned problem, and determine your best work strategy. Let's consider the approaches of two hypothetical students, Jeremy (as a convergent thinker) and Angela (as a divergent thinker).

Using a dictionary, Jeremy begins by analyzing the words *story* and *images.* He finds that a *story* is shorter than a novel, that it may be true or fictitious, that it requires a series of connected events, and that it may take many forms, including a memoir, a play, or a newspaper article. Next, he determines that an *image* is a representation of a person or thing, a visual impression that a reflection in a mirror produces, or a mental picture. This means that photographs from books, magazines, and the Internet are all fair game. Jeremy realizes that he can even include a mirror in the project, to reflect the viewer's own image.

He spends the first hour of class on brainstorming, and then decides to develop a story about Irish immigration to America in the 1890s.

Do Research

Creativity is highly dependent on seeking connections and making new combinations. The more information you have, the more connections you can make. For this assignment, Jeremy reads extensively, then develops a plausible story based on immigrant diaries. He begins to collect images of ships, cities, and people.

Determine Your Objective

Jeremy now has the necessary raw material to solve the problem. However, many questions remain unanswered, including the following:

- What happens in this story? Is it fiction or nonfiction?
- Who is the storyteller? A 12-year-old boy will tell a very different story from a 20-year-old woman.
- What is the best format to use? A dozen letters that fictitious brothers in Dublin and Boston sent to one another? A website describing actual families? A photo album?

At this point, Jeremy pauses to rethink his strategy. What does he really want to communicate? He considers:

- *Does it solve the problem?* He reviews the assignment parameters.
- *Is the solution conceptually inventive?* Is it really intriguing, or is it something that we have all seen before, a cliché?
- *Is the planned solution visually compelling?*
- *Can he complete this solution by the due date?* To meet the due date, it may be necessary to distill a complex problem down to an essential statement. In this case, Jeremy decides to simplify his project by focusing on one main character.

Devise a Strategy

Although Jeremy can complete some assignments in an afternoon, three-dimensional projects and multiple-image works tend to take longer. He determines the supplies that he needs and considers the best time and place to work on the project.

Execute the Strategy

Now Jeremy just digs in and works. He works best with great concentration and determination at this point, rather than second-guessing himself.

Evaluate the Results

At the end of each work session, Jeremy considers the strengths and weaknesses of the work in progress. What areas in each composition seem cluttered or confusing? How can he strengthen those areas? He finally presents the project for a class critique.

Convergent Thinking Applications

Convergent thinking is most effective when

- You can clearly define the problem.
- You can solve the problem rationally.
- You must solve the problem sequentially.
- You must meet firm deadlines.

Because many problems in science and industry fit these criteria, scientists, businesspeople, and graphic designers favor convergent thinking.

Using Divergent Thinking

The advantages of convergent thinking are clarity, control, focus, and a strong sense of direction. For many tasks, convergent thinking is ideal. In some cases, however, convergent thinking can offer *too* much clarity and not enough chaos. Inspiration is elusive. Over-the-edge creativity is often messy and rarely occurs in an orderly progression. If you want to find something completely new, you will have to leave the beaten path.

In **divergent thinking**, the means determines the end. The process is more open-ended, and specific results are hard to predict. Divergent thinking is a great way to generate completely new ideas.

Two major differences exist between convergent and divergent thinking. First, in divergent thinking, we define the problem much more broadly. Research is more expansive and less tightly focused. Second, because the convergent thinker discards weak ideas at the thumbnail stage, the final image is more planned and predictable. The divergent thinker, on the other hand, generates many variables, is less methodical, and may have to produce multiple drafts of a composition to obtain a polished result.

Whereas convergent thinking is usually more efficient, divergent thinking is often more inventive. It opens up unfamiliar lines of inquiry and can lead to a creative breakthrough. Divergent thinking is a high-risk/high-gain approach. By breaking traditional rules, the artist can explore unexpected connections and create new possibilities.

Let's try the same assignment again, now using Angela's divergent thinking.

> *Problem:* Organize up to 20 photocopies or prints from historical sources so that they tell a story. Use any size and type of format. You can enlarge, reduce, crop, or repeat any image.

Realizing that the strength of the source images is critical, Angela immediately heads to a library section or website devoted to historical photography. By leafing through a dozen books or webpages, she finds 40 great photographs, ranging from images of railroad stations to trapeze artists. She scans or prints the photographs, enlarging or reducing them to provide more options. Laying them out on a table or on a large computer screen, she begins to move the images around, considering various stories that they might generate. Angela soon discards 20 of the images. They are unrelated to the circus story that she decides to develop. She then finds 10 more images to flesh out her idea.

At this point, her process becomes similar to the final steps that we described in the preceding section. Like Jeremy, she must clarify her objective, develop characters, decide on a format, and construct the final artwork. However, because she started with such a disparate collection of images, her final story is more likely to be nonlinear. Like a dream, her images may *evoke* feelings rather than *describe* specific events.

Divergent Thinking Applications

Divergent thinking is most effective when

- The definition of the problem is elusive or evolving.
- A rational solution is not required.
- A methodical approach is unnecessary.
- Deadlines are flexible.

Which is better—convergent or divergent thinking? A good problem-solving strategy is one that works. If five people are working on a website design, a clear sense of direction, agreement on style, an understanding of individual responsibilities, and adherence to deadlines are essential. On the other hand, when an artist is working independently, the open-ended divergent approach can lead to a major breakthrough. Combining convergent and divergent thinking is ideal. When you need to expand an idea through open-ended exploration, use divergent thinking. When you need focus or distillation, shift to convergent thinking.

In the following interview, designer Steve Quinn uses both divergent and convergent thinking to efficiently create a simple and straightforward website.

Profile:
Steve Quinn,
Website Designer
Design Thinking

Steve Quinn of Quinn Design develops websites, branding, and advertising for a wide range of public organizations and private companies, such as Kimberly-Clark, Milwaukee Ballet, and the City of Chicago. While teaching at Northern Illinois University, he developed a seven-step problem-solving process that can be applied to all types of design. In the following interview, we discuss the steps in this process and their application.

MS: Let's start with your seven-step ideation to implementation process.

SQ: Sure. This process can be used for large and small projects, and can frame up our entire conversation.

Step One: Develop a Problem Statement. Clients arrive with problems they want designers to solve. However, they may underestimate or misread the real problem, and thus miss the mark completely. For example, just redesigning a logo will not improve sales if poor product design is the real problem. So,

I begin my work by asking a lot of questions and listening carefully. As an advocate for the customer as well as the client, I must view the problem from multiple perspectives.

Step Two: Define Objectives. It is impossible to hit a target I can't see. By defining our objectives, both the client and I can agree on the targets we must hit. This stage further clarifies our overall intention and creates a strong bridge between the problem statement and the solution.

Steve Quinn, Past Basket Kitchen Design website page home page, 2013.
© Steve Quinn

Kitchen Design Portfolio

Award winning kitchen designs from traditional to contemporary. See a sampling of our client's dream kitchens!

Learn More

About Us

Mature professionals comprise our staff with an average Past Basket employee tenure of more than 20 years.

Learn More

Small Kitchens - A Past Basket Design Specialty!

Our Kitchen Design Team loves the challenge that comes with a small kitchen remodel.

Learn More

New Kitchen Showroom Coming Soon!

A new entrance, a new showroom and a new focus on kitchen design. See the Plan!

Learn More

Steve Quinn, Past Basket Kitchen Design website contents portal, 2013.
© Steve Quinn

Step Three: Set Parameters. Every design problem is developed within various restrictions, or parameters. What is the budget? If I am designing a brochure, how large can it be and how many colors can I use? When working on a video advertisement, what is the maximum duration? What is the deadline? Without clear parameters, we could waste a lot of time and money on infeasible proposals. I continue to advocate for both the client and the customer at this stage. We want the best possible solution, delivered on time, within defined parameters.

Step Four: Research. Research provides us with deeper understanding of potential solutions—and of potential obstacles we must overcome. Reviewing existing solutions to similar problems is especially valuable. When we know what already exists, we can deliberately push our solution a bit further. On large, complex projects, research may also include customer surveys, reading up on specific subjects related to the project, and simply tracking customer response to a product.

Step Five: Solution Development. We can focus on the solution once the problem has been defined, the objectives and parameters clarified, and research done. Based on knowledge I gain in the first four steps of this process, I think through or sketch out many ideas before I begin to finalize anything.

Step Six: Evaluation and Feedback. When we have a range of potential solutions sketched out, we can evaluate each one. Does each solution meet the objectives and solve the problem, while still working within the parameters set? Which solutions meet the criteria most fully—and are most visually distinctive? When working on a website, I often test-drive it with actual clients, to identify problem areas and increase ease of navigation.

Step Seven: Execution. I can now finalize the project. Diplomacy is crucial: the client is very eager to see a final result within the budget we have approved. Just as a great idea can be ruined by a weak design, so a great design can be ruined by poor craftsmanship or substandard materials. By seeing the project through from start to finish, I can insure the best quality possible. This always pays off in the long run!

MS: Can you talk us through an actual project, based on this problem-solving sequence?

SQ: In 2012, a kitchen design firm called Past Basket Design hired me to develop new signage, a website, and a brochure. Developed in 1988, this company was best known for offering high-quality and custom products within a very user-friendly sales environment. They wanted to establish themselves as a forward-looking firm—yet had "past" built right into their name.

Rather than starting on a simple redesign of their existing materials, I therefore started with Step One: Problem Statement. I asked lots of questions about their mission and what they really wanted to accomplish as a company.

Moving on to Step Two, I interviewed three customers at some length regarding what they wanted to see in a new design. What attracted them to Past Basket in the first place? What information did they need when considering the investment in a custom-made kitchen design? I found that knowledgeable and friendly marketing staff was a major attraction and that seeing lots of beautiful design examples was essential.

These initial steps set the stage for all the remaining steps. Functionality is always a top priority; customers need easy access to the information they want. I have created complex websites, with motion graphics and other effects. However, flashy effects would not attract Past Basket customers, so I distilled the design as much as I possibly could. We featured beautiful photographs of past projects, each accompanied with a brief description. The friendly sales staff was a major asset, so I featured them in two areas, in a section called "about us" and in a section devoted to the design process itself. A section on testimonials from happy customers and accolades provided even more information and increased confidence in the company.

MS: How many designs does the client need to see?

SQ: Paul Rand, one of the masters of graphic design, presented only one solution to his clients. His design process was very effective and he was able to hit the nail on the head just about every time. I try to follow this model. By making adjustments early in the process, I can generally create an effective design that will be accepted with only minor changes.

MS: The phrase "think outside the box" has become a cliché—but it describes an important idea. When we "think outside the box" we go beyond the ordinary, seeking something challenging and new. To what extent does your design process invite such invention?

SQ: Actually, I start by thinking *inside* the box created by the problem statement, client objectives, and design parameters. Without understanding these essentials, I could create a wonderful design that totally misses the point. I can become really inventive once I understand the limitations. It is like playing a game within various rules.

MS: You've talked and written a lot about the social responsibility of design. Do you have any advice for my students?

SQ: Designers have an important responsibility: to ensure that what we put in that space enhances it, rather than polluting an already cluttered visual environment. Designers must provide a meaningful service to their clients, advocate for the user, proactively solve problems, and provide engaging, effective solutions—no matter who the client may be.

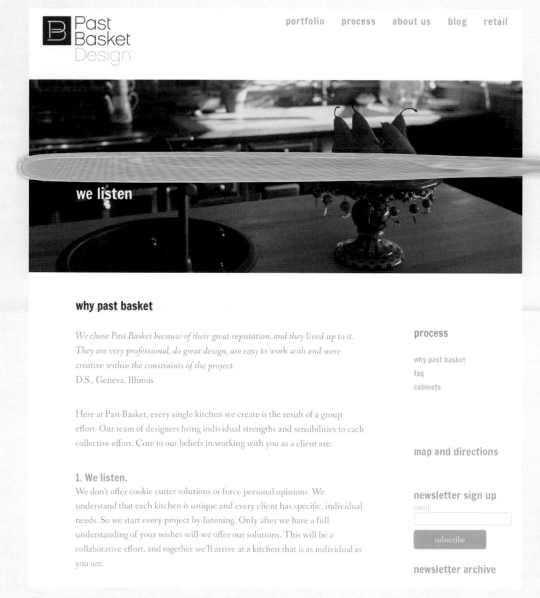

Steve Quinn, Past Basket Kitchen Design "process" page, 2013.
© Steve Quinn

BRAINSTORMING

Brainstorming plays an important role in both convergent and divergent thinking. It is a great way to expand ideas, see connections, and explore implications. Following are four common strategies.

Make a List

Suppose that the assignment involves visualizing an emotion. Start by listing every emotion that you can, regardless of your interest in any specific area. Getting into the practice of opening up and actively exploring possibilities is crucial—just pour out ideas!

By investigating specific kinds of anger and determining the causes and the effects, you now have many specific images that you can develop.

Use a Thesaurus

Another way to explore an idea's potential is to use a thesaurus. Be sure to access a thesaurus that lists words conceptually rather than alphabetically. Use the index in the back to look up the specific word that you need. For example, *The Concise Roget's International Thesaurus* has a section titled "Feelings," including everything from *acrimony* to *zeal*. Here is a list of

synonyms from the section on resentment and anger: *anger, wrath, ire, indignation, heat, more heat than light, dudgeon, fit of anger, tantrum, outburst, explosion, storm, scene, passion, fury, burn, vehemence, violence, vent one's anger, seethe, simmer,* and *sizzle*! Thinking about a wide range of implications and connections to other emotions can give you a new approach to a familiar word.

Explore Connections

By drawing a conceptual diagram, you can create your own thesaurus. Start with a central word. Then, branch out in all directions, pursuing connections and word associations as widely as possible. In a sense, this approach lets you visualize your thinking, as the branches show the patterns and connections that occurred as you explored the idea (5.11).

In *Structure of the Visual Book* (1984), Keith A. Smith demonstrates the value of verbal connections. He seeks immersion in his subject. He wants to know it so well that he can pursue his images intuitively, with all the power and grace of a skilled cyclist. Try to follow the steps in figure 5.12, as he explores the word *bicycle.* Using a single object, he explores movement, friendship, and geometry.

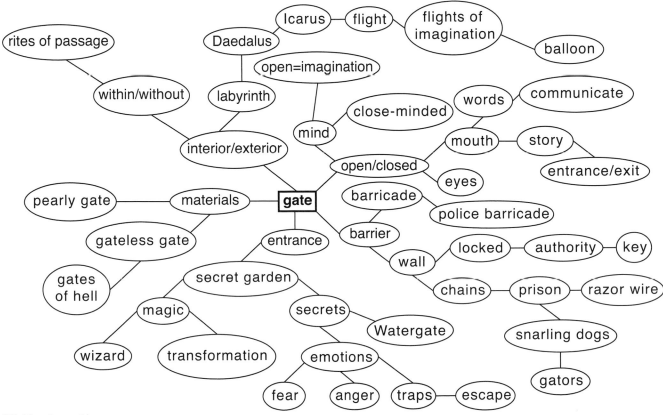

5.11 Mapping an idea.

If I am going to make drawings or photographs which include a bicycle, I might go for a bike ride, but more importantly I would fantasize about a bike. I would picture a bike in my mind. The most obvious depiction is the side view because this is the significant profile. I would then imagine a standing bicycle with no rider, looking from above, directly down on the bike, or from behind or in front of the standing bike with my eye-level midway between the ground and the handlebars. In these three positions the bicycle is seen from the least significant profile. It is a thin vertical line with horizontal protrusions of the pedals, seat and handlebars. The area viewed is so minimal that the bicycle almost disappears.

Before long in examining a bike I would become involved with circles. Looking at the tires, I think about the suspension of the rim and the tire, indeed, the entire vehicle and rider, by the thin spokes. It amazes me that everything is floating in space,

connected only by thin lines. I imagine riding the bike through puddles and the trace of the linear journey from the congruent and diverging water marks left by the tread on the pavement. I might think about two friends together and separated. Symbolism.

I think about cycles of being with friends and apart. And again I would think literally of cycles, circles and tires.

I would think of the full moon as a circle and how in its cycle it turns into a line. I would see the tires from the significant profile and in my mind I would turn it in space and it would become an ellipse.

If I turned it further, until it was on an axis 90 degrees from the significant profile, it would no longer be a circle or an ellipse, but it would be a line. So again, line comes into my thoughts.

A circle is a line.

A circle is a straight line.[1]

5.12 Keith A. Smith. Brainstorming.
© Keith A. Smith, www.keithsmithbooks.com

1. Keith A. Smith, *Structure of the Visual Book* (Fairport, NY: The Sigma Foundation, 1991), pp. 17–18.

Keep a Journal

Keeping a journal or a sketchbook is an ideal way to record your ideas and create connections. In it, you can

- Classify, arrange, and record information
- Develop new ideas
- Examine your current beliefs and analyze the beliefs of others
- Record your responses to critiques
- Make connections among your various classes

Recording your ideas at the end of each class and reviewing them at the beginning of the next can help you construct your own learning process. Anything that expands your thinking is fair game, including

- Plans for projects, such as thumbnail sketches and rough drafts
- Comments on how you can improve your work
- Notes from textbook readings and clippings from magazines
- Notes on visiting artists or gallery visits
- Technical notes or information on class materials
- Questions that you want to pose in the next class meeting

Your record keeping can take many forms, including

- Drawings and diagrams

- Written ideas, descriptions, and lists
- Poetry and song lyrics

Periodically ask yourself the following questions:

- What was the most compelling image that I saw today? What made it compelling?
- What similarities and differences were there among my studio classes this week?
- What connections were there between my lecture classes and my studio classes?
- What do I need to know to push my ideas further?

Viewing the journal as a record of your creative process is liberating. A random idea today can help you solve a specific problem tomorrow. It is wise to review the journal as you move into upper-level classes. Many ideas that were too ambitious for a first-year class are perfectly suited to further development later on.

Collaborative Creativity

Designers generally use group brainstorming. This helps them explore a wider range of possibilities and better meet client needs. In *The Art of Innovation* (2001), IDEO general manager Tom Kelley lists seven characteristics of effective group brainstorming. The following list is based on a chapter titled "The Perfect Brainstorm."

1. Sharpen your focus. A good brainstormer will generate a lot of ideas. When these ideas all address

the same problem, many viable solutions result. On the other hand, when participants don't understand the problem, chaos can result.

2. Use playful rules, such as "write it down" and "think bigger." A visual and verbal record of your ideas is helpful. Premature criticism is not.

3. Number your ideas. Numbers ("Let's aim for 50 ideas in the next hour") can create quantitative targets and provide a record of the order in which ideas occurred.

4. Build and jump. As the momentum builds, more and more ideas burst forth. A thoughtful question can then help the group leap to the next level, rather than getting stuck on a plateau.

5. The space remembers. Fill your brainstorming space with 22 × 30-inch Post-it notes covered with ideas that the group has developed. By *seeing* the information, you can more easily spot bridges and build connections.

6. Warm up. If you are working with a completely new group, it may be necessary to provide an ice-breaker to build trust. This is especially true if the participants are unfamiliar with brainstorming. I often ask each participant to present one succinct question or to draw a quick cartoon of the problem as they see it. It may be an enraged elephant, a tangle of thorns, or a whirling chain saw. Both the questions and the cartoons can reveal participant insights without demanding too much too soon.

7. Get physical. A wide range of simple materials opens up possibilities, especially if you are brainstorming a three-dimensional design problem. Cardboard, plasticine, and canvas all behave very differently. Playing with various materials can lead to a wider range of possibilities.

VISUAL RESEARCH

Thumbnail Sketches

Now let's practice turning ideas into images.

Return to the original list of emotions that you developed in the brainstorming exercise. Circle the most promising words or phrases and look for connections between them. Start working on thumbnail sketches, about 1.5 × 2 inches in size (5.13). Be sure

5.13 Examples of thumbnail sketches.

to draw a clear boundary for the sketches. The edge of the frame is like an electric fence. By using the edge wisely, you can generate considerable power!

As with the verbal brainstorming, move fast and stay loose at this point. It is better to generate 10 to 20 possibilities than to refine any single idea. You may find yourself producing very different solutions, or you may make a series of solutions to the same problem. Either approach is fine—just keep moving!

Model Making

When working two-dimensionally, it is often necessary to make one or more full-sized rough drafts to see how the design looks when enlarged. Refinements that you make at this stage can mean the difference between an adequate solution and an inspired solution.

Prototypes, models, and maquettes serve a similar purpose when you are working three-dimensionally. A **maquette** is a well-developed three-dimensional sketch. Figure 5.14 shows Peter Forbes's maquette for *Shelter/Surveillance Sculpture*. In this chipboard "sketch," Forbes determined the sculpture's size relative to the viewer and developed a construction strategy. As a result, when he constructed the final, 11-foot-tall sculpture, Forbes was able to proceed with confidence. A **model** is a technical experiment. A **prototype** can be quite refined, such as the fully functional test cars that automobile companies develop. As shown in figure 5.15, three-dimensional printing has greatly increased the speed and ease with which complex prototypes can be made. In addition to the aesthetic benefit of such preliminary studies, we can often use models and prototypes to solve specific problems. Is the cardboard that you are using heavy enough to stand vertically, or does it bow? Is your adhesive strong enough? If there are moving parts, is the action fluid and easy, or does the mechanism constantly get stuck? Does the object look good from all sides?

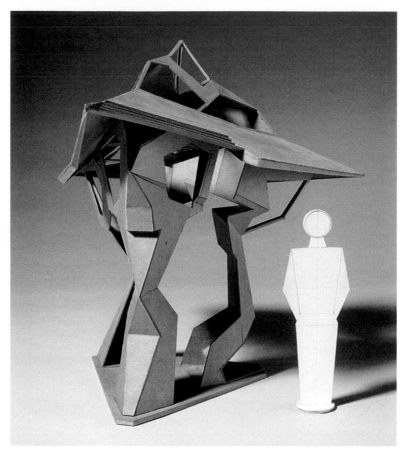

5.14 Peter Forbes, model for *Shelter/Surveillance Sculpture*, 1994. Mixed media, 10½ × 9½ × 9 in. (27 × 24 × 23 cm).
© Peter Forbes

5.15 Prototype of shoe made with 3D printer. Digitally generated image.
Maciej Frolow/Getty Images

By completing these preliminary studies, you can refine the idea, strengthen the composition, and improve the final piece. As with a well-rehearsed performance, the work that you bring to the critique now is ready for discussion.

AN OPEN MIND

The very best artists and designers are often accomplished in more than one field. For example, Michelangelo was acclaimed as a painter, sculptor, and poet, and Leonardo da Vinci was a master of art, biology, and engineering. The study of philosophy has had a major impact on videographer Bill Viola and on installation artist Robert Irwin. As we will see in Chapter Eight, Jim Elniski and Frances Whitehead

researched energy systems, roof gardens, and architecture to create a unique artwork—which is also their home (5.16). Whenever the base of knowledge expands, the range of potential connections increases. When the islands of knowledge are widely scattered, as with interdisciplinary work, we can create transformative connections.

The message is clear: the more you know, the more you can say. Read a book. Attend a lecture. Take a course in astronomy, archaeology, psychology, or poetry. Use ideas from academic courses to expand your studio work. Art and design require conceptual development as well as perceptual and technical skill. By engaging your heart, your eye, your hand, and your mind, you can fully use your emotional, perceptual, technical, and conceptual resources to create your very best work.

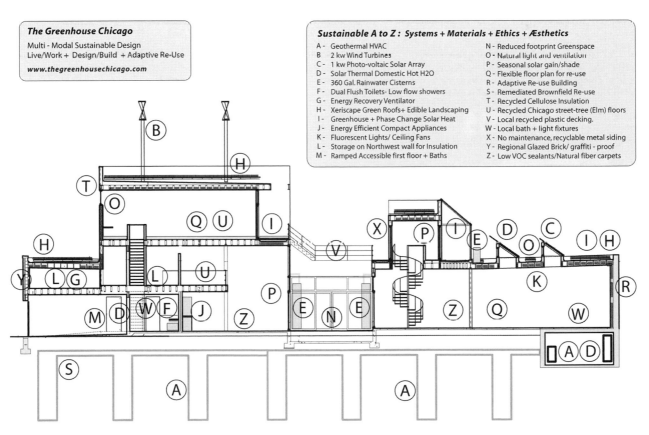

The Greenhouse Chicago
Multi - Modal Sustainable Design
Live/Work + Design/Build + Adaptive Re-Use
www.thegreenhousechicago.com

Sustainable A to Z : Systems + Materials + Ethics + Æsthetics

A - Geothermal HVAC
B - 2 kw Wind Turbines
C - 1 kw Photo-voltaic Solar Array
D - Solar Thermal Domestic Hot H2O
E - 360 Gal. Rainwater Cisterns
F - Dual Flush Toilets- Low flow showers
G - Energy Recovery Ventilator
H - Xeriscape Green Roofs+ Edible Landscaping
I - Greenhouse + Phase Change Solar Heat
J - Energy Efficient Compact Appliances
K - Fluorescent Lights/ Ceiling Fans
L - Storage on Northwest wall for Insulation
M - Ramped Accessible first floor + Baths

N - Reduced footprint Greenspace
O - Natural light and ventilation
P - Seasonal solar gain/shade
Q - Flexible floor plan for re-use
R - Adaptive Re-use Building
S - Remediated Brownfield Re-use
T - Recycled Cellulose Insulation
U - Recycled Chicago street-tree (Elm) floors
V - Local recycled plastic decking.
W - Local bath + light fixtures
X - No maintenance, recyclable metal siding
Y - Regional Glazed Brick/ graffiti - proof
Z - Low VOC sealants/Natural fiber carpets

5.16 Frances Whitehead, *The A to Z*, 2007. Diagram of multimodal sustainable features.
© Jim Elniski

summary

- Concept and composition are equally important aspects of art and design.

- Designers usually solve problems that their clients present. Artists usually invent aesthetic problems for themselves.

- Ideas come from many sources, including common objects, nature, mythology, and history.

- Good problems are significant, socially responsible, comprehensible, and authentic. They provide basic parameters without inhibiting exploration.

- Convergent thinking is highly linear. The word *prose* can help you remember the steps.

- Divergent thinking is nonlinear and more open-ended than convergent thinking. It is less predictable and may lead to a creative breakthrough.

- You can expand or enrich any idea using brainstorming. Making lists, using a thesaurus, making a conceptual diagram, and creating connections are all common strategies.

- Visual and verbal research can provide the background information that you need to create a truly inventive solution.

- The best artists and designers have a wide range of interests and approach new challenges with an open mind.

key terms

brainstorming
convergent thinking
divergent thinking

maquette
model
prototype

Success Story: Elizabeth Nelson, Designer
Shedd Aquarium, Chicago, Illinois

Elizabeth Nelson is a design graduate from the University of Illinois-Chicago. Now Director of Graphic Design at Shedd Aquarium, she established there an in-house advertising and design agency to meet the many communication and design needs of one of Chicago's most popular tourist attractions.

MS: What did you find most challenging in your initial design classes?

EN: The University of Illinois-Chicago department was founded by faculty from the Bauhaus, a pioneering German art school that was closed in 1933 as the Nazis rose to power. Instead of making beautiful paintings, we made geodesic domes, shot weird photos with pinhole cameras, and drew seemingly random lines with messy ink pens. Figurative art was barely tolerated. Everything was "conceptual."

It was like being in outer space with no sense of direction. I had no idea when I was going to be praised or sent back to the drawing board. There was zero understanding of what we were doing or why we were doing it.

And yet, the foundation program transformed the way I thought about experimentation, aesthetics, and the role of design in the world. Art was not about being "pretty." It could shine a spotlight on issues and conditions critical to human culture. The role of a creator was not that of a decorator, but of a provocateur, instigator, and collaborator.

MS: How did you make the transition from your BFA coursework to your current position?

EN: With 25 years of hard work! But it started with learning to assess my own shortcomings and ask for help. After graduating, I realized my portfolio consisted of a few nice projects and a lot of filler. Making the effort to rebuild it would be a time-consuming but necessary investment. I also needed a really tough mentor, so I asked Tad Takano, the teacher who liked me the least. He was known as a take-no-sh*t task-

master. The cigarette literally fell out of his mouth when I asked him.

To my dismay, he tossed my entire portfolio and declared we would start from scratch. It took more than eight months to rebuild all the work. Tad negotiated a talent tuition waiver to help cover my fees, but he also locked me in his basement when I wanted to go out dancing because he thought my typography needed work. "This is illegal!" I banged on the locked door, "It's kidnapping!"

Based on my transformed portfolio, Professor Takano helped me find my first full-time job in a huge public relations firm. He would later occasionally appear like a grumpy guardian angel to help advance my career.

MS: What are the most challenging aspects of your current position?

EN: As a design director, I am often equal parts visionary, diplomat, accountant, logistics expert, therapist, and IT specialist. Maintaining design integrity and organizational priorities is critical, but I also need to manage relationships with clients, upper management, our peers, my team, and our vendors. All this goes on while keeping track of about 50 active projects at any time. There are days when I feel more like an air traffic controller than a designer.

To deal with the volume of work, my team has developed processes that we follow religiously. Real basics, such as consistent file naming, greatly increase efficiency. When I first started in design, I hated having to work in organized systems. Now I realize how liberating constraints can be. They give a solid framework so that we can take care of the business side before leaping into the creative pool.

But designers also have to be ready to abandon frameworks when necessary. Being flexible and adaptable is a valuable and highly underrated skill that is quite difficult to teach. People depend on having a "right" and "wrong" way of doing things as a safety net against risk taking. "I can't do it," they say, "It's against the rules." "Break the rules," I tell them, "We'll live."

Breaking the rules is the only way to make new rules and develop truly creative and innovative solutions. However, there is a fine line between being disruptively innovative and just being obnoxious. It takes a while to learn how to walk that tightrope.

MS: What basic design skills inform your work today?

EN: I spent years honing my understanding of great design. I now find that I often have to put my preconceived notions aside, so that I can see the genius in a truly unexpected solution.

MS: What advice would you give to students starting college today?

EN: Invest in yourself. Ask for help (as often as it takes). Be willing to work hard. Accept opportunities. Work for and with people you respect. Take targeted risks. And embrace kindness. It's different from empathy, which is still about being stuck in your own head. Kindness is acting on empathy. It's thinking and behaving unselfishly.

Aquarium interior
© Vasiliki/Getty Images

Cultivating Creativity

"The heart of all new ideas lies in the borrowing, adding, combining or modifying of old ones. Do it by accident and people call you lucky. Do it by design and they'll call you creative."

Michael LeBoeuf, in *Imagineering*

The convergent problem-solving process described in Chapter Five seems methodical and predictable. Even the more open-ended divergent thinking process is based on a pattern that alternates between idea expansion and idea selection. Why, then, do we need to know anything more about creativity?

The answer is simple. We confront much messier creative challenges whenever we begin our work. Artists and designers often encounter creative blocks or problems that stubbornly resist solution. So, this chapter is designed to help bridge the gap between the ideal situation that we explored in Chapter Five and your actual experience in the studio. In it we consider characteristics of creative people, discuss goal setting, list time-management strategies, and explore habits of mind and habits of work that you can use to increase success.

SEVEN CHARACTERISTICS OF CREATIVE THINKING

"Conditions for creativity are to be puzzled, to concentrate, to accept conflict and tension, to be born every day, to feel a sense of self."

Erich Fromm, in *Creativity and Its Cultivation*

Creativity is inherently unpredictable. Through creative thinking, we break old habits and transform familiar patterns of thought. Anything can happen. Predicting the future based on past experience becomes inadequate when a creative breakthrough occurs. Like a shimmering drop of mercury, creativity eludes capture.

We can actively cultivate creative thinking, however. Rather than waiting for inspiration, we can set up the conditions that favor it. First, let's look at the characteristics of highly creative people, based on the work of many researchers.

Receptivity

Creative people are open to new ideas and welcome new experiences. Never complacent, they question the status quo and embrace alternative solutions to existing problems. Listening more and talking less is helpful. As journalist Larry King says, "I never learn anything new when I'm the one talking!"

chapter six

Curiosity

Researching unfamiliar topics and exploring unusual systems are a source of delight for most creative people. "How does it work?" and "How can it work better?" are questions that creative people frequently ask.

Wide Range of Interests

With a broad knowledge base, a creative person can make a wider range of connections. Consider the number of words that you can quickly create from the letters in the word *image*:

age, game, gem, am, aim, a, I, me

Try the same game with the word *imagination*:

gin, nation, gnat, ton, tan, not, man, again, gain, oat, got, tag, am, aim, ant, no, on, tin, gamin, inn, ingot, main, a, I

With more components, the number of combinations increases. Likewise, an artist who has a background in or knowledge of literature, geology, archery, music, and other subjects can make more connections than can a strict specialist.

Attentiveness

Realizing that every experience is valuable, creative people pay attention to seemingly minor details. Scientists often develop major theories by observing small events, which they then organize into complex patterns. Artists can often see past superficial visual chaos to observe an underlying order. Playwrights develop dramatic stories by looking past the surface of human behavior to explore the comedy (and tragedy) of human existence. By looking carefully, creative people see possibilities that others miss.

Connection Seeking

A creative breakthrough often occurs when we see connections between seemingly random fragments. For example, Egyptian hieroglyphs became readable when a young French scholar realized that they carried the same message as an adjacent Greek inscription on a slab of stone, now called the Rosetta Stone (6.1). By comparing the two and cracking the code, Jean-François Champollion opened the door for all subsequent students of ancient Egyptian culture.

Conviction

Because we often derive new ideas from old ones, it is foolish to ignore or dismiss the past. However, creative people embrace change and actively pursue an alternative path. Never satisfied with routine answers to familiar questions, they invent new possibilities and often challenge the status quo.

Complexity

In lectures, our instructors encourage us to think rationally and write clearly. In studio classes, they encourage us to explore, experiment,

6.1 Rosetta Stone, Egypt, Ptolemaic period, 196 BCE. 5.7 × 28.5 × 11 in. (14.4 × 72.3 × 27.9 cm).
British Museum, London. Leemage/Getty Images

and use our intuition. Synthesis, visualization, spatial perception, and nonlinear thinking are valued highly in art and design.

To be fully effective, a creative person needs to combine the rational and the intuitive. Although we may use intuition to generate a new idea, we often need logic and analysis for its realization. As a result, the actions of creative people are often complex or even contradictory. As psychologist Mihály Csíkszentmihályi[1] noted, creative people often combine

- *Physical energy with a respect for rest.* They work long hours with great concentration, then rest and relax, fully recharging their batteries.

- *Savvy with innocence.* Creative people tend to view the world and themselves with a sense of wonder, rather than clinging to preconceptions or stereotypes. They use common sense as well as intellect in completing their work.

- *Responsibility with playfulness.* When the situation requires serious attention, creative people are remarkably diligent and determined. They realize that there is no substitute for hard work and drive themselves tirelessly when nearing completion of a major project. On the other hand, when the situation permits, they may adopt a playful, devil-may-care attitude. This provides a release from the previous work period.

- *Risk taking with safekeeping.* Creativity expert George Prince noted two behavioral extremes in people.[2] Safekeepers look before they leap, avoid surprises, punish mistakes, follow the rules, and watch the clock. A safekeeper is most comfortable when there is only one right answer to memorize or one solution to consider. Risk takers are just the opposite. They break the rules, leap before they look, like surprises, are impetuous, and may lose track of time. A risk taker loves inventing multiple answers to every question.

  Creative thinking requires a mix of risk taking and safekeeping. When brainstorming new ideas, risk takers use open-ended exploration. However, when implementing new ideas, deadlines, budgets, and feasibility become major concerns. It often seems that the risk taker jump-starts the job and the safekeeper completes it.

- *Extroversion with introversion.* When starting a new project, creative people are often talkative and gregarious, eager to share insights and explore ideas. When a clear sense of direction develops, however, they often withdraw, seeking solitude and quiet work time. This capacity for solitude is crucial. Several studies have shown that talented teenagers who cannot stand solitude will rarely develop their creative skills.

- *Passion with objectivity.* Mature artists tend to plunge into new projects, convinced of the importance of the work and confident of their skills. Any attempt to distract or dissuade them is futile. However, when they complete a model or preliminary study, most pause to assess their progress. At that point, a dispassionate objectivity replaces the emotional attachment required while creating. The artist reworks or discards the work that does not pass this review, regardless of the hours he or she has spent on it. In major projects, this alternating process of creation and analysis may be repeated many times.

- *Disregard for time with attention to deadlines.* Time often dissolves when studio work begins. An artist or a designer can become engrossed in a project: when the work is going well, 6 hours can feel like 20 minutes. On the other hand, attention to deadlines is necessary when preparing an exhibition or working for a client.

- *Modesty with pride.* As they mature, creative people often become increasingly aware of how teachers, family, and colleagues have contributed to their success. Rather than brag about past accomplishments, they tend to focus on current projects. On the other hand, as creative people become aware of their significance within a field, they gain a powerful sense of purpose. They delete distractions from the schedule, and set increasingly ambitious goals.

When the balance is right, all these complex characteristics fuel even greater achievement.

GOAL SETTING

As humans, our behavior is strongly goal-directed. Every action occurs for a reason. When we focus our attention on a specific task, we can channel our energy and better manage our time. When we reach our goals,

1. Mihály Csíkszentmihályi, *Creativity: Flow and the Psychology of Discovery and Invention* (New York: HarperCollins, 1996), pp. 55–76.

2. George Prince, "Creativity and Learning as Skills, Not Talents," *The Philips Exeter Bulletin*, June–October, 1980.

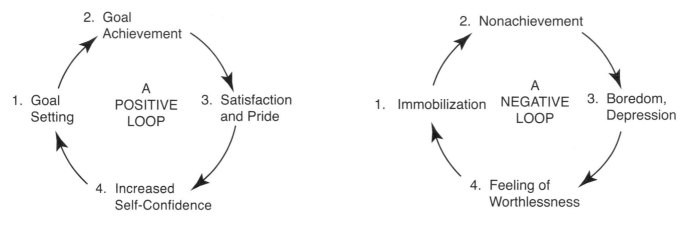

6.2 Michael LeBoeuf, *Imagineering,* **1980.** Achievement feeds self-confidence, while nonachievement induces inertia.

our self-esteem increases. Michael LeBoeuf has diagrammed this effect clearly (6.2). Goal achievement creates a positive loop; procrastination or failure creates a negative loop. Because they are so important, let us now consider ways to develop good personal goals.

Characteristics of Good Goals

Ambitious yet Achievable

Too modest a goal will provide no sense of accomplishment. Too ambitious a goal will reduce, rather than increase, motivation. No one wants to fight a losing battle! Analyzing your strengths and weaknesses can help you set realistic goals.

Compatible

To train for the Boston Marathon while simultaneously trying to gain 20 pounds is unwise, because you will burn off every calorie that you consume. Trying to save a thousand dollars while touring Europe is unrealistic, because travel always costs more than you expect. On the other hand, by taking a dance class or joining a hiking club, you may be able to combine a fitness goal with a social goal.

Self-Directed

It is best to avoid goals that are primarily dependent on someone else's actions or opinions. "I want to earn an A in drawing" is an example. The instructor determines your grade and you can't really control his or her judgment. Instead, try focusing on improving your drawing as much as possible. This will increase your receptivity to learning and will focus your attention on actions that you *can* control. When you do your best work, good grades generally follow.

Temporary

Set clear target dates, get the job done, and move on to the next project. As figure 6.2 shows, each completed task increases your self-confidence and adds momentum. By contrast, unfinished work can drain energy and decrease momentum. If you are overloaded, delete secondary goals so that you can complete primary goals.

TIME MANAGEMENT

Time management can help you achieve your goals. Working smarter is usually more effective than simply working harder. In a world bursting with opportunity, using your work time well can increase the time available for travel, volunteer work, or socializing. Many artists and designers have used the following time-management strategies.

Set the Stage

Choosing when and where to work can significantly increase your output. If you are a lark, bursting with energy and enthusiasm early in the morning, tackle major projects before noon. If you are a fierce and nocturnal owl, work on major projects after dinner. If you are distracted by clutter, clean your desk before beginning your workday, and tidy up your desk before you leave. These seemingly minor actions can really increase your productivity.

Prioritize

Note which tasks are most *urgent* and which tasks are most *important.* Timing can be crucial. When you pay your phone bill on time, you easily complete an urgent but unimportant task. When your phone bill is overdue and the service is cut off, this unimportant task becomes a major headache. Dispense with urgent tasks quickly so that you can focus on more important things.

See the Big Picture

Use a monthly calendar to record your major projects and obligations. Organizing your calendar by months can help you see which weeks will be packed with deadlines and which weeks will be relatively quiet. To avoid all-nighters, distribute large, important tasks over several weeks. To avoid missing a pivotal lecture or critique, schedule out-of-town trips during "slow" weeks.

Work Sequentially

Often, it is most effective to tackle activities in a specific sequence. If you are writing a 20-page paper, you should start with research, craft an outline, complete a rough draft, make revisions, and *then* write the final draft. If you are designing a poster, begin with research, make thumbnail sketches, assess the results, create a full-size rough draft, consult the client, and *then* complete the poster. To eliminate the intermediate steps and move directly to the final draft rarely works. With most large projects, you learn more, save time, and do better work by tackling the problem one step at a time.

Use Parts to Create the Whole

When you look at a major project as a whole, it can become overwhelming. In an extreme case, creative paralysis sets in, resulting in a condition similar to writer's block. Breaking down big jobs into smaller parts helps enormously. In *Bird by Bird* (1998), Anne Lamott provides a wonderful description of this process:

> Thirty years ago my other brother, who was ten years old at the time, was trying to get a report on birds written that he'd had three months to write. [It] was due the next day. . . . He was at the kitchen table close to tears, surrounded by binder paper and pencils and unopened books on birds, immobilized by the hugeness of the task ahead. Then my father sat down beside him, put his arm around my brother's shoulder, and said, "Bird by bird, buddy. Just take it bird by bird."[3]

By breaking the job down into manageable parts, you are likely to learn more and procrastinate less.

Make the Most of Class Time

Psychologists tell us that beginnings and endings of events are especially memorable. An experienced teacher knows that the first 10 minutes of class set the tone for the rest of the session, and that a summary at the end can help students remember the lesson. Similarly, master learners tend to arrive 5 minutes early for class and maintain attention to the end of class.

Be an active learner. You can use that 5 minutes before class to review your notes from the previous session or set up your materials. Try to end the class on a high note, either by completing a project or by clearly determining the strengths and weaknesses of the work in progress. By analyzing your progress, you can organize your thinking and provide a solid beginning point for the next work session.

When in Doubt, Crank It Out

Fear is one of the greatest obstacles to creative thinking. When we are afraid, we tend to avoid action. Consequently, we may miss opportunities.

Both habit and perfectionism feed fear. If you consistently repeat the same activities and limit yourself to familiar friendships, you may become even more anxious about new experiences. Perfectionism is especially destructive during brainstorming, which requires a loose, open approach.

Creativity takes courage. As IBM founder Thomas Watson noted, "If you are not satisfied with your rate of success, try failing more." Baseball player Reggie Jackson is renowned for his 563 home runs—but he also struck out 2,597 times. Thomas Edison's research team tried more than 6,000 materials before finding the carbon-fiber filament used in light bulbs. "When in doubt, don't!" is the safekeeper's motto. "When in doubt, do!" is the risk taker's motto. By starting each project with a sense of adventure, you increase your level of both learning and creativity.

Work Together

Many areas of art and design (including digital media, industrial design, and advertising design) often require collaborative creativity. Together, artists and designers can complete projects that are too complex or time-consuming to be done solo. Furthermore, collaborative thinking helps us break familiar patterns and teaches us to listen to alternative or opposing ideas.

Lexicon (6.3A–C), a year-long project by Lynda Lowe in Washington and Georgiana Nehl in Oregon, beautifully demonstrates the value of collaboration. The artists took turns initiating and responding to

3. Anne Lamott, *Bird by Bird: Some Instructions on Writing and Life* (New York: Anchor Books, 1998), pp. 18–19.

A–Memory

B–Primordial

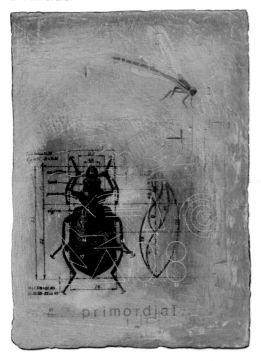

C–Dilemma

6.3A–C Lynda Lowe and Georgiana Nehl, *Lexicon*, 2000. Mixed media on paper, 5 × 7 in. (13 × 18 cm).
© Lynda Lowe and Georgiana Nehl, www.lyndalowe.com

each other's images as they sent small groups of paintings back and forth through the mail. Despite distinct stylistic differences, the artists share a mutual fascination with the unconscious, commitment to the power of symbols, and mastery of composition. By working together, Lowe and Nehl were able to complete a remarkable series of 100 paintings that have been shown nationally.

This process greatly expands when the collaborative team is multidisciplinary. In the following interview, painter Sara Mast describes the challenges and opportunities of a collaboration between art and science.

Profile:
Sara Mast, Painter
Applying Art to Science

© Sara Mast

Sara Mast's paintings have been exhibited nationally and internationally in *The Art of Encaustic Painting: Contemporary Expression in the Ancient Medium of Pigmented Wax* (2001), *Art & Science Now* (2010), and *Encaustic Art in the Twenty-First Century* (2016). Her collaborative art and science installation *Black (W)hole* is now traveling worldwide.

MS: Your father, noted inventor Gifford Morrison Mast, was educated in physics and mechanical engineering. His projects ranged from a robot he built as a child to his work in the design of optical and measuring devices. Your brother is a marine biologist and president of the Oceanic Society. Other relatives have excelled in the fields of educational psychology and engineering. Where do you fit into this family of scientists?

SM: We all bring an open-minded curiosity to our work. However, I see the world through an aesthetic and interdisciplinary lens and am most interested in ways that language, images, and experience can be connected to communicate ideas. In a sense, mathematics and prose are the languages of science. Both require the distillation of complex information into correct answers or concise theories. My work is more poetic. It relies on metaphors to multiply and expand meaning.

MS: How did you get started?

SM: In 2011, I began collaborating with physicists Nico Yunes, Joey Shapiro Key, and Charles Kankelborg on a project dealing with black holes. Scientific accuracy was a primary concern as we began to develop the installation. To communicate more broadly, I soon proposed a more intuitive and expansive approach. I wanted to immerse the viewer in a powerful experience, rather than try to simply illustrate scientific content.

MS: An immersive environment requires many collaborators and work within an unfamiliar realm. What inspired you to shift from painting to pursue this route?

SM: My paintings are built using encaustic, which employs layers of melted wax to create the image. Made of fragments of information, they are designed to suggest possibilities rather than illustrate events. Recently, I noticed that fewer and fewer people take the time to stand quietly before a painting, contemplating the layers of meaning. So, for this project, I decided to expand my practice and engage a broad audience in a way that does not require the viewer to "speak" the language of painting.

MS: Please describe *Black W(hole)*.

SM: In this installation, the viewer enters a laser field of stars and stands on the edge of an accretion disk, which visually swirls into a supermassive black hole. Suddenly, the viewer zooms to the edge of the first black hole as a second, smaller black hole is captured and begins to orbit. The sounds that gravitational waves produce in such an encounter surround the viewer. A film of morphing images plays in a continuous loop on the back wall of the space, referencing Einstein's 1915 General Relativity equations scrawled in chalk on his blackboard, the solutions of which predicted the existence of black holes 100 years ago.

MS: Painting is usually a solitary and individual activity. How did you transition into collaborating?

SM: For this project, I was the collaborative leader of a richly diverse team that included a solar physicist and optics expert, an architect, an artist-animator, a composer, an experimental filmmaker, and two science advisors, both of whom were physicists and experts in gravitational wave astronomy. This synergy of disciplines required an ability to bridge languages and seek common ground, which was my job. Although the idea of working alone in a studio seems very different from working with a group of multidisciplinary collaborators, the skill set is the same. How can we unify a range of ideas into one coherent and powerful work?

MS: The team is even larger for *Cave,* your current project. How can you get 10 people from different disciplines working together well?

SM: The NeuroCave Collaborative includes a visual team, a computer science team, and a sound team. Our neuroscientist works across all the teams. The project focuses on the use of neurofeedback devices to generate individual sound and color "readings," allowing the viewer-participant to interact and respond to others in the space. The gallery becomes a scientific instrument from which we collect data on "co-variance," a trending area of neuroscience research. Bi-weekly meetings keep everyone moving in the same direction, provide updates, and integrate the work by various teams into the larger vision.

MS: As an art student, why study science?

SM: Science is our society's dominant paradigm. In a way, it is our culture's secular religion. Whenever one paradigm reigns supreme, there is value in questioning its authority and exploring its pervasive myths. As an artist, I embrace the awe and wonder of science, and am fascinated by the speed at which discoveries are made and ideas implemented. But that is also why it is important for artists to challenge science and ask the questions that scientists may not ask in the rush of progress.

MS: As a scientist, why study (or make) art?

SM: As a violinist, Einstein noted: "If . . . I were not a physicist, I would probably be a musician. I often think in music." The fact that he was often "thinking in music" (the most highly abstract of all art forms) implies that an intuitive approach to problem solving played an important role in his scientific work. If more scientists engaged in the deeper philosophical questions of art while practicing the scientific method, they might bring even wider-ranging insight to their complex and demanding work.

Sara Mast, *Black (W)hole,* **2013.** Installation view, animation and video, size variable.
© Sara Mast

VARIATIONS ON A THEME

Both *Lexicon* and Sara Mast's collaborative installations developed gradually. As a project evolves, we can reveal new possibilities that explore ideas and go well beyond our initial intentions. By pursuing these implications, we can exceed our original expectations. Just as the landscape appears to expand when we climb a mountain, so an idea can expand as our understanding increases.

One way to get more mileage out of an idea is through variations on a theme. Professional artists rarely complete just one painting or sculpture from a given idea; most do many variations before moving to a new subject.

Thirty-Six Views of Mount Fuji is one example. Japanese printmaker Katsushika Hokusai was 70 years old when he began this series. The revered and beautiful Mount Fuji appeared in each of the designs in some way. Variations in the time of year and the size of the mountain helped Hokusai produce dramatically different variations on the same theme (6.4A–C).

Variations on a theme can also help us explore our own ideas. For figures 6.5 A, B, and C, Elizabeth

6.4A Katsushika Hokusai, *Thirty-Six Views of Mount Fuji: Under the Mannen Bridge at Fukagawa*, **Edo period, c. 1830.** Color woodblock print, 10 1/16 × 14 11/16 in. (25.7 × 37.5 cm).
Open access, courtesy of the British Library

6.4B Katsushika Hokusai, *Thirty-Six Views of Mount Fuji: The Great Wave off Kanagawa*, **Edo period, c. 1830.** Color woodblock print, 10 3/16 × 14 15/16 in. (25.9 × 37.5 cm).
Open access, courtesy of the British Library

6.4C Katsushika Hokusai, *Thirty-Six Views of Mount Fuji: Near Umezawa in Sagami Province*, **Edo period, c. 1830.** Color woodblock print, 10 1/16 × 14 7/8 in. (25.6 × 37.8 cm).
Open access, courtesy of the British Library

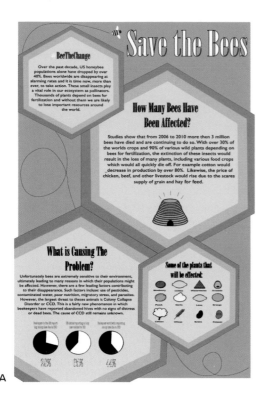

A

C

6.5A–C Elizabeth Kelly, *#Save the Bees* poster and T-shirt series.
© Elizabeth Kelly

B

Kelly selected the topic of "Save the Bees" and created a series of posters about the importance of bees to our environment through a combination of text and graphics. And she even created a T-shirt.

Similarly, figure 6.6 shows many variations on a cube. Submitted by beginning architecture students at Auburn University, they further demonstrate one advantage of studying art and design in a classroom

6.6 Cubes from above, study models from Auburn University School of Architecture.
Courtesy of Rusty Smith, Auburn University School of Architecture

setting. The cube created by each class member provides another possible solution to the problem set.

ACTIVELY SEEK SUCCESS

Personal initiative is powerful. Indeed, a highly motivated person with average ability can surpass an unmotivated genius. Consider these final success strategies.

Habits of Mind

Dr. Arthur L. Costa and Dr. Bena Kallick have identified 16 "habits of mind" essential to success. Four attributes that are especially important in art and design follow.

Flexibility

Convergent, divergent, and collaborative problem-solving strategies present distinct advantages and disadvantages. Limiting yourself to just one approach reduces your ability to solve a wide range of problems. Flexibility, on the other hand, allows you to question existing assumptions, adopt new ideas, and shift strategies as needed.

Analytical Thinking

In general, designers are hired to solve a client's problem. Complications arise when time is limited and expenses increase. An analytical mindset helps the designer continue to focus on the real problem rather than wasting time on an imagined one.

Capacity for Synthesis

We can define *synthesis* as the capacity to combine separate parts to create a coherent whole. Two aspects of synthesis are particularly important for artists and designers. First, they must be able to combine visual elements to create unified designs. Second, they must be able to apply past knowledge to new situations. You can accumulate a vast storehouse of knowledge by simply remembering past solutions to similar problems.

Responsible Risk Taking

Risk takers are willing to risk failure to achieve success. They view setbacks as opportunities for growth rather than occasions for despair. Irresponsible risk takers leap before they look. Responsible risk takers weigh benefits and hazards, gather their energy, and then leap.

Habits of Work

To provide beginners with a realistic checklist, Professor Rusty Smith and his colleagues at the School of Architecture at Auburn University have developed the following "habits of work."

Self-Reliance

Essentially, self-reliance creates an active approach to work. Rather than waiting for directions or blaming others for delays, each person actively generates possibilities, weighs options, and makes choices. To a substantial degree, self-reliant students drive their own learning process.

Organized Persistence

Beating your head against a brick wall is an example of mindless persistence. It is impressive but ineffective. Chiseling away at the mortar between the bricks until the wall falls apart is an example of organized persistence. Organized persistence gives us the ability to prevail, even when we are faced with the most daunting task.

Daily Practice

Momentum is extremely powerful when you are working on a difficult problem. Daily practice helps maintain momentum. Working an hour a day on a project is sometimes better than working for eight hours in a single day.

Appropriate Speed

Some tasks are best completed quickly, with brisk decision making and decisive action. Slowing down to reframe a question and weigh alternative solutions is necessary in other cases.

Incremental Excellence

Most art and design problems are best developed in a series of stages. Ideas evolve, skills improve, and compositions are distilled. Rather than trying for the "perfect solution" on the first day of work, it is better to start with a "funky junky" draft.

Direct Engagement

Talk is cheap. Work is hard. The only way to solve most art and design problems is to get involved. It is impossible to win a race when you are standing on the sidelines.

summary

- Creative people are receptive to new ideas, are curious, have a wide range of interests, are attentive, seek connections, and work with great conviction.

- A combination of rational and intuitive thinking feeds creativity. Although we can use intuition to generate a new idea, we may need logic and objective analysis for its completion.

- Good goals are ambitious yet achievable, compatible, self-directed, and temporary. Intermediate deadlines can help us meet our goals.

- Completing tasks in an appropriate sequence, making the most of each work period,

  maintaining momentum, and reducing stress are major aspects of time management.

- Collaborative work can help us expand ideas, explore new fields, and pursue projects that are too complex to do alone.

- We can explore ideas more fully using variations on a theme.

- Flexibility, analytical ability, the capacity for syntheses, and responsible risk taking are crucial habits of mind.

- Self-reliance, organized persistence, daily practice, appropriate speed, and direct engagement are crucial habits of work.

Success Story:
Jane Parkerson Ferry, Curator of Education
Orlando Museum of Art, Orlando, Florida

© Jane Parkerson Ferry

Jane Parkerson Ferry manages the Education department at the flagship art museum in Central Florida. She and her staff help visitors of all ages to have enriching and engaging experiences with art.

MS: Please describe the work of the Education department.

JPF: Education department programming helps to advance the OMA's mission to inspire creativity, passion, and intellectual curiosity by connecting people with art and new ideas. Our main job is to make art accessible to the widest possible range of visitors and stimulate an interest in lifelong learning by offering programs to complement the museum's collections and temporary exhibitions. We offer tours, lectures, workshops, studio classes, professional development workshops for teachers, family days, outreach programs, art appreciation series, and community access programs.

MS: Contemporary art can be especially challenging to visitors. How have you helped them understand difficult artworks?

JPF: Contemporary art is the art of our time. Never before has there been such a diversity of materials, approaches, and ideas. Learning the stories behind contemporary art can help visitors think about their world, make meaning, and discover why it matters. We always use an inquiry-based approach. To alleviate visitor confusion about unfamiliar artworks, we start by asking open-ended questions such as "What do you see?" If we start with the known and make connections, we can then move beyond to ask the "how" and "why" questions. Building bridges between the known and unknown helps make the art relevant and understandable.

MS: How do the basic skills you developed as an undergraduate at Dickinson College inform your OMA work?

JPF: I use two areas of foundational knowledge every day in my work at OMA. They are:

- **Visual literacy.** How to read works of art, learning the basic vocabulary of the elements of art and principles of design, how to put it all together to make meaning in works of art, helping visitors be visually literate.

- **Creative thinking and problem solving.** Learning to look at different possibilities, learning from multiple viewpoints, recognizing different learning styles, finding the best fit or solution.

MS: What advice would you give to art and design majors starting their education today?

JPF: • **Know your audience.** Learn expectations and tailor your message appropriately. Just as your professors have different requirements, expectations, and needs, so will your clients and colleagues in the real world.

- **Pay attention to details.** Aim for results,

not perfection, but the way you handle the small details along the way may reflect how you handle the bigger ones.

- **Be flexible and adaptive to changing conditions.** Change is necessary for growth. If things aren't changing, things aren't moving forward. Embrace change and evolve with it!

- **Don't be afraid of failure.** Innovation requires risk taking. Some of the best lessons are those that are learned from mistakes. Be a risk taker!

- **Good communication skills are crucial.** Whether it's verbal, visual, or written, being able to get your message across effectively is vital for success.

- **Be passionate about what you do.** To be successful and happy, you need to truly love your work and believe in it.

Stephen Knapp, *Celebration*, Orlando Museum of Art, 2013.
© Stephen Knapp

Developing Critical Thinking

Critical thinking challenges us to

- Analyze visual relationships
- Evaluate our conceptual and compositional choices
- Invent alternative solutions

Using critical thinking, we can determine what to keep and what to change in a composition. By enhancing the best aspects of a design and deleting the weak areas, we can dramatically increase both communication and expression.

ESTABLISHING CRITERIA

Let's begin by establishing the criteria on which we will make judgments. For example, craftsmanship is highly valued when we take a technical workshop, while brainstorming is highly valued in a concepts course. More specifically, if we are given a complementary color problem, a black-and-white painting will not meet the criteria, no matter how well it is composed. By determining the major questions in an assignment, we can understand the basis on which judgments will be reached.

So, when starting an assignment, consider the following questions:

- What is the assignment's purpose? What new knowledge can we gain?
- What are the parameters of the assignment? Are there limitations in the size, style, content, or materials?
- When is the assignment due, and in what form must it be presented?

It is important to distinguish between determining assignment criteria and seeking the "right answer." By understanding assignment criteria, we can effectively direct our energy as we begin to work. Just as we can use a magnifying glass to focus sunlight into a powerful beam, so assignment parameters can help to focus creative energy. On the other hand, students who try to determine the "right answer" to a problem may just want to know the instructor's solution. Such knowledge is rarely helpful. The assignment simply sets a learning process in motion: we learn through the work we do.

FORM, SUBJECT, CONTENT

We may define **form** as the physical manifestation of an idea or emotion. We can construct two-dimensional forms using point, line, shape, texture, value, and color. The building blocks of three-dimensional forms are point, line, plane, volume, mass, space, texture, and color. We can combine duration, tempo, intensity, scope, setting, and chronology to create time-based art forms. For example, *Star Wars*, a classic science-fiction movie, appears in the art form that we call film.

The **subject**, or topic, of an artwork is most apparent when it clearly represents a person, an object, an event, or a setting. For example, the war between the rebels and the Empire provides the subject for *Star Wars*.

An artwork's emotional or intellectual message provides its **content**, or underlying theme. The theme of *Star Wars* is the journey into the self. Luke Skywalker's gradual understanding of himself and his acceptance of the villainous Darth Vader as his father provide an essential emotional undercurrent to the entire series.

Each artwork also occurs within a geographical and temporal **context**. This context can substantially affect the artwork's meaning. For example, Mary Lucier's video showing a fragile monarch butterfly's death is astonishing and poignant when we see it in Times Square, the bustling theater district in the heart of New York City (7.1). If we viewed the same event while hiking, we would consider it a normal occurrence rather than a statement about the fragility of life.

STOP, LOOK, LISTEN, LEARN

We typically discuss artworks using a critique process. During a **critique**, our peers and professors analyze our work and offer advice. They identify compositional strengths and weaknesses, and reveal areas that need revision. We can use these insights to improve the current design or to generate possibilities for the next assignment.

Depending on the amount and type of student involvement, critiques can be extremely helpful, extremely destructive, or really boring. Specific recommendations are most helpful. Be sure to substantiate each recommendation you offer so that the rationale is clear.

Whether we are giving or receiving advice, it is important to arrive with our minds open, rather than with our fists closed. A critique is not a combat zone! We must listen carefully to explanations and generously offer our insights to others. Likewise, we must receive suggestions gracefully rather than defensively. Each of us will make the final decision on revisions: thus, if someone gives us bad advice, we can quietly discard it. Because a substantial and supportive critique is the best way to determine the effect our design has on an audience, it is best to speak thoughtfully and weigh every suggestion seriously.

OBJECTIVE AND SUBJECTIVE CRITIQUES

When beginning a critique, it is useful to distinguish between objective and subjective criticism. We use **objective criticism** to assess how well a work of art or design uses the elements and principles of design. Discussion generally focuses on basic compositional concerns, such as:

- The type of balance that the artist used in the composition and its effect
- The spatial depth of a design and its compositional effect
- The degree of unity in a design and how the artist achieved it

7.1 Mary Lucier, *Migration (Monarch)*, Times Square, New York.
© Mary Lucier. Courtesy of Lennon, Weinberg, Inc., New York. Photograph by Charlie Samuels

We base objective criticism on direct observation and a shared understanding of assignment parameters. Discussion is usually clear and straightforward. We may discuss alternative compositional solutions in depth.

We use **subjective criticism** to describe the personal impact of an image, the narrative implications of an idea, or the cultural ramifications of an action. Discussion generally focuses on the design's subject and content, including:

- The artwork's meaning
- The feelings it evokes
- Its relationship to other cultural events
- The artist's intent

Because we do not base subjective criticism on simple observation, it is more difficult for most groups to remain focused on the artwork itself or to reach clear conclusions on possible improvements. The

7.2A Gustave Caillebotte, *Place de l'Europe on a Rainy Day*, **1877.** Oil on canvas, 83½ × 108¾ in. (212.2 × 276.2 cm).
Erich Lessing/Art Resource, New York

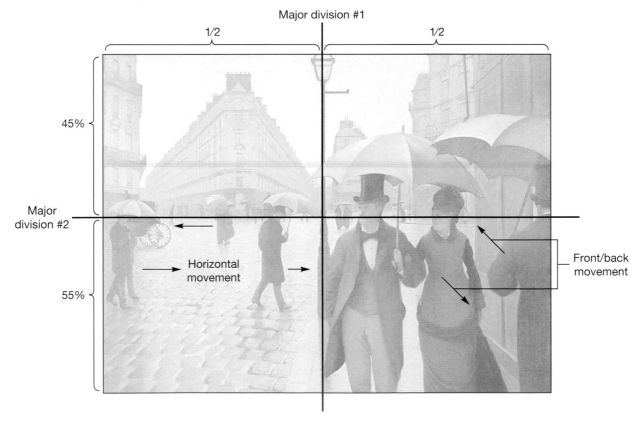

7.2B Gustave Caillebotte, *Place de l'Europe on a Rainy Day*, **1877.** Compositional diagram.
Erich Lessing/Art Resource, New York

discussion may range widely, as we analyze political or social questions that the works of art and design raise.

CRITIQUE STRATEGIES

Description

The first step is to look carefully and report clearly. Without evaluating, telling stories, drawing conclusions, or making recommendations, we can simply describe the work's visual organization. A **descriptive critique** can help us to see details and heighten our understanding of the design. We can identify which design aspects are most eye-catching and which areas are muddled and require work.

This is a particularly useful exercise when analyzing a complex piece, such as figure 7.2A. In an art history class, we might write:

> French Impressionist painter Gustave Caillebotte's *Place de l'Europe on a Rainy Day* is a rectangular painting depicting a street in Paris. A vertical lamppost and its shadow extend from the top edge to the bottom edge, neatly dividing the painting in half. A horizon line, extending from the left side and three-quarters of the way to the right, further divides the painting, creating four major quadrants. Because this horizon line is positioned just above center, the composition's bottom half is slightly larger than the top half. A dozen pedestrians with umbrellas occupy the painting's bottom half. At the right edge, a man strides into the painting, while next to him a couple moves out of the painting, toward the viewer. To the left of the lamppost, most of the movement is horizontal, as people cross the cobblestone streets.

When using description in a spoken studio-class critique, it is useful to note these essential compositional characteristics:

- What is the shape of the overall composition? A circle or sphere presents a different compositional playing field from a square or a cube.
- What range of colors has the artist used? A black-and-white design is different from a full-color design.

- What is the size of the project? Extremes are especially notable. A sculpture that is 10 feet tall or a painting that is 1 inch square will immediately attract attention.
- Is the visual information tightly packed, creating a very dense design, or is the design more open and spacious?

The Key Questions that appear throughout this book can provide a springboard for a descriptive critique.

Cause and Effect

A descriptive critique helps us analyze an artist's compositional choices. A **cause-and-effect critique** (also known as a **formal analysis**) builds on this description. In a simple description, we might say that diagonal shapes dominate a design. Using cause and effect, we might conclude that *because* of the many diagonals, the design is very dynamic. Essentially, in a cause-and-effect critique, we discuss *consequences* as well as choices. Here is an example:

> *Place de l'Europe on a Rainy Day* depicts a city street in Paris near the end of the nineteenth century.
>
> A lamppost, positioned near the center, vertically bisects the painting. The horizon line creates a second major division, with roughly 45 percent of the space above and 55 percent below this line. When combined, these vertical and horizontal divisions create a focal point near the painting's center.
>
> A dozen pedestrians in dark clothing cross the cobblestone streets from left to right, creating a flowing movement. To the right of the post, the pedestrians move in and out of the painting, from background to foreground. Both types of movement add compositional energy. Two men and one woman are the most prominent figures. The man at the far right edge pulls us into the painting, while the couple to his immediate left moves toward us, pushing out of their world and into ours.

As figure 7.2B shows, a visual diagram can support your written comments.

Mary Cassatt's *The Boating Party* (7.3) can provide a second example of a cause-and-effect critique. It is

7.3 Mary Cassatt, *The Boating Party*, **1893/94.** Oil on canvas, 46⁷⁄₁₆ × 108³⁄₁₆ in. (90 × 117.32 cm).
© National Gallery of Art, Washington, DC, Chester Dale Collection 1963.10.94. © NGA Washington

a remarkable example of the coloristic push and pull described in Creating the Illusion of Space on page 55:

> A dark blue oarsman fills the right half of the frame. Surrounded by the bright yellow boat interior and light blue water, he creates a strong counterbalance to the woman and child positioned near the center of the painting. The warm yellow boat interior pushes the dark blue figure toward us: it seems that we can almost reach out and touch him.

> Dressed in a light blue frock and white hat, the woman seems more luminous and less solid than the oarsman. She is framed by the white sail at left and the horizontal shoreline in the distance.

Overlapping both the sail and the shoreline, the woman tends to push forward, yet the blue water to her right and left tends to pull her backward, into the painting. As a result, a seemingly simple composition is charged with energy. Placed near the compositional center and dressed in pink, the squirming child becomes the compositional focal point and creates a bridge between the two adults.

Compare and Contrast

In a compare/contrast critique, we identify similarities and differences between two images. Let's return to the Caillebotte painting one more time, now comparing it to Italian Renaissance painter Raphael's *The School of Athens* (7.4).

7.4 Raphael, *The School of Athens*, 1509–11. Fresco, 26 × 18 ft (7.92 × 5.49 m). Stanza della Segnatura, Vatican, Rome.
Stanza della Segnatura, Vatican Palace, Vatican State. Scala/Art Resource, New York

The city streets in *The School of Athens* and *Place de l'Europe* demonstrate many differences between the Renaissance and Impressionist perspective.

The one-point perspective that Raphael uses in his painting leads our eyes to Plato and Aristotle, positioned just below the center of the composition. The other figures in the painting are massed in a horizontal band from the far right to the far left side and in two lower groups, to the right and left of the central figures. A man sprawled on the steps to the right and the scribes' tables on the left direct our attention back to the philosophers at the center. Like a proscenium arch in a theater, a broad arch in the foreground frames the scene. Overlapping arches add to the painting's depth. This composition combines the stability of one-point perspective with a powerful illusion of space.

Both *The School of Athens* and *Place de l'Europe on a Rainy Day* are carefully divided both vertically and horizontally. However, in the Caillebotte painting a lamppost occupies center stage, rather than a philosopher. The perspective in the cobblestone street and in the building on the right is complicated by the perspective the artist uses for a triangular building to the left of the lamppost. This unusual illusion of space, combined with the pedestrians' movement, creates a feeling of instability.

Art history classes often use compare-and-contrast essays. This form of analysis helps demonstrate differences in historical periods or artistic styles. We can

7.5 Cally Iden, ***Crouse College as a Labyrinth.*** Student work, 18 × 24 in. (45.7 × 61 cm).
Cally Iden. Courtesy of the author

use the same approach in the studio, for either spoken or written critiques. The following, written by Cally Iden and Tricia Tripp when they were two students in a basic design class, is an example. The assignment was to complete an 18 × 24-inch design, transforming the music building (Crouse College) into a labyrinth. Looking at Cally's design (7.5), Trish wrote:

> Cally's artwork uses strong black-and-white contrast, with both negative and positive space clearly defined. In contrast, my design is brightly colored, representing a kaleidoscope based on the stained-glass windows in the building.
>
> We both use the staircase as a major element. Cally's stair leads you in and around the building, creating a way to explore the space. My stair becomes part of a complex overall pattern.
>
> I thought of the labyrinth as an abstract puzzle, a design you could draw your pencil through to find the end. I wanted my design to be playful.

Cally's design focuses on the psychological, creating an entry into the human mind. Cally's design is mysterious and somewhat ominous.

> We both use lines very deliberately. Where one line ends, another begins. Without lines in a labyrinth, it wouldn't be as puzzling or mysterious. It would just be another design, rather than a puzzle to solve or a fun house to explore.

Looking at Trish's design (7.6), Cally wrote:

> My labyrinth uses black and white to form a high-contrast composition; Trish uses color to transform the building into a complex pattern. My vertical format helps suggest the height of the building, which is dominated by two amazing staircases. Trish's horizontal format contains a design that is as abstract as a computer circuit board.
>
> There are also conceptual differences in our solutions. My drawing is representational, depicting a psychological labyrinth, whereas Trish's turns the labyrinth into a puzzle. The space is generally flat in her design. Color is used to create a balanced composition rather than being used to create any illusion of space. On the other hand, because my design is representational, I used size variation to create a convincing interior space.
>
> One similarity between our drawings is in the inclusion of the staircase. Trish used the stairs as a background shape that adds dynamism to the composition. I used the stair as a primary motif, a means by which people using the building can explore their own minds.
>
> For me, Trish's design creates a sense of alienation. There is no evidence of human experience here—it is a purely visual world, made up of complex shapes. It is as beautiful as an image in a kaleidoscope.
>
> On the other hand, there are hints of "the human" in my composition, but it is lost within the maze of repetitive stairs: only traces remain. I want to convey the feeling of being caught in a labyrinth, solving a mystery, and finding one's self.

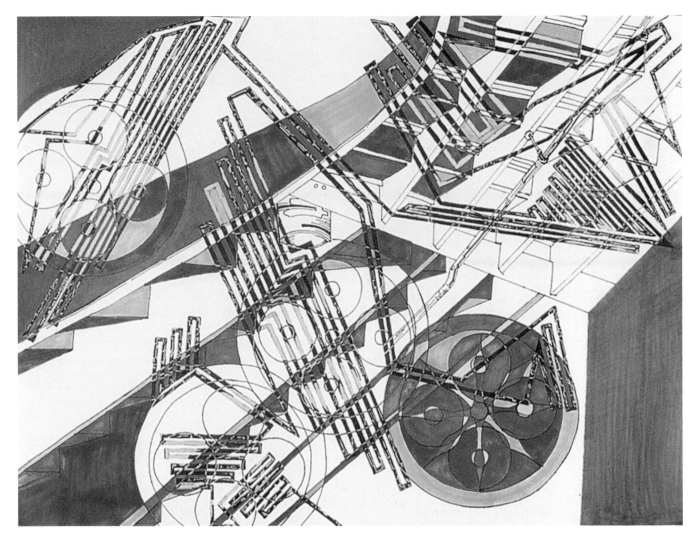

7.6 Tricia Tripp, *Crouse College as a Labyrinth*, **1999.** Student work, 24 × 18 in. (61 × 45.7 cm).
Tricia Tripp. Courtesy of the author

The critiques are honest, but not abusive, and offer a discussion of both concept and composition. Although the critiques are very different, each student clearly respects the other's approach.

Greatest Strength/Unrealized Potential

Many projects have several notable strengths and one glaring weakness. To create a positive atmosphere, we can begin by pointing out the strengths using the following list:

- What is the level of unity in the design, and how did the artist achieve it?

- How much variety is there, and does it generate visual energy?

- What type of balance did the artist use? What is its emotional effect?

- Is the artwork brash and bold, or more subtle and quiet? This could include a discussion of craftsmanship, conceptual nuance, or compositional economy.

- Is there an unexpected conceptual spark? We all love to see an unexpected solution that redefines a project's imaginative potential.

Weaknesses tend to undermine compositional strengths. Thus, by removing a weakness, we can enhance compositional strengths. Using figure 7.7A as an example, we could say:

7.7A Initial design.

7.7B Design variation.

The primary strength of this project is unity. The use of black marker throughout gives the design a simple, clean, and consistent look. The repetition of the arches helps tie it all together. Vertical and horizontal lines dominate, creating a type of grid.

Next, we might consider ways to improve the project. Mentally we can arm ourselves with a magic wand. If we could instantly transform the design, what single aspect would we change? How can we more fully realize the project's potential? Here are some basic questions:

- Is it big enough? Is it small enough?
- Is it bold enough? Is it subtle enough?
- How rich is the concept? Can it be expanded?
- Can the concept be communicated more clearly?
- Can the concept be communicated more fully?

The assignment was to create a labyrinth. Figure 7.7A is spatially shallow. To strengthen the composition, we might suggest:

When I think about a labyrinth, I think of a mysterious place that I can enter and explore. Right now, this design is spatially flat: it gives me no place to go. Greater size variation in the arches, with larger ones in the front and smaller ones in the back, would increase the illusion of space. Overlapping some of the arches could increase the space even more and add visual rhythm. Have you considered using gray marker for the background shapes? This would reduce the contrast and push those shapes back in space. By increasing the illusion of space, you could provide an entry into your labyrinth.

The resulting design (7.7B) is more spatially complex.

DEVELOPING A LONG-TERM PROJECT

Critiquing is useful at many points in a project, not just at the end. When working on a project for 10 hours or more, it is useful to assess progress at the beginning or the end of each work period. We can facilitate this in a large-group critique, in small teams, in discussion with the instructor, or on our own. Several effective strategies follow.

Week One Assessment

Determine Essential Concept

As a project begins to evolve from brainstorming thumbnails to rough drafts, the concept may also evolve. Our initial idea may expand or shift as we translate it from the mind to the hand to the page. Stopping to reconsider the central concept and refine our image can bring great clarity and purpose to the work. What is the design *really* about? We can speak more forcefully when we know what we want to say.

Explore Polarities

Sometimes, the best way to strengthen an idea is to present the exact opposite. For example, if we want to show a political prisoner's *joy* upon release from jail, we may need to show the *despair* that she felt before her release. To increase the *dynamism* in a design, we can add some emphatically *static* elements. The contrast that polarities create can heighten communication.

Move from General to Specific

"Be specific!" demands the writing instructor. The vague generalities that weaken our writing can also weaken our designs. Details are important. "A bird watched people walk down the street" is far less compelling than "Two vultures hovered over University Avenue, hungrily watching the two hapless interns stagger from bar to bar." Specifying the kind of bird, type of people, and exact location makes the image come alive.

Move from Personal to Universal

Autobiography is a rich source of images and ideas. The authenticity of personal experience is extremely powerful. However, if we cling too tightly to our own families, friends, and experiences, the viewer can feel like a bystander rather than a participant. Using a personal story to express a universal experience can help. We can expand a story about a pivotal experience in our first year away from home to say something about *all* rites of passage from childhood to adulthood.

Week Two Assessment

A well-developed rough draft or a full-scale model may be presented at this stage. The purpose of this critique is to help the artist or designer determine ways to increase the visual and conceptual impact of an existing idea. Three major strategies follow.

Develop Alternatives

By helping a friend solve a problem, we can often solve our own problem. Organize a team of four or five classmates. Working individually, design 5 to 10 possible solutions to a visual problem using 2 × 3-inch thumbnail sketches. Then have one person present his or her ideas verbally and visually. Each team member must then propose an alternative way to solve the problem. We can do this verbally; however, once we get going, it is more effective and stimulating if everyone (including the artist) draws alternative solutions. This process helps the artist see the unrealized potential in his or her idea. Because of the number of alternatives, the artist rarely adopts any single suggestion. Instead, the exercise simply becomes a means of demonstrating ways to clarify, expand, and strengthen already formed intentions.

Edit Out Nonessentials

Have you ever found it difficult to determine the real point of a lengthy lecture, and thus lost interest? Seeking to communicate fully, teachers sometimes provide so many examples and references that students get lost. Likewise, if our designs are overloaded with nonessential detail, or if we give a secondary visual element the starring role, the result will be cluttered. Clutter reduces impact. Look carefully at your design, focusing on visual relationships. Are there any elements that you can delete?

Amplify Essentials

Just as it is necessary to delete extraneous information, so it is equally important to strengthen the most important information. We can review the section on emphasis in Chapter Three and

7.8A Linear design.

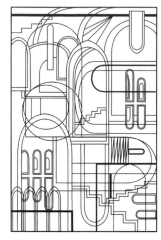

7.9A Visual clutter.

7.10A Completed labyrinth design

7.8B Adding invented texture.

7.9B Visual clarity.

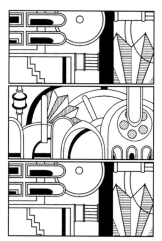

7.10B Divided labyrinth design.

then consider ways to heighten compositional impact. By "going too far" and wildly exaggerating the size, color, or texture of a visual element, we can transform the composition. By making extraordinary compositional choices, we can create extraordinary images.

TURN UP THE HEAT: PUSHING YOUR PROJECT'S POTENTIAL

Some compositions are so bold that they seem to explode off the page. Other compositions have all the right ingredients but never really take off. By asking the following questions, we can more fully realize the potential of any assignment.

Basic Arithmetic

1. Should we *add* anything to the design? If our composition lacks energy, we might add another layer of information or increase the illusion of space. Notice how texture changes the composition in figures 7.8A and 7.8B.

2. Should we *subtract* anything? If the composition is cluttered, we might discard 25 percent of the visual information. We can then use the remaining shapes more deliberately (7.9A and B). Let's get as much as possible from every visual element. Economy is a virtue.

3. What happens when we *multiply* any component?

Figures 7.7A and 7.7B show that repetition can unify a design, add rhythm, and increase the illusion of space.

4. Can we *divide* the design into two or more separate compositions? When a design is too complicated, it may become impossible to resolve. Packing 20 ideas into a single composition can diminish rather than improve communication. In figures 7.10A and 7.10B, the artist has separated a complicated source image into several designs, creating a group of stronger images.

Transformation

Works of art and design present ideas in physical form. The materials that we use, the relationships that we create, and the viewing context that we select strongly influences each composition. Let's consider the following alternatives:

1. What happens when the artist changes the material? Even when the shapes stay the same, a silver teapot is very different from a glass, steel, or ceramic teapot. Sculptors Claes Oldenburg and Coosje van Bruggen have extensively used transformations in material, often changing hard, reflective materials into soft vinyl. This form of transformation is especially effective when the new material brings structural qualities and conceptual connotations that challenge our expectations.

2. What is the size relationship between the artwork and the viewer? What happens when an artist reduces a chair to the size of a salt shaker, or when there is a 19-foot-tall badminton shuttlecock installation in front of a museum (7.11)?

3. When working three-dimensionally, are we creating compositions that are interesting from all viewpoints?

7.11 Claes Oldenburg and Coosje van Bruggen, *Shuttlecocks*, 1994. South facade of the Nelson-Atkins Museum of Art and the Kansas City Sculpture Park. Aluminum, fiberglass-reinforced plastic, and paint. 19 ft 2⁹⁄₁₆ in. × 15 ft 11⅞ in. (585.63 × 487.36 cm).
Claes Oldenburg and Coosje van Bruggen. Donald J. Hall Sculpture Park at the Nelson-Atkins Museum of Art, Kansas City, Missouri. Purchase: acquired through the generosity of the Sosland Family, F94-1/3-4. Photograph by Louis Meluso

4. Will a change in viewing context increase meaning? The badminton shuttlecocks immediately added whimsical energy with their placement in front of the very serious-looking art museum.

Reorganization

We generally construct time-based work, such as visual books, comic books, film, and video, from multiple images. Changing the organization of the puzzle pieces can completely alter the meaning. For example, let's say that Angela contemplates entering a mysterious building in the sequence in figure 7.12. By reorganizing the same three images, in figure 7.13, we can show that Angela now wonders what

will happen when she opens the door at the top of the stairs. By repeating Angela's image, we can present a dilemma: she is now in a labyrinth—which route should she take (7.14)?

Although this strategy is most dramatic when we are working with film or video, we can apply the idea of reorganizing existing information to all kinds of objects and images. Such reorganization often occurs in website design, such as the Genomics Digital Lab (7.15). The home page typically provides an overview of the entire site. By scanning a collection of thumbnail images, viewers can understand the range and type of information available. Each specific page within the site then provides information on an activity in greater

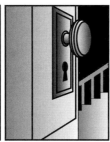

7.12

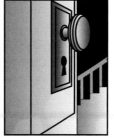

7.13

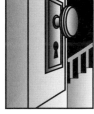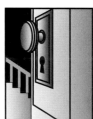

7.14

depth. As the site unfolds, general information reorganizes and represents itself in increasing detail.

Developing a Self-Assignment

Independent thinking is the ultimate goal. As we end this chapter, Jason Chin describes the development of a month-long self-assignment that he completed at the end of his freshman year. The original project proposal is at the top of the first page. The rest of the text is devoted to Jason's analysis of his actual work process. This type of personal assessment can bring an extended project to a memorable conclusion. The more self-directed you are, the more independent you become.

TAKING RESPONSIBILITY

Regardless of the critique strategy used, two facts are inescapable. First, we will learn only what we want to learn. If we reject all advice or if we avoid responsibility for our conceptual and compositional choices, we will gain nothing from the experience. Second, there are no free rides. Everyone in the class is responsible for the success of a critique. When we receive a superficial response to a project, insisting on further clarification is not easy. Yet, we are all responsible. We can greatly improve our artwork when others offer substantial advice. Professor Jim Elniski from the School of the Art Institute of Chicago sums it up beautifully:

"Speak with the expectation of being heard, and listen with the possibility of being changed."

The greatest responsibility and the most dramatic changes occur when we create our own assignment. We must identify a topic to visually research, select the medium that will communicate our ideas most fully, develop a timetable for completing the project, and then dig in and work. As the commentary by Jason Chin demonstrates, the initial proposal provides a framework for a project that evolves over time.

7.15 Genomics Digital Lab.
© Spongelab video game, www.spongelab.com

Self-Assignment: Jason Chin
The Mythological Alphabet

Original Proposal

Description: I plan to make an illustrated alphabet book with 32 pages and a cover. The theme of the book will be myths and heroes. I am interested in illustrating the essence of each hero's story. Specifically, how can I visually communicate the story of a tragic hero versus a triumphant one? Further concerns with the book will be making it work as a whole. That means keeping it balanced and making it flow: I don't want the images to become disjointed.

Primary Concerns

1. How do I communicate the individual nature of the characters?
2. How do I connect each hero to all the others?
3. How will the book affect the reader? I want to get the reader fully involved in the book.
4. How can I best use the unique characteristics of the book format?

Time Management

Week 1: Research myths and heroes. Identify possible characters for the book.

Week 2: Bring at least 20 thumbnail sketches to the first team meeting.

Week 3: Bring finalized design/layout for the book. Each page must have a final design in the form of thumbnails.

Week 4: Complete half of the pages.

Week 5: Finish remaining pages and present at the critique.

Commentary

The independent project was both a blessing and a curse. Being given the freedom to do what I chose was liberating, but the burden of what to do with that freedom was great. Ultimately, it became one of the best learning experiences of my freshman year.

I had decided to pursue illustration as my major, because of my interest in storytelling. This interest in stories led me to choose to make a book for my project. The next step was to find a story to tell. To limit my workload, I looked for a story that had already been told, one that I could reinterpret, as opposed to writing my own story. At this point, I came across two books—one of Greek myths, and the other an alphabet book illustrated by Norman Rockwell—and my initial concept was born.

Once the idea was initiated, I set to work researching Greek myths. The idea was to find one character for each letter of the alphabet. It proved more difficult than I had first thought. I found about 20 names with no problem, but I soon realized that several letters in our alphabet did not exist in the Greek alphabet. To overcome this hurdle, I took some liberties with the original problem and did not limit myself strictly to characters from myths (for example, I included the White Island for the letter W). Once the subject of each illustration was chosen, I set about the task of creating the images and designing the format of the book.

Doing the illustrations and designing the format of the book all came together at about the same time. As I was working out the drawings, I made several key decisions that heavily influenced the outcome of the project. First, I decided that each picture would have to be black-and-white if I was going to pull this whole thing off. Second, I knew that they would have to be relatively small. Through my art history class, I gained a strong interest in Japanese woodblock prints and was especially attracted to their strong compositional sensibility. This became the focus of my

attention while working out the illustrations. Finally, the decision to make the illustrations small helped determine the way I used text in the book, because it all but eliminated the possibility of overlaying text on image.

I designed each image in my sketchbook, doing thumbnails and comp sketches of all sizes and shapes, until I found the image that I felt best represented the character. For example, Zeus has the biggest and busiest frame in the book because he is the king of the gods, while the image of the White Island is quite serene because it is a burial ground.

When I had each individual image worked out, I redrew them in order in the pages of my sketchbook as if they were in the real book. I could now see how each image would work as a double-page spread, and also how well the book could flow visually. With this mockup of the book in front of me, it was very easy to see

Jason Chin, *A Is for Apollo*, 2000. Student work.
© Jason Chin

obvious mistakes and correct them before going to final art.

I did the final illustrations in pen and ink, on illustration board, and when they were finished, it was time to drop in the text. My first concept for the text was to be very minimal; each page would read, "A is for," "B is for," and so on. However, I soon realized that making each page rhyme would drastically increase the reader's interest in the book. So I wrote a more extensive text and put the rhyming parts on opposite pages in order to give the reader one more incentive to turn the page.

The final touch for the book was putting the colored paper down. The decision to do this came when I went to place the type. The only means I had to get good type was to print it out on the computer, but I had no way to print it on the illustration board. So I had to put it on printer paper and cut and paste it. No matter how carefully I cut the paper and pasted it on, it just didn't look right. I came up with two solutions: one, print the words on colored paper and paste it on; or two, cut frames of colored paper to cover the entire page except for the image and the text. I chose the latter, and was pleased to discover that the local art store had a vast selection of handmade and colored papers.

Today I look back on this project as a pivotal experience in my art education, because I had free range to pursue storytelling, something that has since become an essential aspect of my art. In the professional world, bookmaking is rarely an individual process. It is a collaborative process, involving editors, artists, and writers, so for me to be able to pursue it on my own was in fact a blessing. I got to make a book the way that I thought it should be done, and to pursue my own personal vision of what a Mythological Alphabet should be. By making this book, I discovered something that I love to do, and want to make a career of doing, and to me the vision I have gained from this experience is invaluable.

U
IS FOR URANIA THE MUSE OF
CELESTIAL FORCES IS SHE

Jason Chin, *U Is for Urania*, **2000.** Student work.
© Jason Chin

summary

Critical thinking helps us identify strengths and weaknesses in a project and determine the improvements that we need to make.

- Understanding the criteria on which one will judge a project helps focus critical thinking.
- We can analyze many artworks in terms of four basic aspects: form, subject, content, and context.
- Objective critiques focus on observable facts. Subjective critiques focus on feelings, intentions, and implications.
- Four common critique methods are description, cause and effect, compare and contrast, and greatest strength/unrealized potential.
- When working on long-term projects, in-progress critiques can help us to explore alternatives, delete nonessentials, and strengthen essentials.
- Basic arithmetic, transformation, and reorganization can increase compositional impact.
- An open mind combined with a willingness to share ideas can strengthen any critique.

key terms

cause-and-effect critique
content
context
critique
descriptive critique

form
formal analysis
objective criticism
subject
subjective criticism

Success Story: Jason Chin, Illustrator

© Jason Chin

Jason Chin studied illustration at Syracuse University in New York. After graduation, he moved to New York City and worked in a children's bookstore, continuing to develop his own illustration. He has now published a series of children's books about encountering and exploring nature, winning multiple awards in the process.

MS: What attracted you to illustration in the first place?

JC: I have always enjoyed drawing, and in high school I met a local artist who was a children's book illustrator. She became my mentor, and showed me what the life of a successful illustrator could be like. I witnessed both her passion and her frustration with her work. Importantly, I saw how she overcame self-doubt and created meaningful art.

MS: How do you use critical thinking to extend your creativity?

JC: For me, making art is a continuous loop of creation and evaluation. As creator, it's important that I be emotionally invested in the art, but as evaluator, I must turn around and honestly critique that work. The process involves repeatedly changing my relationship with the artwork, from invested creator to distanced critic. It's not always easy, but learning to do it has been important for my artistic growth.

MS: Your freshman year final project appeared earlier in this chapter. It is great to see now that you've been very productive since receiving your BFA from Syracuse University in 2001. Can you expand on your working process?

JC: My working process is well structured. For each painting I start with a small, rough sketch that I revise before moving to a larger sketch. I revise this, then move on to a full-size drawing. Finally, I turn the drawing into a painting. This process allows me to work on one aspect of the image at a time. In the thumbnails I can work on the composition without considering details; in the large drawing I can work on details, with confidence that the composition will hold up.
The process gives me space to switch from creator to evaluator after each revision. It's much easier to emotionally divest, and then reinvest, with a rough sketch than with a final painting. After the painting is finished, I begin distancing myself from it by

putting it away and moving on to the next piece. Emotional distance helps me to take advantage of criticism, and recognize that critiques are directed at the painting and not at me. All artists need to find processes that allow them to have a healthy, productive relationship with their artwork. My mentor had her way, my professors had their ways, and I have mine. I encourage young artists to seek and develop their own. Glean what you can from your professors, not just how to make art, but how to relate to the art that you make.

MS: We "met" you as a freshman through your Mythological Alphabet (page 156). Beyond the critique/creation process you have already described, what were three basic skills you learned in your first year of college that most help with your work today?

JC: **Image construction:** I learned to identify individual visual elements and how artists manipulate them to produce a desired effect.

Life drawing: Through life drawing I developed my seeing skills and visual memory.

Clean workspace: I found that my art came out better when I wasn't wasting time looking for my pencils! I developed productive habits that serve me well today.

Jason Chin, *Grand Canyon*, 2017
© Jason Chin

Constructing Meaning

Seeking and solving visual problems, cultivating creativity, and developing critical judgment all require hours of hard work. Why do artists, designers, and college teachers value these skills so strongly?

The answer is simple. At a professional level, art and design projects communicate ideas and express emotions. Turning elusive concepts into effective communication is not easy. Clay, ink, metal, paint, and other physical materials must somehow stimulate an audience to see, understand, and respond. In this chapter, we explore the essentials of visual communication and identify some of the strategies that artists and designers use to construct meaning.

BUILDING BRIDGES

Shared Language

A shared language is the basis on which we build all communication. For example, if you are fully fluent in English and I am effective as a writer, the ideas that I want to communicate in this chapter should make sense to you. On the other hand, if English is your second language, some of the vocabulary may be unfamiliar. In that case, you may have to strengthen the bridge between us by looking up some words in a dictionary.

Figure 8.1 demonstrates the importance of shared language. For a reader of Chinese, the graceful brushstrokes form characters that communicate specific ideas. For those of us who don't know Chinese, the calligraphy is visually engaging, but conveys no information. We cannot understand the meaning of the characters.

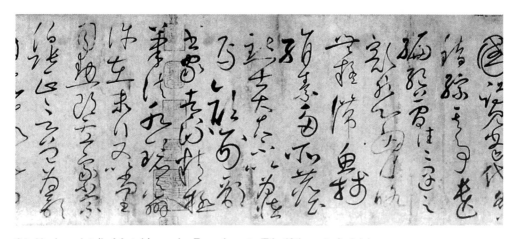

8.1 Huai-su, detail of *Autobiography*, Tang dynasty (7th–10th centuries). Ink on paper.
National Palace Museum, Taipei, Taiwan/Werner Forman Archive/The Bridgeman Art Library

Historical and cultural "literacy" can create another type of bridge. As an American, I live within a framework that is driven by a capitalist economic structure, a two-party political system, and social systems dominated by Judeo-Christian values. South African artist William Kentridge brings a different frame of reference to his artwork. Born in 1951 as the son of white civil rights lawyers, he observed apartheid (state-sponsored racism) at first hand. Kentridge has extensive knowledge of the history of many African genocides. In *Black Box/Chambre Noir* (8.2), he used a miniature theater to tell the story of one such genocide, which nearly wiped out the Herero people. Powered by an inkjet printer mechanism, six robotic figures enter and exit the stage. Projections of historical documents, combined with fragments of music from Mozart's opera *The Magic Flute* and Namibian songs, tell the tragic story. Although any viewer may be attracted to the fascinating structure and the intriguing projections, we must understand African history if we want to fully understand the meaning of Kentridge's story.

8.2 View of William Kentridge's *Black Box/Chambre Noire*, 2005. Miniature theater with mechanized objects, projections, and sound, dimensions variable.
© William Kentridge. Courtesy of Marian Goodman Gallery, New York

Iconography

Many artworks depend on cultural and historical references to build meaning. **Iconography** (literally, "describing images") is the study of such symbolic visual systems.

Deborah Haylor McDowell's *The Serpent Didn't Lie* (8.3) is loaded with references. Leonardo da Vinci's anatomical diagram of a fetus appears in the upper left corner, and the nude couple near the center is based on *The Kiss*, a sculpture by Auguste Rodin. Albert Einstein's computations for the theory of relativity appear in the upper right corner, and in the foreground a baby takes his first steps. A detailed snakeskin border surrounds the image. What does it all mean? Haylor McDowell says:

> Ignorance may spare us the pain of difficult decisions. However, we pay a high price. Can humankind's greatest gifts, emotion and intellect, mature in a world that is free of suffering? In

8.3 Deborah Haylor McDowell, *The Serpent Didn't Lie*, 1997. Etching, 15 × 23 in. (38.1 × 58.42 cm).
© Deborah Haylor McDowell

8.4 Milton Glaser, *Art is . . . WHATEVER*, **1996.**
Poster.
Courtesy of Milton Glaser Studio

8.5 René Magritte, *Golconde*, **1953.** Oil on canvas, 31¾ × 38⅝ in. (80.65 × 98.11 cm).
The Menil Collection, Houston; © 2017 C. Herscovici, London/Artists Rights Society (ARS), New York

8.6 Poster design by Catherine Kanner, photo by Reed Hutchinson, *Serenade* **by George Balanchine, Los Angeles Ballet, 2009.**
Balanchine® is a Trademark of The George Balanchine Trust; Permission granted for LA Ballet

the absence of adversity, will our humanness be lost? *The Serpent Didn't Lie* is based on a biblical text dealing with good and evil in the Garden of Eden. What is the price we pay for knowledge? The images I used in the composition deal with the complexities and responsibilities of our pursuit of knowledge.

Through a sophisticated use of iconography, Haylor McDowell created a puzzle that is filled with ideas for us to explore. For those who understand the cultural references, this elegant print represents many forms of knowledge. However, for those who do not understand the references, the print is simply a beautifully crafted collection of architectural and figurative fragments.

Graphic designers are especially aware of the importance of iconography. On a purely visual level, Milton Glaser's 1996 poster for the School of Visual Arts (8.4) is intriguing and evocative in itself. The hovering hat, shadowy figure, and curious text raise many questions. When we compare the poster with surrealist René Magritte's *Golconde* (8.5), the ideas expand much further. In this and other paintings by Magritte, the man in the bowler hat represents anyone who is courageously navigating the chaos of contemporary life. By connecting Glaser's floating bowler hat to Magritte's painting, we begin to understand the complexity of this seemingly simple poster. Like the man in the bowler hat, each art student must pursue a personal path in order to develop a meaningful and distinctive approach to his or her work.

Audience

Just as films are targeted and rated for specific audiences, so many forms of visual communication are designed for specific viewers. George Balanchine was a master choreographer renowned for his love of classical ballet as well as his commitment to endless invention. The poster in figure 8.6 is powerful yet restrained. Traditional text on a blue background carefully balances the dancers in blue.

By contrast, Saul Bass's poster for *West Side Story* (8.7) is gritty and bold. This modern retelling of Shakespeare's *Romeo and Juliet* combines gang warfare, racism, and romance in a tragic love story. The silhouetted figures dance on fire escape ladders between their apartments, not on a traditional stage. In the film itself, male dancers often wear blue jeans, T-shirts, and street shoes. The music is powerful and percussive. Both shows attracted diverse audiences, but the marketing minds behind the publicity targeted the Balanchine poster at those seeking more traditional ballet, while they pitched the *West Side Story* poster to those seeking modern dance.

Immediacy

When the bridge between the image and the audience is explicit, communication can occur almost instantaneously. When the iconography is elusive or complex, communication takes longer and may vary more. Each approach can be effective in the right time and place. When we are driving a car, our lives depend on the immediate message that we receive when a traffic light turns red. The "Stop!" is clear and emphatic. However, when visiting a museum, we often seek greater complexity and emotional resonance.

Graphic designers generally aim for a combination of immediacy, clarity, and resonance. Their goal is to create effective visual communication that viewers can understand at a glance. Figure 8.8 is an excellent example. The bold shape of a hanged man immediately attracts attention, and the book title itself is simple and direct. The position of the figure's head adds another layer of meaning to this critique of capital punishment.

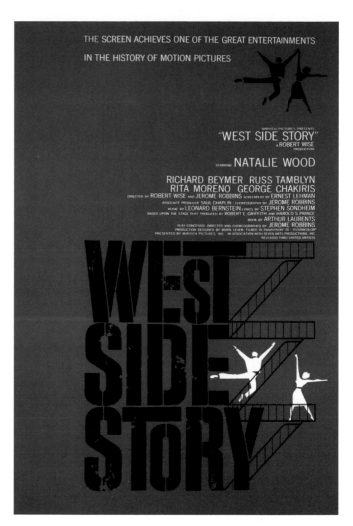

8.7 Saul Bass, *West Side Story* poster, 1961. Written by Ernest Lehman, directed by Jerome Robbins, Robert Wise, music by Leonard Bernstein.

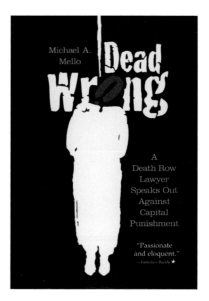

8.8 Mark Maccaulay, book jacket design and illustration for *Dead Wrong: A Death Row Lawyer Speaks Out Against Capital Punishment* by Michael A. Mello, 1997.

8.9 Markus Schaller, *Some Words*, 2007. Steel, 157½ × 354⅜ × ⅝ in. (400 × 900 × 1.5 cm).
© Markus Schaller, Berlin

By contrast, *Some Words* (8.9) by the German artist Markus Schaller requires extended viewer involvement. Created from a sequence of stream-of-consciousness texts inscribed onto 70 iron panels, the installation was designed as a meditation on the very process of thinking. Viewers entering a visual labyrinth had to be willing to puzzle over the words and explore their own cognitive responses. The message was neither explicit nor immediate. In fact, forcing the viewer to think was the main objective. As with Haylor McDowell's work (see figure 8.3), the viewer must piece together a complex set of clues, then reach his or her own conclusions about the nature of knowledge and the development of language.

Stereotypes

A **stereotype** is a fixed generalization based on a preconception. When we use a stereotype, we ignore individual characteristics and emphasize group characteristics. For example, shipping crates often feature a broken wine glass (8.10) to communicate fragility. Glass is actually a versatile material that can be cast as bricks, spun into fiber-optic cables, and polished to create lenses. Nonetheless, we are most familiar with

fragile wine glasses and bottles. Relying on this *general* perception, the shipping label designer used a stereotype to communicate fragility.

Racial stereotyping tends to exaggerate negative generalizations. Even when people positively make an assumption (such as "Asian Americans are brainy overachievers"), the overall effect is demeaning. Rather than learning about an individual person, we are making judgments based on our preconceptions.

Confined to a World War II internment camp as a young child, Roger Shimomura and his family have had very direct experience with racism. Following the Japanese attack on Pearl Harbor, the American government removed roughly 110,000

8.10 "Fragile" pictogram.
Kevkhiev Yury/Alamy Stock Photo

8.11 Roger Shimomura, *Florence, South Carolina*, from *Stereotypes and Admonitions*, 2003. Acrylic on canvas, 20 × 24 in. (51 × 61 cm).
© Roger Shimomura. Private collection

In l969, after graduating from Syracuse University, Roger and his first wife visited their good friend Alvin, in Florence, South Carolina. Alvin's mother threw a dinner party for her friends and relatives, all long-time residents of Florence. The purpose of the party was for everyone to meet Alvin's "friends from Japan" despite Roger and his wife's repeated insistence that they were Americans who happened to be of Japanese descent.

During pre-dinner cocktails, Roger was introduced to Fran, one of Alvin's favorite aunts. Fran was a schoolteacher and college graduate, often referred to as the "intellectual" of the family. As introductory pleasantries were exchanged, Fran asked Roger his name. Roger said his first name and then, in very crisp English, Fran repeated her question to Roger. After Roger repeated his first name, Fran commented very slowly, so as not to be misunderstood, "Well, I guess my name sounds as weird to you as yours does to me."

Japanese Americans living along the West Coast from their homes and sent them to remote camps in Idaho, Wyoming, and other states. In his *Stereotypes and Admonitions* series (8.11), Shimomura used this experience and subsequent encounters with stereotypes as a primary theme. A story accompanies each image. In this example, Shimomura recounts an awkward social encounter. No matter how many times he said "Roger," the woman he was meeting was still convinced that he was an exotic foreigner with an unpronounceable first name. In the painting, he exaggerated her perception by portraying himself as a fierce, yellow Japanese warrior. The text that accompanies the image follows:

Yet, despite the potential hazards, designers may deliberately use stereotypes to create the bridge on which communication depends. Because they are based on preconceptions, stereotypes require little thought. The viewer responds automatically. In some situations, an automatic response is ideal. Figure 8.12 shows four airport pictograms. Can you determine the meaning of each? If the designer is successful, even an exhausted traveler will be able to determine at a glance where to find a baggage locker, an elevator, or a toilet. Notice, in particular, the use of the male and female stereotypes for the toilet pictograms. Despite the wide range of clothing that female travelers wear, the designers used a dress to create a stereotypical female.

Baggage lockers   Elevators   Toilet, men   Toilet, women

8.12 Roger Cook and Don Shanosky, images from a poster introducing the signage symbol system developed for the U.S. Department of Transportation, 1974.

8.13 Asher & Partners for the California Department of Public Health, *I miss my lung, Bob*, poster, 2003.
California Department of Health

Clichés

A **cliché** is an overused expression or a predictable treatment of an idea. Phrases such as "Let's level the playing field" and "Think outside the box" are powerful the first time. However, when we hear them repeatedly, they lose their impact and become clichés. Visual clichés are equally predictable. Skulls representing death and seagulls representing tranquility may be effective at first, but tend to become worn out when we use these images repeatedly.

Surprise

A shift in a stereotype or cliché upsets our expectations and challenges our assumptions. The resulting shock can surprise or delight an audience, making the message more memorable. Originally based on the American cowboy stereotype, the "Marlboro Man" was an early advertising icon. Television and print ads showed this rugged individual confidently riding across a Western landscape. Of course, the Marlboro was his cigarette of choice. The Adbusters spoof in figure 8.13 suggests that "cowboys are a dying breed" because of the cancer caused by their smoking. By breaking the stereotype, the designers attracted viewers' attention, challenged the conventional cigarette ad, and strengthened their nonsmoking message.

Na Zha Cradle (8.14) is equally surprising. Cradles are "supposed" to be soft, safe, and comforting. This cradle is metallic, threatening, and dangerous. Metaphorically commenting on the aggressive capitalism that has driven the Chinese economy in recent years, Shi Jinsong suggests that we pay a price when society progresses too quickly.

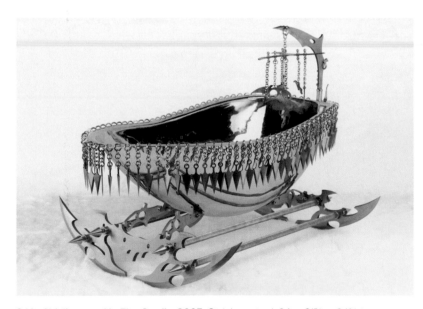

8.14 Shi Jinsong, *Na Zha Cradle*, 2005. Stainless steel, 24 × 31⅞ × 24⅜ in. (61.4 × 81.7 × 62.2 cm).
© Shi Jinsong. Courtesy of Chambers Fine Art

key questions

BUILDING BRIDGES

- Are there any symbolic or cultural meanings embedded in your composition? Are these meanings consistent with the message that you want to convey?

- Have you used a stereotype or a cliché? If so, does that add to or subtract from your message?

- What audience do you want to reach? Are the form and content of your design appropriate for that audience?

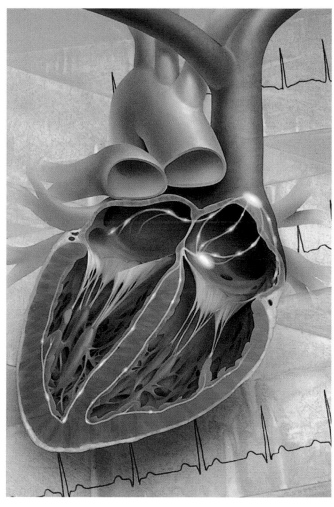

8.15 Kim Martens, *Arterial Fibrillation*, 2000. Photoshop.
© Kim Martens

PURPOSE AND INTENT

Any number of approaches to visual communication can be effective. We simply choose the style, iconography, and composition best suited to our purpose.

Let's consider five different uses of human anatomy. *Arterial Fibrillation* (8.15) was developed for the cover of a medical journal. With equal training in art and science, medical illustrator Kim Martens combined anatomical accuracy with artistic imagination to create this design. To increase sales, the magazine's art director requested an image that was both physically accurate and visually attractive.

Figure 8.16 shows an extensive online training system developed by the National Cancer Institute. Despite the encyclopedic amount of information, this website is visually simple and easy to navigate. Rather than introduce flashy effects, the designers used a methodical structure that presents each lesson very clearly. As a result, readers can focus on the content of the course, from the conducting respiratory passages to the complexities of the cardiovascular system.

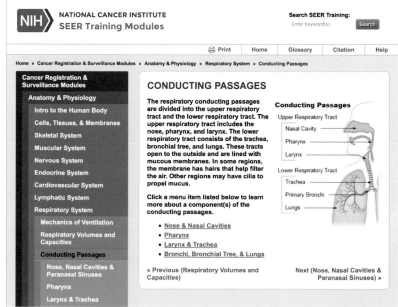

8.16 SEER Training Modules, National Cancer Institute, Conducting Passages, 2013.
http://training.seer.cancer.gov/

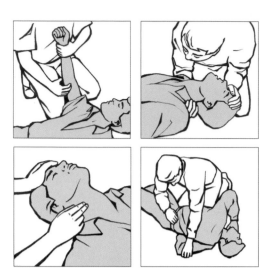

8.17 Medical illustration, directions for first responders.
dieKleinert/Alamy Stock Photo

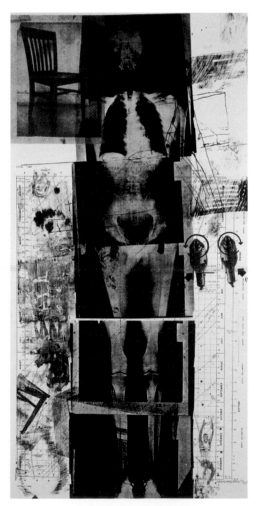

8.18 Robert Rauschenberg, *Booster*, 1967.
Lithograph and serigraph, printed in color, composition,
5 ft 11⁹⁄₁₆ in. × 2 ft 11⅛ in. (181.7 × 89.1 cm).
From an edition of 38, published by Gemini G.E.L., Los Angeles
Art © Robert Rauschenberg /Licensed by VAGA, New York.
Princeton University Art Museum/Art Resource, NY

8.19 Kiki Smith, *Virgin Mary*, 1992.
Beeswax, microcrystalline wax, cheesecloth,
and wood on steel base, 67½ × 26 × 14½ in.
(171.5 × 66 × 36.8 cm).
© Kiki Smith. Courtesy of Pace Gallery, New York.
Photograph by Ellen Page Wilson

Figure 8.17 requires even greater clarity and economy. Designed to demonstrate a life-saving emergency procedure, this graphic relies on simple line drawings. A close-up view of the essential hand position is more important than attractive colors or anatomical detail.

Shifting our attention to fine art, Robert Rauschenberg's *Booster* (8.18) presents his body as a series of X-rays. This unconventional self-portrait combines the personal X-rays with images of an astronomer's chart, diagrams of hand drills, arrows, graphs, and an empty chair. The title adds further meaning, suggesting a connection to booster shots, booster rockets, and booster seats, which increase the height of an ordinary chair so that young children can sit at a table comfortably. Reduced to an X-ray image and surrounded by fragments of technological information, the artist becomes a cog in the technological machinery. By contrast, the woman in Kiki Smith's *Virgin Mary* (8.19) seems both vulnerable and graceful. She displays her flayed body unapologetically, extending her open hands in a type of blessing.

DEGREES OF REPRESENTATION

Nonobjective or **nonrepresentational shapes**, such as circles, rectangles, and squares, are **pure forms**. Pure forms are shapes that we create without direct reference to reality. Artists often use pure form to embody elusive emotions or express universal meaning. For example, in *Several Circles* (8.20), Wassily Kandinsky sought to express his complex spiritual feelings. For him, the simple circular shapes were as poignant and expressive as music.

We derive **representational shapes** from specific subject matter that is strongly based on direct observation. Most photographs are representational and highly descriptive. For example, in Ansel Adams's *Monolith, The Face of Half Dome, Yosemite Valley* (8.21), each variation in the cliff's surface is clearly defined.

Between these two extremes, **abstract shapes** are derived from visual reality but are distilled and transformed, reducing their resemblance to the original source. In *Seventh Sister* (8.22), Robert Moskowitz deleted surface details from the rocky mountain. His abstracted cliff is a general representation of a vertical surface rather than a descriptive painting of a specific cliff.

Reference to reality is a traditional way to increase meaning in an artwork. Drawing on their experience in the physical world, viewers can connect to the illusion of reality presented in the painting. In a nonobjective image, lines, shapes, textures, and colors must generate all of the meaning. Because there is no explicit subject matter, some viewers find it more difficult to understand nonobjective images.

Abstract images can combine the power of association with the power of pure form. Charles Demuth's *... And the Home of the Brave* (8.23) demonstrates the power of abstraction. He has transformed a factory into a series of lines and geometric shapes. Variations on red, white, and blue add a symbolic connection to the American flag. The image was painted during a period of nationwide unemployment, and the factory

is dark and forbidding. The ironic title (which is taken from the concluding words of the American national anthem) adds a pointed political statement.

DEGREES OF DEFINITION

Definition is the degree to which we distinguish one visual component from another. **High definition** creates strong contrast between shapes and tends to increase clarity and immediacy of communication. For this reason, the diagrams in this book generally feature black figures on a white background. **Low-definition** shapes, including soft-edged shapes, gradations, and transparencies, can increase the complexity of the design and encourage multiple interpretations.

Definition is an inherent aspect of photography. In addition to variations in focus, the photographer can choose finer-grained film and slick paper to create a crisper image, and coarser-grained film and textured paper to create a softer image.

Variations in photographic definition can substantially affect meaning. We normally expect to see high definition in the foreground and low definition in the background. In *Gun 1, New York* (8.24), William Klein reversed this expectation. Pointed directly at the viewer's face, the gun itself is blurred, menacing, and monstrously large. Even more disturbing, however, is the scowling face of the boy holding the gun. Fierce and sharply focused, his face epitomizes both fear and rage.

> ▶ key questions
>
> DEFINITION AND REPRESENTATION
>
> - Which will best express your idea—representation, nonrepresentation, or abstraction?
>
> - Variations in definition can increase the illusion of space. Will your design benefit from greater depth?
>
> - Definition can also direct the viewer's attention to specific areas in the design. How can definition enhance meaning in your design?

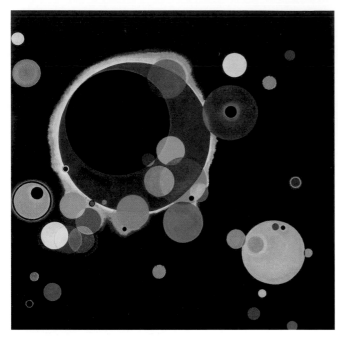

8.20 Wassily Kandinsky, *Several Circles*, 1926. Oil on canvas, 55¼ × 55⅜ in. (140.3 × 140.7 cm).

The Solomon R. Guggenheim Museum, New York. Gift, Solomon R. Guggenheim, Founding Collection. 41.283. © 2017 Artists Rights Society (ARS), New York

8.21 Ansel Adams, *Monolith, The Face of Half Dome, Yosemite Valley*, 1927. Photograph.
© Ansel Adams Publishing Rights Trust

8.22 Robert Moskowitz, *Seventh Sister*, 1982. Oil on canvas, 108 × 39 in. (274.3 × 99 cm).
© Robert Moskowitz

8.23 Charles Demuth, . . . And the Home of the Brave, 1931. Oil on composition board, 29½ × 23⅝ in. (74.8 × 59.7 cm).
© The Art Institute of Chicago/Giraudon/The Bridgeman Art Library

8.24 William Klein, Gun 1, New York, 1955. Gelatin silver print, 15¾ × 11¾ in. (40 × 29.8 cm).
© William Klein. Courtesy of Howard Greenberg Gallery, New York

CONTEXT

As we noted in Chapter Seven, the context in which any image appears profoundly influences its meaning. Viewers tend to connect informational fragments. For example, in figure 8.25, the juxtaposition of discouraged flood survivors with a propagandistic billboard makes us rethink the phrase "There's no way like the American way."

The social context in which an image appears is equally important. In figure 8.26, Winston Churchill, the prime minister who led Britain to victory in World War II, extends two fingers to create the famous "V for victory" gesture that he used throughout the war. If we are familiar with Churchill and know about the British people's desperate struggle during the war, we immediately make the correct connection. In figure 8.27, the same gesture communicates a different idea. As part of the signage for the Minnesota Children's Museum, the extended fingers now communicate the number 2. Because children may not be able to read, this icon can help them find their way in the museum. Finally, in Sean O'Meallie's *Out-Boxed Finger Puppets Perform the Numbers 1 Through 5 in No Particular Order* (8.28), the same gesture becomes a playful piece of sculpture, as well as an indication of the number 2. We now see the extended fingers in the context of a series of whimsical forms. In each of these three cases, the meaning of the two fingers depends on the context.

CONNECTIONS

Analogies, similes, and metaphors are figures of speech that link one thing to another. An **analogy** creates a general connection between unrelated objects or ideas, whereas a **simile** creates the connection using the word *as* or *like,* as in "She has a heart as big as Texas." A **metaphor** is more explicit: Speaking metaphorically, we would say "Her heart *is* Texas." As we can see, a substantial shift in meaning occurs when we use a metaphor.

In all cases, we give the original word the qualities of the linked word. For example, when Robert Burns wrote the simile "My love is like a red red rose," he gave the abstract concept of "love" the attributes of a glorious, colorful, fragrant, thorny, and transient rose.

We can use **metaphorical thinking** to connect an image and an idea. Take the phrase "I have butterflies in my stomach." We widely use this phrase to

8.25 Margaret Bourke-White, *At the Time of the Louisville Flood*, 1937. Gelatin silver print.
Margaret Bourke-White/TimePix/Getty Images

describe nervousness. Let's substitute other insects for butterflies, such as bees or wasps. How does this change the meaning? To push it even further, start with the phrase "My mind was full of clouds." What happens when you replace "clouds" with mice on treadmills, rats in mazes, shadowy staircases, beating drums, screaming children—or even butterflies? When my mind is full of butterflies, I am happy, but butterflies in my stomach indicate fear. In addition to expanding ideas, metaphors can help provide specific images for elusive emotions.

8.26 Alfred Eisenstaedt, *Winston Churchill*, Liverpool, 1957. Gelatin silver print.
Alfred Eisenstaedt/TimePix/Getty Images

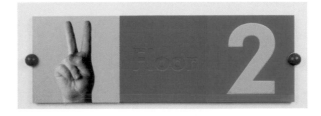

8.27 Pentagram design, Minnesota Children's Museum signage, New York. Tracey Cameron and Michael Bierut, designers.
Courtesy of Pentagram

8.28 Sean O'Meallie, *Out-Boxed Finger Puppets Perform the Numbers 1 Through 5 in No Particular Order*, **1999.** Polychromed wood, 17½ × 42 × 11 in. (44.5 × 106.7 × 27.9 cm).
© Sean O'Meallie. Photograph by Ric Helstrom

8.29 Jimmy Margulies, editorial cartoon, 2006.
© Jimmy Margulies

To strengthen communication, artists and designers have always used metaphorical thinking. Editorial cartoons offer many examples. In figure 8.29, a congressional hand puppet vows independence from the very lobbyist who is controlling his vote.

Painter Carrie Ann Baade is a master of metaphor. The figures and objects in her meticulously rendered paintings are never simple representations of reality or displays of technical mastery. There is alway more to the story. In *Explaining Death to a Dead Rabbit* (figure 8.30), she references both Richard Adams's *Watership Down* (a book that was popular in her childhood) and the artwork of Joseph Beuys, a German performance art pioneer. In one of his most famous works, Beuys cradled a dead hare while he discussed the complexities of contemporary art. The combined references suggest ways in which art can be used to help us consider connections between life and death.

The following interview with Jim Elniski describes a further use of connections. Rather than create exhibitions for museums, Elniski and his partner, Frances Whitehead, typically seek ways to connect their art and design projects to the social and architectural fabric of the neighborhoods they inhabit. As the interview unfolds, the possibilities for connection expand to encompass the environment more broadly.

8.30 Carrie Ann Baade, *Explaining Death to a Dead Rabbit*, **2011.** Oil on panel, 24 × 30 in. (60.9 × 76.2 cm).
© Carrie Ann Baade

Profile:
Jim Elniski, Artist
Creating Sustainable Architecture

© Jim Elniski

Between 2003 and 2007, Jim Elniski and his partner, Frances Whitehead, envisioned and constructed *The Greenhouse Chicago*. This home and studio combines cutting-edge energy technology with locally sourced materials to create sustainable architecture that is also a work of art.

Elniski is a social practice artist, educator, and clinical social worker. His work with groups and communities employs a hybrid approach, linking individual and collective expressions to create socially engaged artworks. Frances Whitehead, a self-proclaimed "designist," explores the juncture of art, science, and design. Trained as a studio artist, she has established a collaborative design studio for hybrid public projects that are driven by her commitment to place-based research and biologic communities.

MS: Please describe this project.

JE: *The Greenhouse* is a 4,000-square-foot residence with studios in the West Town neighborhood of Chicago. Reclaimed from an outmoded, underused brick warehouse, it combines sustainable technology, adaptive reuse, and affordable green design. A geothermal heating and cooling system produces 50 percent of the energy we use, and there are two wind turbines, solar photovoltaic, and solar thermal roof panels. Radiant heating in the floor, dual-flush toilets, energy star appliances, rainwater cisterns, and a green roof further reduce our carbon footprint. We also grow vegetables and maintain beehives on the rooftop.

MS: This project was extraordinarily labor-intensive, taking more than four years to plan and complete. What inspired you to start?

JE: We had been living and working in a very large and energy-inefficient loft building. Since we are both strongly committed to sustainability and systems thinking, we decided to design a smaller and smarter place to live.

MS: What is adaptive reuse, and why is it important?

JE: Adaptive reuse is the process of transforming an outmoded existing building for a new purpose. This approach required us to work creatively with what we found, rather than building a new ideal structure from scratch. It challenged us to clearly assess the strengths and weaknesses of the site and then make choices that will produce the results we seek. We must maximize opportunities within those limitations. As artist/designers, this critical-thinking process is very familiar—we analyze, assess, discard, and rethink every project as it evolves through multiple iterations.

MS: You've described this as a "design/build" project. What does that mean?

JE: The design/build approach helped us to embrace new ideas and make adjustments as the building was constructed. For example, once construction began, we could more clearly see the dialog between the interior and the exterior spaces, and could better understand the number of distinct and interrelated systems the structure could incorporate.

MS: Can you take us through the major steps in the process?

JE: We asked a seemingly simple question: How could we create a smaller, smarter, and sustainable live/work space? Next, we conducted extensive research.

What technology was being used in sustainable architecture, and how could it be applied to our project? Then, working with architect William James and his associate Mhairi McVicar, we developed a layout of how the various spaces would relate to one another. The central open-air courtyard was at the heart of our vision. Beyond that point, the process became more fluid. As with any of our art projects, we planned, built, evaluated, reconsidered, and revised our plans. Because the architect was also our general contractor, he was able to respond to unexpected changes we had to make along the way. For example, while we were trying to decide with the systems engineer whether to have either solar photovoltaic panels (for electricity) or solar thermal panels (for hot water), we realized that our home could incorporate a complete set of sustainable building elements. That's when we realized that *The Greenhouse* was becoming an art project.

MS: Frances created a graphic linking the many systems you incorporated. Can you talk us through this image?

JE: Let's focus on the way the solar thermal panels and the geothermal system work together. In the winter months, the fluid pumping through our geothermal heating system collects the heat of the earth (about 55 degrees F) and is augmented by the heat from our solar thermal panels (about 120 degrees F). It then passes through the heat pump that uses electricity (generated in part from our solar photovoltaic panels and wind turbines) to extract the heat from the fluid into our radiant floor. We viewed this multi-systemic interconnectedness not as a problem to be solved but rather as a condition to be explored.

MS: *The Greenhouse* has been featured on the Discovery Channel and in various architecture magazines. Professionals from the American Institute of Architects and entire classes of architecture students often tour the site. What is its significance, and why are people so drawn to this project?

JE: The house is very deliberate, in every sense of the word. Every choice has been made to maximize the ecology of the house as a whole and to position it elegantly within its urban setting. As artists, we were especially sensitive to the form and the function of our chosen materials, including the corrugated siding, glass, concrete, and wood.

In many ways, *The Greenhouse* is experienced as kind of a Rubik's cube puzzle. This live/work space is a series of interlinked systems: heat, ventilation, light, water, ADA accessible, and so on. Each discrete space frames each adjacent space, and the central courtyard animates the entire building.

As a machine for urban living, *The Greenhouse* continues to evolve. Recently, I installed two beehives on the roof over my studio space. These colonies gracefully contribute to the nested layers of their ecology and sustainably use their living space. Likewise, *The Greenhouse* reflects how essential it is for us, as artists, to situate our work in the space between art and life. Viewed in this way, art helps to reveal the miraculous in everyday life.

Jim Elniski and Frances Whitehead, *The Greenhouse Chicago*, Chicago, 2004–07.
© Jim Elniski

AESTHETICS

Cultural Values

In *Design in the Visual Arts* (1984), Roy Behrens noted the difference between the words *anesthetic* and *aesthetic*. We use an **anesthetic** to induce insensitivity or unconsciousness. In an anesthetic state, we are numbed and disoriented. We may not be able to determine the size or location of objects or the sequence of events. On the other hand, **aesthetics** is the study of human responses to beauty. An aesthetic experience enhances our feelings, and our understanding expands. As a result, an aesthetic experience tends to heighten meaning, whereas an anesthetic experience tends to dull meaning. Dentists use anesthetics; artists and designers use aesthetics.

Aesthetic theories reflect social values and thus vary greatly from culture to culture. For example, an exalted conception of Christianity dominated civic life during the Middle Ages in Europe. To express their faith, architects developed ingenious building strategies to create the soaring Gothic cathedrals that we associate with that period (8.31).

8.31 Interior of Notre-Dame Cathedral, 13th century.
Paris, France. chienmuhou/123RF.com

8.32 Frank Lloyd Wright, interior of Unity Temple, 1906. Oak Park, Illinois.
© 2017 Artists Rights Society (ARS), New York View Pictures/UIG via Getty Images

By contrast, the Unitarian congregation that commissioned Frank Lloyd Wright's Unity Temple (8.32) most valued a sense of community. As a result, their sanctuary is essentially a cube, with rows of seats facing inward from three sides. Congregants face one another while simultaneously maintaining close contact with the minister. The Pompidou Center (8.33), by Renzo Piano and Richard Rogers, offers a third approach to public architecture. From the outside, it looks more like a rollercoaster than a major art museum. To emphasize the importance of technology in contemporary life, the architects highlighted the blue ventilation ducts, red elevators, and green water pipes, rather than hiding them.

Because cultural values are so variable, before we conclude our discussion of visual communication, we must delve into contemporary aesthetics.

Modern and Postmodern

Postmodernism was the dominant art movement from about 1975 through 2005, and remains a powerful force in contemporary art. The word itself emphasizes the extent to which artists and designers often seek solutions that challenge or exceed modernism. Thus, to understand contemporary aesthetics, we must first examine the essential characteristics of both these aesthetic periods.

In the arts, **modernism** is a general term that encompasses a wide range of individual movements. Beginning in Europe in the latter part of the nineteenth century, modernism became the dominant force in art and design from around 1860 to 1960.

In a sense, modernism rose from the ashes of World War I. After this devastating conflict, traditional

8.33 Renzo Piano and Richard Rogers, **Pompidou Center, 1976.** Paris, France.
© GM Photo Images/Alamy

attitudes and images seemed inadequate and out of date. Architects began to strip away traditional ornamentation to reveal the underlying structures and spaces in their buildings. Designers such as Marcel Breuer (see figure 5.1), Raymond Loewy, and Charles and Ray Eames (see figure 5.4) used plastic, metals, and glass to mass-produce objects and images for an expanding consumer market. Artists such as Wassily Kandinsky (see figure 8.20), Barnett Newman, and Mark Rothko (8.34) valued abstraction over traditional representation. The international art world became a hotbed of experimentation.

Many modernists shared four fundamental beliefs. First, they were fascinated by **form**, meaning the physical manifestation of an idea. "Less is more" became a mantra for designers, and "the form is the content" became a catchphrase for many painters. Second, modernists readily embraced new materials and production methods. Concrete, plastic, and glass began to replace traditional materials such as wood, brick, and stone, especially in architecture. Third, the early modernists believed strongly in the social significance of the arts. They wanted to bring art and design to the general population, rather than working for the elite. Finally, many modernists sought to understand and express universal truths. No longer satisfied with a conventional representation of reality, they began to develop a new visual language based on distillation and abstraction.

These fundamental beliefs stimulated innovation in all areas of art, architecture, and design, thus producing an enormous amount of brilliant work. Over time, however, many modernists became trapped by their own

success. Constructed from hard, reflective materials and dominated by right angles, modernist buildings could seem cold and uninviting. Based on an underlying grid and typographical conventions, modernist posters could become stale and predictable. Reduced to essential forms, late modernist painting and sculpture became detached from the chaos and complexity of contemporary life. Artists and designers seemed to have answered all the questions of modernism. Something had to change.

The publication in 1966 of *Complexity and Contradiction in Architecture* set the stage for postmodern architecture. In it, architect Robert Venturi extolled the energy and ambiguities of Renaissance architecture:

> I like elements which are hybrid rather than "pure," compromising rather than "clean," distorted rather than "articulated," perverse as well as impersonal, boring as well as "interesting," conventional rather than "designed," accommodating rather than excluding, redundant rather than simple, vestigial as well as innovating, inconsistent and equivocal rather than direct and clear. I am for messy vitality over obvious unity.

At the same time, philosophers Jean-François Lyotard, Jacques Derrida, Michel Foucault, and Roland Barthes began to challenge previous aesthetic theories. They argued that both knowledge and communication change constantly: there *are* no universal truths. Because the audience rather than the artist ultimately responds to the artwork, interpretation is inherently open-ended. Furthermore, postmodern theorists tended to see knowledge as cyclical rather than progressive. They argued that we are pursuing a complex path with multiple branches rather than a grand journey leading to human perfection.

Influenced by these theorists and seeking fresh ideas and approaches, many contemporary artists and designers reject the central tenets of modernism. For the postmodernist, context and content are as important as pure form. Postmodern use of materials tends to be open-ended and often irreverent. For example, an artist may construct an artwork from trash, or manipulate fiberglass to mimic steel.

Interested in all forms of experience, postmodernists tend to question distinctions between "high art" (such as painting and sculpture) and "low art" (such as advertising and crafts). Since various aspects of visual culture are intertwined, the postmodernist may recycle images and ideas, deliberately "appropriating" them for use in a new context. Finally, for the postmodernist there are multiple rather than universal truths—and all truths change continually. As a result, where late modernism tended to be stable and reductive, postmodernism tends to be expansive and dynamic. As Venturi suggested, we can view complexity and contradiction as strengths.

Since 1990, the collision between modernism and postmodernism has released an enormous amount of energy. Artists have broken taboos repeatedly, and the criteria for excellence continue to evolve.

Postmodern Strategies

Five common characteristics of postmodern art and design follow.

We often use **appropriation** (the reuse of an existing artwork) to create a connection between past and present cultural values. In *We Don't Need Another Hero* (8.35), Barbara Kruger borrowed a Norman Rockwell illustration in which a young girl admires her male counterpart's muscles. The emphatic text shifts the meaning from the original gender stereotype to a powerful feminist statement.

Recontextualization is another postmodern strategy. Constructed from steel pins and placed in a gallery, Mona Hatoum's *Doormat II* (8.36) forces us to rethink a commonplace object. As part of a series on racism, this artwork suggests that the opportunities offered by civil rights legislation may be as ironic as a welcome mat made of pins.

Artists often use **layering** to create complex or even contradictory meanings. In *The Red Mean: Self-Portrait* (8.37), Jaune Quick-to-See Smith reinterprets Leonardo da Vinci's famous drawing of ideal human proportions (8.38). As a Renaissance man, Leonardo was fascinated by both perfection and the grotesque. In this drawing, he mapped out an idealized figure radiating from the navel in the center. Despite its superficial similarity, the aesthetic basis for Smith's self-portrait is entirely different. Her circular outline simultaneously suggests a target, cancellation, and the

four directions emphasized by many Native American spiritual practices. A sign proclaiming "Made in the USA" combined with the artist's tribal identification number covers the figure's chest, and tribal newspapers fill the background. While the Leonardo drawing is simple and elegant, Smith's self-portrait provides a rich commentary on the complexities of her life as a Native American.

These examples demonstrate a fourth postmodern characteristic: we often integrate words and images to expand emotional impact or to create conflict. The postmodernist celebrates contradiction and complexity as facts of life and sources of inspiration.

Finally, we can define **hybridity** as the creation of artworks using disparate media and meanings to create a unified conceptual statement. Jaune Quick-to-See Smith constructed her *Self-Portrait* from newspapers, posters, and identity cards, as well as paint. Kathryn Frund combined government documents and a carpenter's plumb bob with paint on aluminum to create *Radical Acts* (see figure 3.21). William Kentridge's *Refusal of Time* (8.39) is a 30-minute meditation on time and space, the complex legacies of colonialism

8.35 Barbara Kruger, *Untitled (We Don't Need Another Hero)*, 1987. Photographic silkscreen, vinyl lettering on Plexiglas, 109 × 210 in. (276.9 × 533.4 cm).
© Barbara Kruger. Collection: Fisher Landau Center for Art, Long Island City, NY. Courtesy of Mary Boone Gallery, New York

8.36 Mona Hatoum, *Doormat II*, 2000–01. Steel and rubber, 1 × 28 × 16 in. (2.5 × 71 × 40.6 cm).
© Mona Hatoum. Courtesy of Alexander and Bonin, New York. Photograph by Orcutt & Van Der Putten

8.37 Jaune Quick-to-See Smith, *The Red Mean: Self-Portrait*, **1992**. Mixed media.
© Jaune Quick-to-See Smith (Salish member of the Confederated Salish and Kootenai Nation, MT) and Accola Griefen Gallery

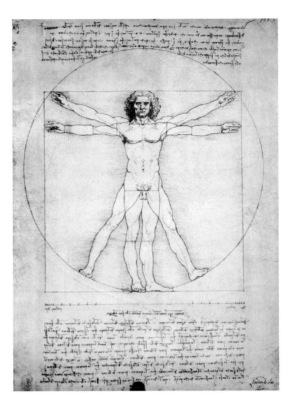

8.38 Leonardo da Vinci, *Proportions of the Human Figure (after Vitruvius)*, **c. 1485–90**. Pen and ink, 13½ × 9¾ in. (34.3 × 24.8 cm).
INTERFOTO/Alamy Stock Photo

8.39 William Kentridge, *Refusal of Time*, **2012**. Installation view of five-channel video with sound, 30 min., with steel megaphones and breathing machine "elephant," dimensions variable.
Collection SFMOMA, Jointly owned by the Metropolitan Museum of Art, New York, and the San Francisco Museum of Modern Art (purchase, by exchange, through an anonymous gift and the K. Hart Smith Trust); Marian Goodman Gallery, New York. © 2012 William Kentridge. All rights reserved

and industry, and the artist's own intellectual life. It combines video, sound, and sculpture, and requires a sustained commitment on the part of the viewer. For the postmodernist, visual impact and conceptual meaning are more important than technical purity.

DRAMA

Regardless of the medium or the message, we can strengthen all communication through dramatic delivery. Even Martin Luther King, Jr.'s "I Have a Dream" speech loses much of its power when one delivers it in a flat, monotonous tone of voice. Just as a playwright sets the stage for the story that he or she seeks to tell, so an artist can set the stage for visual communication.

We can use all the design elements and principles that we describe in this book to increase *compositional* drama. To increase *conceptual* drama, we can:

- *Personify the idea.* When we identify with a character in a play, we become more empathetic and involved in the story. Likewise, when we identify with a character in a painting or a poster, we are much more likely to remember the idea or emotion. Figure 8.40 represents one of the most effective campaigns used by those opposed to drunk driving. These posters combine before and after photographs of young drivers to show the devastating results of traffic accidents.

- *Focus on essentials.* Some say that theater is "life with the boring parts left out." To be meaningful to an audience, the characters and events in a play must have a strong relationship to direct experience. However, a playwright rarely shows a character flossing his or her teeth. Too much detail clutters the composition, confuses the audience, and muddles the message. Including the right amount of information in just the right way can add drama to even the simplest idea.

- *Seek significance.* We can use any event, character, or time period to create an effective play. For example, in figure 8.28, Sean O'Meallie turned a simple sequence of numbers into a witty series of sculptures. A unique approach to a familiar subject or an insightful interpretation of personal and political events can add significance and increase impact.

8.40 Drink driving magazine advertising, "Not Everyone Who Drives Drunk Dies," 1987.
© Advertising Archive 1980s

summary

- A shared language is the basis on which we build all communication.
- Iconography (the study of symbolic visual systems) provides us with a way to analyze the meaning of images and objects.
- Just as films target specific audiences, artists and designers use different forms of visual communication for different audiences.
- Graphic designers often seek visual immediacy. By comparison, many paintings require extended viewer involvement and longer viewing time.
- A stereotype is a fixed generalization based on a preconception. Stereotypes can easily create a bridge between the image and the audience.
- A cliché is an overused expression or predictable treatment of an idea. Even the most interesting image will lose its power if we overuse it.
- A shift in a stereotype or cliché challenges our assumptions and can increase impact.
- Artists and designers choose the style, iconography, and composition best suited to their purpose. A mismatch between the type of image and its purpose creates confusion.
- The visual and social context in which an image appears will profoundly affect its meaning.
- Analogies, similes, and metaphors are figures of speech that link one thing to another. Visual communication, especially, widely uses metaphors.
- Appropriation, recontextualization, layering, word/image integration, and hybridity are five common strategies that we use to create postmodern meaning.
- Dramatic delivery of a message enhances meaning.

key terms

abstract shapes	hybridity	postmodernism
aesthetics	iconography	pure form
analogy	layering	recontextualization
anesthetic	low definition	representational
appropriation	metaphor	shapes
cliché	metaphorical thinking	simile
definition	modernism	stereotype
high definition	nonobjective shapes	

© Dennis Montagna

Success Story:
Dennis Montagna,
Historian
National Park Service, Northeast Region Office, Philadelphia

Dr. Dennis Montagna directs the National Park Service's Monument Research & Preservation Program. The program provides comprehensive assistance in the care and interpretation of historic cemeteries, outdoor sculpture, and public monuments to managers of National Park sites and to other constituents nationwide.

MS: How did you make the transition from printmaking and photography to your current position?

DM: Actually, I'd see it as more a process of accretion than one of transition. Spending part of my sophomore year at Florida State University's Study Center in Florence was a game changer for me. Taking art history courses there allowed me to bring together my passions for art, history, and writing. So I double-majored in Art and Art History, and then completed MA and Ph.D degrees in Art History, specializing in American Sculpture and Architecture.
I was then hired by the National Park Service in a job that included work with Historic Preservation. A six-month period of study at the International Centre for the Study of the Preservation and Restoration of Cultural Property in Rome prepared me to create a program that would help people better care for commemorative monuments, sculpture, and historic cemeteries. Thus, I've been able to meld my training in studio art, history, and preservation into a career that allows me to use them all.

MS: How does your design background inform your current work?

DM: Day to day, my work often requires me to design or oversee the creation of new memorials. On a larger scale, my design training was especially valuable when I chaired the committee that selected from among the five designs shortlisted for the African Burial Ground Memorial in New York City. The committee had to identify strengths and weaknesses in the various submissions, and once the project was approved, I had to provide critical advice during its implementation.

My training also helps me to plan conservation projects that require knowledge of the artist's initial intent. I can then advocate for treatments that seek to recapture a creator's vision and, more importantly, plan the maintenance that will preserve it over time.

MS: What advice would you give to students starting college today?

DM: I would suggest that students resist the urge to focus their education too tightly. Depth of knowledge in a discipline is helpful; narrow job training is much less so. I was fortunate to develop a dual-major approach that let me integrate studio art, history, and writing into a rich and engaging career. While universities talk a good game about providing a broad "liberal" education, in practice it is often an education marked by a narrowing of interests. Embrace life as fully as you can—and travel abroad when your time and budget allows!

Dennis Montagna (left, in white cap) working with Conservator Ronald Harvey on Frederick C. Hibbard's 1915 bronze sculpture *The Rifleman* in front of Barton County Courthouse, Great Bend, Kansas. The monument was created in commemoration of soldiers who fought for the Union during the American Civil War.
Photograph: Karen Neuforth

Visual Organization

Arnheim, Rudolph. *Power of the Center*. Berkeley: University of California Press, 1999.

Berger, Arthur Asa. *Seeing Is Believing: An Introduction to Visual Communication*, 3rd ed. New York: McGraw-Hill, 2007.

Berger, John. *Ways of Seeing*. London: British Broadcasting Corporation, 1987.

Dondis, Donis. *A Primer of Visual Literacy*. Cambridge, MA: MIT Press, 1973.

Two-Dimensional Design

Lupton, Ellen, and Jennifer Cole Phillips. *Graphic Design: The New Basics*. Princeton, NJ: Princeton Architectural Press, 2008.

Myers, Jack Fredrick. *The Language of Visual Art: Perception as a Basis for Design*. Orlando, FL: Holt, Rinehart and Winston, 1989.

Ocvirk, Otto G., Robert E. Stinson, Philip R. Wigg, Robert O. Bone, and David L. Cayton. *Art Fundamentals: Theory and Practice*, 11th ed. New York: McGraw-Hill, 2009.

Wong, Wucius. *Principles of Form and Design*. New York: John Wiley and Sons, 1993.

Color Theory

Albers, Josef. *Interaction of Color*. New Haven, CT: Yale University Press, 1963.

Gerritsen, Frans. *Theory and Practice of Color*. New York: Van Nostrand Reinhold, 1975.

Hornung, David. *Color: A Workshop Approach*. New York: McGraw-Hill, 2005.

Itten, Johannes. *The Art of Color*. New York: Van Nostrand Reinhold, 1974.

Koenig, Becky. *Color Workbook*. Upper Saddle River, NJ: Pearson Education, 2010.

Kuppers, Harald. *Color: Origin, Systems, Uses*. New York: Van Nostrand Reinhold, 1972.

Munsell, Albert H. *A Grammar of Color: A Basic Treatise on the Color System of Albert H. Munsell*. New York: Van Nostrand Reinhold, 1969.

Norman, Richard B. *Electronic Color*. New York: Van Nostrand Reinhold, 1990.

Theroux, Alexander, *The Primary Colors: Three Essays*. New York: Henry Holt and Company, 1994.

Wong, Wucius. *Principles of Color Design*. New York: John Wiley and Sons, 1997.

Creativity

Bohm, David. *On Creativity*. New York: Routledge, 2000.

Briggs, John. *Fire in the Crucible: Understanding the Process of Creative Genius*. Grand Rapids: Phanes Press, 2000.

Csikszentmihalyi, Mihaly. *Creativity: Flow and the Psychology of Discovery and Invention*. New York: HarperCollins, 1996.

Dewey, John. *Art as Experience*. New York: Capricorn Books, 1958.

Gardner, Howard. *Art, Mind and Brain: A Cognitive Approach to Creativity*. New York: Basic Books, 1982.

Gardner, Howard. *Creating Minds: An Anatomy of Creativity Seen Through the Lives of Freud, Einstein, Picasso, Stravinsky, Eliot, Graham, and Gandhi*. New York: Basic Books, 1993.

Gardner, Howard. *Frames of Mind: The Theory of Multiple Intelligences*. New York: Basic Books, 1985.

Lamott, Anne. *Bird by Bird: Some Instructions on Writing and Life*. New York: Anchor Books, 1998.

Le Boeuf, Michael. *Imagineering*. New York: McGraw-Hill, 1980.

Prince, George. "Creativity and Learning as Skills, Not Talents," *The Philips Exeter Bulletin*, June–October, 1980.

Root-Bernstein, Robert and Michele. *Sparks of Genius: The Thirteen Thinking Tools of the World's Most Creative People*, New York: Houghton Mifflin Harcourt, 2013.

Shekerjian, Denise. *Uncommon Genius: How Great Ideas Are Born*. New York: Penguin Books, 1991.

Tharp, Twyla. *The Creative Habit: Learn It and Use It for Life*. New York: Simon and Schuster, 2006.

Wallace, Doris B., and Howard E. Gruber, eds. *Creative People at Work*. New York: Oxford University Press, 1989.

Concept Development

Adams, James L. *Conceptual Blockbusting*. Reading, MA: Addison-Wesley, 1986.

de Bono, Edward. *Lateral Thinking*. London: Ward Educational Limited, 1970.

Grear, Malcolm. *Inside/Outside: From the Basics to the Practice of Design*. New York: Van Nostrand Reinhold, 1993.

Johnson, Mary Frisbee. *Visual Workouts: A Collection of Art-Making Problems*. Englewood Cliffs, NJ: Prentice Hall, 1983.

Kelley, Tom. *The Art of Innovation: Lessons in Creativity from America's Leading Design Firm*. New York: Doubleday, 2001.

Lakoff, George, and Mark Johnson. *Metaphors We Live By*. Chicago: University of Chicago Press, 1981.

Shahn, Ben. *The Shape of Content*. Cambridge, MA: Harvard University Press, 1957.

Von Oech, Roger. *A Kick in the Seat of the Pants*. New York: Harper and Row, 1963.

Von Oech, Roger. *A Whack on the Side of the Head*. New York: Harper and Row, 1986.

Wilde, Judith and Richard. *Visual Literacy: A Conceptual Approach to Graphic Problem Solving*. New York: Watson-Guptil, 2000.

bibliography

Critical Thinking

Barrett, Terry. *Interpreting Art*. New York: McGraw-Hill, 2003.

Tucker, Amy. *Visual Literacy: Writing About Art*. New York: McGraw-Hill, 2002.

Three-Dimensional Design

Andrews, Oliver. *Living Materials: A Sculptor's Handbook*. Berkeley: University of California Press, 1988.

Bachelard, Gaston. *The Poetics of Space*, trans. Maria Jolas. Boston: Beacon Press, 1969.

Beardsley, John. *Earthworks and Beyond: Contemporary Art in the Landscape*. New York: Abbeville Press, 1998.

Ching, Frank. *Architecture: Form, Space, and Order*, 2nd ed. New York: Van Nostrand Reinhold, 1996.

de Oliveira, Nicolas, Nicola Oxley, and Michael Petry. *Installation Art*. Washington, DC: Smithsonian Institution Press, 1994.

Dormer, Peter, and Ralph Turner. *The New Jewelry: Trends and Traditions*. London: Thames and Hudson, 1985.

Frantz, Suzanne. *Contemporary Glass: A World Survey from the Corning Museum of Glass*. New York: Harry N. Abrams, 1989.

Koplos, Janet. *Contemporary Japanese Sculpture*. New York: Abbeville Press, 1991.

Lane, Peter. *Ceramic Form: Design and Decoration*, rev. ed. New York: Rizzoli, 1998.

Lewin, Susan Grant. *One of a Kind: American Art Jewelry Today*. New York: Harry N. Abrams, 1994.

Lidstone, John. *Building with Wire*. New York: Van Nostrand Reinhold, 1972.

Luecking, Stephen. *Principles of Three Dimensional Design*. Upper Saddle River, NJ: Pearson Education, 2002.

Lynn, Martha Dreyer. *Clay Today: Contemporary Ceramicists and Their Work*. Los Angeles: Los Angeles County Museum of Art; San Francisco: Chronicle Books, 1990.

Manzini, Ezio. *The Material of Invention: Materials and Design*. Cambridge, MA: MIT Press, 1989.

Miller, Bonnie J. *Out of the Fire: Contemporary Glass Artists and Their Work*. San Francisco: Chronicle Books, 1991.

Nunley, John W., and Cara McCarty. *Masks: Faces of Culture*. New York: Harry N. Abrams in association with the Saint Louis Art Museum, 1999.

Penny, Nicholas. *The Materials of Sculpture*. New Haven, CT: Yale University Press, 1993.

Selz, Peter Howard. *Barbara Chase-Riboud, Sculptor*. New York: Harry N. Abrams, 1999.

Wallschlaeger, Charles, and Cynthia Busic-Snyder. *Basic Visual Concepts and Principles for Artists, Architects and Designers*. New York: McGraw-Hill, 1992.

Williams, Arthur. *Sculpture: Technique, Form, Content*. Worcester, MA: Davis, 1993.

Wyatt, Gary. *Spirit Faces: Contemporary Native American Masks from the Northwest*. San Francisco: Chronicle Books, 1994.

Time Design

Baldwin, Huntley. *How to Create Effective TV Commercials*, 2nd ed. Lincolnwood, IL: NTC Business Books, 1989.

Bordwell, David, and Kristin Thompson. *Film Art: An Introduction*, 8th ed. New York: McGraw-Hill, 2008.

Eisner, Will. *Comics and Sequential Art*. Tamarac, FL: Poorhouse Press, 1985.

Goldberg, Roselee. *Performance: Live Art Since 1960*. New York: Harry N. Abrams, 1998.

Johnson, Lincoln F. *Film: Space, Time, Light and Sound*. Orlando, FL: Holt, Rinehart and Winston, 1974.

Katz, Stephen D. *Film Directing, Shot by Shot: Visualizing from Concept to Screen*. Studio City, CA: Michael Wiese Productions, 1991.

McCloud, Scott. *Understanding Comics*. New York: HarperPerennial, 1994.

McKee, Robert. *Story: Substance, Structure, Style, and the Principles of Screen Writing*. New York: HarperCollins, 1997.

Riordan, Steve, ed. *Clio Awards: A Tribute to 30 Years of Advertising Excellence, 1960–1989*. Glen Cove, NY: PBC International, 1989.

Ross, David et al. *Bill Viola*. New York: Whitney Museum of American Art, 1998.

Vogler, Christopher. *The Writer's Journey: Mythic Structure for Storytellers and Screenwriters*. Studio City, CA: Michael Wiese Productions, 1991.

Zettl, Herbert. *Sight, Sound, Motion: Applied Media Aesthetics*, 4th ed. Belmont, CA: Wadsworth, 2004.

Book Arts

Drucker, Johanna. *The Century of Artists' Books*. New York: Granary Books, 1995.

Gordon, Stephen F. *Making Picture-Books: A Method of Learning Graphic Sequence*. New York: Van Nostrand Reinhold, 1970.

La Plantz, Shereen. *Cover to Cover*. Asheville, NC: Lark Books, 1995.

Lyons, Joan. *Artists' Books: A Critical Anthology and Sourcebook*. Rochester, NY: Visual Studies Workshop Press, 1985.

Smith, Keith A. *Structure of the Visual Book*. Fairport, NY: The Sigma Foundation, 1992.

Smith, Keith A. *Text in the Book Format*. Fairport, NY: The Sigma Foundation, 1991.

bibliography

glossary

Glossary by Mary Stewart and Peter Forbes

A

abstract artwork; abstract form 1. an artwork or form derived from visual reality that has been distilled or transformed, reducing its resemblance to the original source. 2. a multiple-image structure, such as a film, in which the parts are related to each other through repetition and visual characteristics such as shape, color, scale, or direction of movement.

abstract shape a shape that is derived from a visual source, but is so transformed that it bears little visual resemblance to that source.

accent a specific shape, volume, color, musical note, etc., that has been emphasized. Using an accent, a designer can bring attention to part of a composition and increase rhythmic variation within a pattern.

achromatic a color (such as black and white) that has no hue.

act a major division in a film or theatrical event. Acts are generally constructed from a group of sequences that increase in intensity.

action-to-action transition in comic books, the juxtaposition of two or more panels showing a sequence of actions.

actual lines lines that are physically present in a design.

actual time the duration of an actual temporal event. For example, it takes less than a minute for the bowling ball to roll down the ramps in Jean Tinguely's *Chaos 1.*

additive color color created by combining projected beams of chromatic light. The additive color primaries are red, green, and blue, and the secondaries are cyan, magenta, and yellow.

additive sculpture a physical object constructed from separate parts that have been connected using glues, joints, stitching, welds, and so on.

aesthetics the study of human responses to art and beauty.

afterimage in color theory, a ghostly image that lingers after the actual image has been removed.

ambient light the quality of light within an entire space or setting. For example, when we enter an open courtyard on a sunny summer afternoon, we are surrounded by warm ambient sunlight. Everything we see is colorful and bright.

amplified perspective the exaggerated use of linear perspective to achieve a dramatic and engaging presentation of the subject. Amplified perspective is often created using an unusual viewing position, such as a bird's-eye view, accelerated convergence, or some form of distortion.

analogous a color scheme based on hues that are adjacent on a color wheel, such as red, red-orange, and orange.

analogy a similarity or connection between things that are apparently separate and dissimilar. For example, when a teacher describes wet plaster as having the "consistency of cream," he or she is using an analogy.

anesthetic a chemical or action used to induce insensitivity or unconsciousness.

anomaly an obvious break from the norm in a design.

appropriation a postmodern practice in which one artist reproduces an image created by another and claims it as his or her own.

approximate symmetry a form of balance that occurs when roughly similar imagery appears on either side of a central axis.

armature an internal structure created to strengthen and support a three-dimensional object.

array a collection of points.

assemblage an additive method in which the artist or designer constructs the artwork using objects and images that were originally created for another purpose. Essentially, assemblage can be defined as three-dimensional collage.

asymmetrical balance equilibrium among visual elements that do not mirror each other on either side of an axis.

atmospheric perspective a visual phenomenon in which the atmospheric density progressively increases, hazing over the perceived world as one looks into its depth. Overall definition lessens, details fade, contrasts become muted, and, in a landscape, a blue mist descends.

attached shadow a shadow that directly defines a form.

B

balance the equal distribution of weight or force among visual units.

beat 1. a unit of musical rhythm that creates the pulse of a sound. 2. in acting, the most basic element in a story. A beat is an exchange of behavior, based on action and reaction.

bend one of the five major forces affecting structural strength.

brainstorming any of a number of problem-solving techniques that are designed to expand ideas and encourage creativity. List making, mapping, associative thinking, and metaphorical thinking are common strategies used.

C

calligraphic line derived from the Greek words for beautiful and writing, a flowing and expressive line that is as personal as handwriting. Calligraphic lines generally vary in thickness and velocity.

cast shadow a dark shape that results from the placement of an opaque object in the path of a light source.

categorical (form) in film, a multiple-image structure that is based on categories, or subsets of a topic. For example, a film on predators might begin with a discussion of wolves, then move on to lions, and conclude with a discussion of hawks.

causality the interrelation of cause and effect, based on the premise that nothing occurs without cause. Narrative film is based on causality: because the starting pistol was shot, the footrace began.

cause-and-effect critique (or formal analysis) a critique in which the viewer seeks to determine the cause for each visual or emotional effect in a design. For example, the dynamism in a design may be caused by the diagonal lines and asymmetrical balance used.

centricity as identified by Rudolf Arnheim, a compressive compositional force.

character-driven narratives in which something about the character's essential self, aesthetics, or feelings leads to a particular action or event.

chiaroscuro from Italian, meaning "light-dark." The gradual transition of values to create the illusion of light and shadow on a three-dimensional form.

chroma the purity, intensity, or saturation of a color.

chromatic gray a gray made from a mixture of various hues, rather than a simple blend of black and white.

chronology the order in which events occur.

cliché an overused expression or a predictable visual treatment of an idea.

close-up in film, a type of framing in which the scale of the object shown is relatively large, as in a close-up of an actor's face.

closure the mind's inclination to connect fragmentary information to produce a completed form. Closure is an essential aspect of Gestalt psychology.

codex traditional bound-edged format used for modern books, with separate pages normally bound together and given a cover.

collage an image constructed from visual or verbal fragments initially designed for another purpose.

color harmony use of compatible colors to help unify a composition.

color interaction the way colors within a composition influence one another.

color key a color that dominates an image and heightens its psychological and compositional impact.

color overtone a secondary hue "bias" in a primary color. For example, alizarin crimson is a red with violet overtones, while scarlet is a red with orange overtones.

color theory the art and science of color interaction and effects.

complementary (colors) hues that oppose one another on a color wheel. When paired in a composition, complementary colors create contrast; when mixed, complementary colors produce a wide range of browns.

composite a new material created when two or more materials of differing strengths are fused. Examples are fiberglass and foamcore.

composition the combination of multiple parts into a harmonious whole

compression the forcing or crushing of material into a smaller, denser condition and its visual dynamics and implied psychological effects.

cone of vision in perspective drawing, a hypothetical cone of perception originating at the eye of the artist and expanding to include whatever he or she wishes to record in an illusionistic image, such as a perspective drawing. The cone's maximum scoping angle is 60 degrees; anything outside the cone of vision is subject to distortion.

containment a unifying force created by the outer edge of a composition, or by a boundary within a composition.

content the emotional and/or intellectual meaning or message of an artwork.

context in art, the set of circumstances or facts that surround when a work of art was made, where, how, and for what purpose.

continuity the degree of connection or flow among compositional parts.

contour line a line that describes the edges of a form and suggests three-dimensional volume.

contrast the degree of difference between compositional parts or between one image and another. Contrast is created when two or more forces operate in opposition.

convergent thinking a problem-solving strategy in which a predetermined goal is pursued in a linear progression using a highly focused problem-solving process. Six steps are commonly used: 1. define the problem; 2. do research; 3. determine your objective; 4. devise a strategy; 5. execute the strategy; 6. evaluate the results.

critique any means by which the strengths and weaknesses of designs are analyzed.

cross-contours multiple lines running over the surface of an object horizontally and/or vertically that describe its surface configuration topographically, as in mapping. This process is much like wire-framing in three-dimensional computer modeling. Cross-contours can also be used in drawing to suggest three-dimensional form through tonal variation.

crosscutting alternating between two or more events.

cross-hatching a technique used in drawing and printmaking to shade an object using two or more networks of parallel lines. Darker values are created as the number of networks increases.

curvilinear shape a shape whose contour is dominated by curves and flowing lines.

cut in film, the immediate change from one shot or frame to another.

D

definition 1. the degree to which a shape is distinguished from both the ground area and other shapes within the design. 2. the degree of resolution or focus of an entire image. Sharply defined shapes tend to advance, while blurred shapes tend to recede.

denouement the outcome, solution, or point of clarification in a story.

descriptive critique a critique in which the viewer carefully describes what he or she sees when observing a design.

diegetic describes the world created in a film or video.

directed light localized and focused light, such as a spotlight on a singer.

direction actual or implied movement of an element within a design.

disharmony a combination of colors that clash with one another and appear to be jumping out of the picture.

displacement a forming method in which a solid material is physically forced into a new configuration. The stamping process used to mint coins is an example of displacement.

dissolve in film, a transition between two shots during which the first image gradually disappears while the second image gradually appears.

divergent thinking an open-ended problem-solving strategy. Starting with a broad theme, the artist or designer expands ideas in all directions.

dominant describes the principle of composition in which certain elements assume greater importance than others. Also see **emphasis**.

duration 1. the length of time required for the completion of an event, as in the running time of a film, video, or performance. 2. the running time of events depicted in the story (plot duration). 3. the overall span of time the story encompasses (story duration). 4. the overall span of time a sound endures (sound duration).

dynamic forms forms that imply change.

dynamic space compositional organization that emphasizes movement or the illusion of movement.

E

earth colors colors made primarily from pigments found in soil, including raw and burnt sienna, raw and burnt umber, and yellow ochre.

earthwork commonly, an artwork that has been created through the transformation of a natural site into an aesthetic statement.

eccentricity as identified by Rudolf Arnheim, an expansive compositional force.

editing in film, selecting and sequencing the details of an event to create a cohesive whole.

elements (of design) basic building blocks from which designs are made. For example, the essential elements of two-dimensional design are line, shape, texture, color, and value.

emotional advertising advertising that uses emotion to sell a service, product, or idea. This strategy is often used when a product is neither unique nor demonstrably better than a competing product.

emphasis special attention given to some aspect of a composition to increase its prominence.

engraving a printmaking process in which lines are carved into a metal plate or wooden board, then filled with ink and printed.

environmental work (or environment) an artwork that must be entered physically. Installations (which are usually presented indoors) and earthworks (which are usually presented outdoors) are two major types of environmental work.

ephemera materials that decay rapidly.

exaggerated advertising pushing an idea to an extreme in order to make a point.

exoskeleton an external support structure.

eye level (or horizon line) in linear perspective, the eye level is determined by the physical position of the artist. Sitting on the floor creates a low eye level, while standing at an easel creates a higher eye level. All vanishing points in one- and two-point perspective are positioned on the eye level.

F

fade a gradual transition used in film and video. 1. in a fade-in, a dark screen gradually brightens as a shot appears. 2. in a fade-out, the shot gradually darkens as the screen goes black.

fidelity the degree of connection between a sound and its source. For example, when we hear the sound of a helicopter and see a helicopter on the screen, the sound matches with the image, creating tight fidelity.

figure/ground reversal an arrangement in which positive and negative shapes alternately command attention.

flashbacks in film, alternations in chronology in which events that occur later in a story are shown first.

flying buttress a type of exoskeleton commonly used by medieval architects in designing cathedrals.

focal point primary point of interest in a composition. A focal point is often used to emphasize an area of particular importance, or to provide a strong sense of compositional direction.

form 1. the physical manifestation of an idea, as opposed to the content, which refers to the idea itself. 2. the organization or arrangement of visual elements to create a unified design. 3. a three-dimensional composition or unit within a three-dimensional composition. For example, a sphere, a cube, and a pyramid are all three-dimensional forms.

formal analysis a type of critique in which compositional causes are connected to compositional effects.

fractured space discontinuous space that is created when multiple viewpoints are combined within a single image.

frame a single static image in film or video.

freestanding work an artwork that is self-supporting and is designed to be viewed from all sides.

function the purpose of a design, or the objective that motivates the designer. For an industrial designer, the primary purpose of a design is often utilitarian. For example, he or she may be required to design a more fuel-efficient automobile. For a sculptor, the primary purpose of a design is aesthetic: he or she seeks to create an artwork that engages the viewer emotionally and intellectually.

fusion the combination of shapes or volumes along a common edge.

geometric forms three-dimensional forms derived from or suggestive of geometry. Examples include cubes, spheres, and tetrahedrons.

geometric shapes shapes derived from or suggestive of geometry. Geometric shapes are characterized by crisp, precise edges and mathematically consistent curves.

Gestalt psychology a theory of visual perception that emphasizes the importance of holistic composition. According to this theory, grouping, containment, repetition, proximity, continuity, and closure are essential aspects of visual unity.

gesture drawing a vigorous drawing that captures the action, structure, and overall orientation of an object, rather than describing specific details. Often used as a basis for figure drawing.

gloss 1. in writing, words of explanation or translation inserted into a text. 2. a secondary text within a manuscript that provides comments on the main text.

gradation any gradual transition from one color to another or from one shape or volume to another.

graphic relationship the juxtaposition of two or more separate images that are compositionally similar. For example, if a basketball is shown in the first panel, an aerial view of the round free-throw zone is shown in the second, and the hoop of the basket itself is shown in the third, a graphic relationship based on circles has been created.

grid a visual or physical structure created from intersecting parallel lines.

grisaille a gray underpainting, often used by Renaissance artists, to increase the illusion of space.

group in sequential structure, a collection of images that are related by subject matter, composition, or source. For example, the trombone, trumpet, and tuba are all members of the group known as the brass section in an orchestra.

grouping visual organization based on similarity in location, orientation, shape, color, and so on.

handheld a small-scale object that can be held in your hands.

Happening an assemblage of improvised, spontaneous events performed by artist and audience alike, based on a general theme. There is no rehearsal, and any location, from a parking lot to a factory interior, can be used. The Happening is most commonly associated with Allan Kaprow and is a precursor to performance art.

hard-sell an advertising approach in which a major point is presented in a clear, direct manner. The narrative is usually linear, and the message is usually explicit.

harmony a pleasing or soothing relationship among colors, shapes, or other design elements.

hatching a technique used in drawing and printmaking to create a range of gray tones using multiple parallel lines.

high definition sharply focused visual information that is easily readable. High definition creates strong contrast between shapes and tends to increase the clarity and immediacy of communication.

hue the name of a color (such as red or yellow), which distinguishes it from others and assigns it a position in the visual spectrum.

human scale a design that is roughly our size.

humorous advertising use of humor to sell a service, product, or idea. By entertaining the viewer, the designer can make the message more memorable.

hybridity the creation of artworks using disparate media to create a unified conceptual statement.

iconography the study of symbolic visual systems.

imbalance the absence of balance.

implied line 1. a line that is suggested by the positions of shapes or objects within a design. 2. a line that is suggested by movement or by a gesture rather than being physically drawn or constructed.

implied time the suggested location or duration of an event.

installation an artwork or a design that presents an ensemble of images and objects within a three-dimensional environment.

intensity 1. the purity, saturation, or chroma of a color. For example, fire-engine red is a high-intensity color, while brick red is a low-intensity color. 2. in time design, the power, concentration, and energy with which an action is performed, or the quality of observation of an event.

interdisciplinary art the combination of two or more different disciplines to create a hybrid art form.

invented texture a form of visual texture that has been created without reference to perceptual reality.

K

kinesthetics the science of movement.

kinetic forms forms that actually move.

L

lap dissolve in film, a dissolve in which two shots are temporarily superimposed.

layered space compositional space that has been deliberately separated into foreground, middle ground, and background.

layering a postmodern practice in which an accumulation of multiple (and often contradictory) visual layers is used to create a single artwork.

line 1. a point in motion. 2. a series of adjacent points. 3. a connection between points. 4. an implied connection between points. Line is one of the basic elements of design.

linear perspective a mathematical system for projecting the apparent dimensions of a three-dimensional object onto a flat surface. Developed by artists during the Renaissance, linear perspective is one strategy for creating the illusion of space.

long shot in film, a type of framing in which the scale of the subject shown is relatively small, as with an image of a human figure within a landscape.

loudness the amplitude of a sound wave; the volume of a sound.

low definition describes blurred or ambiguous visual information. Low-definition shapes can increase the complexity of the design and encourage multiple interpretations.

M

maquette a well-developed three-dimensional sketch, comparable to a two-dimensional thumbnail sketch.

mass a solid three-dimensional form.

matrix a three-dimensional grid.

mechanical forms gears, belts, hoses, and other forms suggestive of machinery.

medium shot in film, a type of framing in which the scale of the subject shown is of moderate size, as in a view of an actor from the waist up.

metaphor a figure of speech in which one thing is directly linked to another, dissimilar thing. Through this connection, the original word is given the qualities of the linked word. For example, when we say "She's a diamond in the rough," we attribute to a woman the qualities of an unpolished gem.

metaphorical thinking the use of metaphors or analogies to create visual or verbal bridges.

model in three-dimensional design, a technical experiment or a small-scale version of a larger design.

modeling the process of manipulating a pliable material (such as clay) to create a three-dimensional object.

modernism a collection of artistic styles, most prominent from around 1860 to 1960, that emphasized the importance of form, introduced new materials and production methods, and sought to express universal truths.

monochromatic a color scheme based on variations in a single hue. For example, a light pastel blue, a medium navy blue, and a dark blue-black may be used in a room interior.

montage time-based structure constructed from multiple and often seemingly unrelated sources; a temporal collage.

monumental scale of objects that are much larger than humans.

movement in design, the use of deliberate visual pathways to help direct the viewer's attention to areas of particular interest.

myth a traditional story collectively composed by many members of a society. The creation of the world, sources of evil, the power of knowledge, and even the nature of reality may be explained through these grand expressions of the imagination.

N

negative shape (or ground) 1. a clearly defined area around a positive shape or form. 2. a shape created through the absence of an object rather than through the presence of an object.

negative space space surrounding a positive form or shape.

nonobjective artworks artworks that have no reference to perceptual reality.

nonobjective shapes shapes created without reference to specific visual subject matter.

non-sequitur transition the juxtaposition of multiple frames or shots that have no obvious conceptual relationship.

O

objective criticism the assessment of strengths and weaknesses in a design, based solely on the visual information presented.

one-point perspective a form of linear perspective in which the lines receding into space converge at a single vanishing point on the eye level or horizon line.

glossary

opponent theory an explanation for the electric glow that occurs when two complementary colors are placed side by side.

organic forms forms that are derived from nature.

organic shapes shapes that visually suggest nature or natural forces. Also known as **biomorphic shapes**.

organizational lines lines used to create the loose linear "skeleton" on which a composition can be built. Also known as **structural lines**.

orientation the horizontal, vertical, or diagonal position of a composition or design element.

orthographic projection a drawing system widely used by artists and designers to delineate the top, bottom, and four side views of a three-dimensional object. Unlike perspective drawing, which is designed to create the illusion of space, an orthographic projection is constructed using parallel lines that accurately delineate six surfaces of an object.

P

pace the rate of change in a temporal event.

pattern a design created through systematic repetition. Many patterns are based on a module, or a repeated visual unit.

pedestal a vertical support for a sculptural object.

performance art a live presentation, often including the artist and usually combining elements from a variety of art forms, such as film, video, theater, and dance.

physical texture actual variation in a surface.

picture plane in linear perspective, the flat surface on which a three-dimensional image is mentally projected.

pitch in music, the relative highness or lowness of a sound. Pitch is determined by wave frequency, as compression and expansion occur within the sound wave.

plane a three-dimensional form that has length and width but minimal thickness.

plinth a horizontal support for a sculptural object.

plot duration the running time of the events depicted in a story.

point a basic mark, such as a dot, a pixel, or a brushstroke. A point is used to create a dialog with the surrounding space.

polyhedra (or polyhedrons) multifaceted volumes.

positive forms areas of physical substance in a three-dimensional design.

positive shape (or figure) the principal or foreground shape in a design and the dominant shape or figure in a figure/ground relationship.

postmodernism a collection of artistic styles that arose in the 1970s as a reaction to modernism. Notable characteristics include conceptual emphasis, social commentary, irreverence, and skepticism about universal truths.

primary colors colors from which virtually all other colors can be mixed. The additive (or light) color primaries are red, green, and blue. The subtractive (or pigment) color primaries are yellow, magenta red, and cyan blue.

process colors in four-color process printing, the subtractive primary colors: yellow, magenta, and cyan, plus black.

proportion the relative size of visual elements within an image.

prototype a well-developed model, as with the fully functional prototype cars developed by automobile companies.

proximity the distance between visual or structural elements, or between an object and the audience.

pure form a circle, sphere, triangle, cube, or other form created without reference to specific subject matter.

R

radial symmetry a form of balance that is created when shapes or volumes are mirrored both vertically and horizontally, with the center of the composition acting as a focal point.

rational advertising a type of advertising in which logic and comparisons of quality are used to sell a service, product, or idea. A rational approach is most effective when the message is compelling in itself or the product is unique.

realistic advertising the use of a familiar setting or situation to involve the viewer and relate a product, service, or idea to everyday life.

recontextualization a postmodern practice in which the meaning of an image or object is changed by the context in which it is placed.

rectilinear shape a shape composed from straight lines and angular corners.

reflective a surface that bounces light back into space.

refracted (of light) bent as it passes through a prism.

relief sculpture in which forms project from a flat surface. The degree of projection ranges from low to high relief.

repetition the use of the same visual element or effect a number of times in the same composition.

representational artworks commonly, the lifelike depiction of persons or objects.

representational shapes shapes derived from specific subject matter and strongly based on visual observation.

rhetorical a type of sequential organization in which the parts are used to create and support an argument. Often used in documentary films.

rhythm 1. presentation of multiple units in a deliberate pattern. 2. in filmmaking, the perceived rate and regularity of sounds, shots, and movement within the shots. Rhythm is determined by the beat (pulse), accent (stress), and tempo (pace).

rhythmic relationship the juxtaposition of multiple visual elements or images to create a deliberate pulse or beat.

S

saturation the purity, chroma, or intensity of a color.

scale a size relationship between two separate objects, such as the relationship between the size of the Statue of Liberty and a human visitor to the monument.

scene in film, continuous action in continuous time and continuous space.

scene-to-scene transition in comic books, the juxtaposition of two or more frames showing different scenes or settings.

scope conceptually, the extent of our perception or the range of ideas our minds can grasp. Temporally, the range of action within a given moment.

screenplay the written blueprint for a film, commonly constructed from multiple acts.

secondary colors hues mixed from adjacent primaries. In paint, the secondary colors are violet, green, and orange.

sequence 1. in filmmaking, a collection of related shots and scenes that comprise a major section of action or narration. 2. in narrative structure, any collection of images that have been organized by *cause and effect*. In a simple sequence, action number two is caused by action number one. In a complex sequence, there may be a considerable delay between the cause and the effect.

series in sequential structure, a collection of images that are linked simply, like cars in a train.

serious advertising advertising that treats a topic in a somber or solemn manner. Often used for public service announcements, such as drunk-driving commercials.

setting the physical and temporal location of a story, the props and costumes used in a story, and the use of sound.

shade a hue that has been mixed with black.

shading In drawing, shading is created through gradation of tones to suggest three-dimensional form.

shape a flat, enclosed area created when a line connects to enclose an area, an area is surrounded by other shapes, or an area is filled with color or texture.

shear a force that creates a lateral break in a material.

shot in film, a continuous group of frames.

sight line 1. a viewing line that is established by the arrangement of objects within one's field of vision. 2. a straight line of unimpeded vision.

simile a figure of speech in which one thing is linked to another, dissimilar thing using the word *like* or *as*. Through this connection, the original word is given the qualities of the linked word. For example, when we say "He's as strong as an ox," we attribute to a man the strength of an animal.

simultaneous contrast the optical alteration of a color by a surrounding color.

site-specific an artwork specifically designed for and installed in a particular place.

skeleton (or endoskeleton) a structure that provides internal support.

soft-sell an advertising approach that uses emotion, rather than reason, to sell a service, product, or idea. The narrative is often nonlinear, and ideas or actions may be implied.

solidification a forming method in which a liquid material is poured into a mold or extruded through a pipe, then allowed to harden.

space the area within or around an area of substance. The artist/designer defines and activates space when constructing a three-dimensional object.

spatial context the space in which a sound is generated. A sound that is played outdoors behaves differently from a sound that is played in a small room.

spatial relationship the juxtaposition of two or more images that are spatially different, such as a close-up, a medium shot, and a long shot.

split complementary a complementary color plus the two colors on either side of its complement on the color wheel.

static forms forms that appear to be stable and unmoving.

stereotype a fixed generalization based on a preconception.

stippling a technique for producing an image from multiple dots.

story duration the overall length of a story.

style the recurring characteristics that distinguish one historical period or particular group of artists from another.

subject the person, object, event, or idea on which an artwork is based.

subjective criticism the assessment of strengths and weaknesses in a design based on nonobjective criteria, such as the narrative implications of an idea, the cultural ramifications of an action, or the personal meaning of an image.

subject-to-subject transition in comic books, the juxtaposition of two or more frames showing different subject matter.

subordinate of secondary importance. See emphasis.

subtractive color hue created when light is selectively reflected off a colored surface.

subtractive sculpture a forming method in which materials are removed from a larger mass. Carving, drilling, cutting, and turning on a lathe are all subtractive processes.

symbolic color a color that has been assigned a particular meaning by the members of a society. For example, in the United States, the white color of a wedding gown symbolizes purity, while in Borneo white symbolizes death.

symmetrical balance a form of balance that is created when shapes are mirrored on either side of a central axis, as in a composition that is vertically divided down the center.

glossary

T

take in film or video, one version of an event.

temperature the physical and psychological heat suggested by a color's hue.

tempo the pace at which change occurs. A fast tempo is generally used in action films, while a slow tempo is commonly used in a dramatic film.

temporal relationship how the shots in a film are related in time.

tension the extension of an object through stretching or bending.

tertiary color a hue that is mixed from a primary color and an adjacent secondary color.

testimonial in advertising, use of a trustworthy character or celebrity to endorse a product, service, or idea.

texture the visual or tactile quality of a form. Texture can be created visually using multiple marks, physically through surface variation, or through the inherent property of a specific material, such as sand as opposed to smooth porcelain.

three-point perspective a form of linear perspective in which the lines receding into space converge at two vanishing points on the eye level (one to the left of the object being drawn and one to the right of the object being drawn) plus a third vanishing point above or below the eye level. Used when the picture plane must be tilted to encompass an object placed above or below the eye level.

three-quarter work a physical object that is designed to be viewed from the front and sides only.

timbre the unique sound quality of each instrument. For example, a note of the same volume and pitch is quite different when it is generated by a flute rather than a violin.

tint a hue that has been mixed with white.

tone a hue that has been mixed with black and white.

torque the distortion of an object through a twisting movement. Also known as torsion.

translucent a surface that partially permits the passage of light.

transparent a surface that permits the passage of light, such as clear plastic or glass.

triadic describes a color scheme based on three colors that are equidistant on a color wheel.

tromp l'oeil a flat illusion that is so convincing that the viewer believes the image is real. A French term meaning "to fool the eye."

two-point perspective a form of linear perspective in which the lines receding into space converge at two vanishing points on the eye level (or horizon line), one to the left of the object being drawn and one to the right of the object being drawn.

U

unity compositional similarity, oneness, togetherness, or cohesion.

V

value the relative lightness or darkness of a color.

value contrast the degree to which values in a composition differ from one another.

value distribution the proportion and arrangement of lights and darks in a composition. Also known as value pattern.

value scale a range of grays that are presented in a consistent sequence, creating a gradual transition from white to black.

vanishing point in linear perspective, the point or points on the eye level at which parallel lines appear to converge.

variety the differences that give a design visual and conceptual interest, notably, use of contrast, emphasis, differences in size, and so forth.

viewing time the time an audience devotes to watching or exploring an artwork.

visual book an experimental structure that conveys ideas, actions, and emotions using multiple images in an integrated and interdependent format. Also known as an artist's book.

visual texture texture created using multiple marks or through a descriptive simulation of physical texture.

visual weight 1. the inclination of shapes to float or sink compositionally. 2. the relative importance of a visual element within a design.

volume 1. an empty three-dimensional form. 2. in two-dimensional design, a three-dimensional form that has been represented using the illusion of space. 3. in time design, the loudness of a sound.

volume summary a drawing that communicates visual information reductively, using basic volumes such as spheres, cubes, and cylinders to indicate the major components of a figure or object.

volumetric three-dimensional in nature.

W

wipe in film, a transition in which the first shot seems to be pushed off the screen by the second. Wipes were used extensively in *Star Wars*.

glossary

D

E

F

G

H

index

I

J

K

L

index

M

N

O

P

R

Q

S

T

U

V

index